Corporate Culture

Corporate Culture

THE ULTIMATE STRATEGIC ASSET

Eric G. Flamholtz and Yvonne Randle

STANFORD BUSINESS BOOKS

An Imprint of Stanford University Press

Stanford, California

Stanford University Press
Stanford, California

Special discounts for bulk quantities of Stanford Business Books are available to
corporations, professional associations, and other organizations. For details and
discount information, contact the special sales department of Stanford University
Press. Tel: (650) 736-1782, Fax: (650) 736-1784

Printed in the United States of America on acid-free, archival-quality paper

Library of Congress Cataloging-in-Publication Data

Flamholtz, Eric.
  Corporate culture : the ultimate strategic asset / Eric G. Flamholtz and
Yvonne Randle.
     p. cm.
  Includes bibliographical references and index.
  ISBN 978-0-8047-6364-6 (alk. paper)
  1. Corporate culture. 2. Industrial management. I. Randle, Yvonne. II. Title.
  HD58.7.F585 2011
  658.4—dc22
                              2010040855

Typeset at Stanford University Press in 10.5/15 Minion

Contents

Preface

It is increasingly recognized by researchers, practitioners, and managers alike that corporate culture is of critical importance to organizational success.[1] Even though this is the case, there are many organizations where the corporate culture is not managed, and in some cases the concept is not even understood.

Corporate Culture: The Invisible Strategic Asset

For some companies—such as Google, Southwest Airlines, Johnson & Johnson, and many others described in this book—a strong positive culture is a true asset, if not in the strict accounting sense then in the real economic sense. Flamholtz (one of the authors of this book) has suggested that culture actually is an asset or form of organizational human capital in the accounting sense as well.[2] At the other extreme, are companies—such as GM, Reuters, AIG, and others to be described throughout this book—where corporate culture is a true economic liability, not in the technical accounting sense but in the colloquial sense of this term.

This dichotomy (asset or liability) and the critical importance of corporate culture is shown clearly in the case of two companies: Starbucks Coffee Company and General Motors. The former is a classic entrepreneurial success story with a strong positive culture that is an economic asset; the latter is a classic case of corporate decline attributable at least in part to a dysfunctional culture, lacking in entrepreneurship behavior for decades, even as its decline persisted.

Although its significance is recognized, the concept of corporate culture as well as how to manage it in a practical way in organizations has remained tantalizingly elusive. There is a substantial amount of literature on the concept of corporate culture, but much of it can be described as academic or theoretical. The focus tends to be on the concept of corporate culture as a social-psychological construct or as a dimension of organizational health.[3] The literature does not fully recognize the importance of culture as a driver of financial performance and as a component of corporate strategy. Further, little emphasis is placed on providing a systematic practical method for managing culture as a key dimension of corporate performance. As a result, there is a serious gap in the exiting literature.

Purpose of This Book

This book is intended to build on and complement, while at the same time fill the gap in, the existing literature. It is based on a different perspective from previous, competing books. Specifically, it views culture as a driver or determinant of corporate financial performance (the so-called bottom line) and as a source of sustainable competitive advantage. This book offers a theoretically sound but practical (user-friendly) method for managing corporate culture.

In brief, the rationale for this book, its ultimate goals, and its content orientation are different from the existing literature. Accordingly, this book:

1. Explains why corporate culture is a critical factor in organizational success and failure, a key driver or determinant of the bottom line of financial performance of business enterprises, and a critical source (and possibly the ultimate one) of sustainable competitive advantage in organizations (that is, a stealth competitive weapon)

2. Presents methods for measuring corporate culture to facilitate its management

3. Describes the current state-of-the-art in corporate culture management as well as the limitations, challenges and opportunities associated with developing this field

4. Offers a framework for understanding corporate culture

5. Identifies the five elements of corporate culture determined by empirical research to be the key drivers of organizational performance[4]

6. Introduces a six-step framework (model) for management of corporate culture as an ongoing process

7. Provides a set of tools for managing corporate culture in actual organizations

Throughout this book, we present examples of companies that are dealing with the issues involved with managing corporate culture and identify the lessons that can be learned from their experiences—that is, how they have used or are using the specific tools to identify, communicate, and reinforce their culture.

Overview

The focus of *Corporate Culture: The Ultimate Strategic Asset* is to help people actually manage corporate culture. It is not just a treatise about corporate culture. In this book, we instruct managers and students in how to manage corporate culture as a source of competitive advantage and as a means of influencing the bottom line of financial performance. We also give in-depth examples describing what actual companies do to manage their corporate culture.

The book is organized into three parts. Part I discusses the nature and importance of corporate culture, presents a framework for better understanding culture, and describes a process for managing it. Part II deals with management of the key dimensions of corporate culture, identified through our own empirical research and practical experience. Part III focuses on culture management leadership, including the important roles that senior executives and those in the human resource function need to play.

Part I: The Role of Corporate Culture and Culture Management in Organizational Success

Part I contains three chapters. Together, they constitute a foundation for understanding and managing corporate culture.

Chapter 1 deals with the concept of corporate culture and the many reasons it is a critical aspect of organizational performance—with special emphasis on its role as a source of sustainable strategic advantage and a key factor that has an impact on the financial success of business enterprises.

Together, Chapters 2 and 3 are designed to present a theoretically sound, but practical (usable), framework for management of corporate culture. In Chapter 2, we (1) define corporate culture operationally, (2) identify the key dimensions of corporate culture, (3) examine how to identify what a company's culture really is, and (4) present a method for measuring corporate culture. The chapter also includes a case study illustrating how organizations can use the culture measurement methods presented as a practical tool. It contains a technical appendix summarizing research using the measurement methods and showing that culture affects financial performance. Chapter 3 describes a systematic (six-step) process for managing corporate culture and presents a set of culture management tools. It also examines the need for culture management at different stages of organizational growth.

Part II: Management of the Key Dimensions of Corporate Culture

The second part consists of six chapters. Chapters 4 through 8 each deal with one of the five key dimensions of culture—customer orientation, employee (or people) orientation, performance standards and accountability, innovation and openness to change, and company process orientation. Each chapter draws on several examples of actual companies and how they accomplish management of these factors. Chapter 9 is titled "The Dark Side of Corporate Culture"; it deals with examples of dysfunctional cultures. This set of chapters also illustrates how the various tools for culture management (identified and described in Chapter 3) have actually been used by companies.

Part III: Leading Culture Management and Transformations

The third part is one final chapter, focusing on the process of culture management and change from the perspective of senior leadership, as well as the human resource function. We also examine the need for cultural transformation in response to overall changes in company size (growth-related changes), vision changes, and changes due to business combinations (mergers and acquisitions).[5]

Our Approach and Perspective

The approach underlying this book is based on a combination of inputs. Our perspective is infused, of course, by prior research and writing in this field. There have been some very important contributions to the literature of culture management prior to our book.[6] In addition to the usual sources of academic literature on this topic, there are frequently useful insights to be obtained from in-depth articles about actual companies found in professional magazines (such as *Fortune* and *Barron's*). Sometimes, this literature is actually more grounded in reality than academic literature is; but both serve a useful purpose. To a great extent, our approach and perspective are based on our own research, our personal experience in managing our own firm, and our experience as consultants helping companies understand, define, and manage their corporate culture.[7]

Corporate Culture: A True Invisible Asset

Corporate culture: you cannot see it, touch it, smell it, taste it, or hear it, but it is there. It pervades all aspects of organizational life, and it has a profound impact on organizational success and failure. If managed effectively, it is a real economic asset. If managed ineffectively or allowed to deteriorate, it can become a true economic liability and even lead to organizational failure.

As we shall see, management of corporate culture is quite complex. But there are clear examples of companies that have mastered the process of culture management. We show that corporate culture can have a significant impact on various aspects of organizational operations. We also show how companies can master aspects of corporate culture management and create competitive advantage as well as enhance their bottom line. We will also see that if culture management is done well, then a company will reap significant rewards.

For these companies, large and small, wherever they are located in the world, in whatever industries they operate, corporate culture is a true asset. And as an invisible asset, it is a significant source of their competitive advantage as well as a contributor to their long-term success.

It is our hope that this book will help companies and their leaders better understand how to master the process of culture management and transform their culture into a true invisible asset and source of sustainable competitive advantage.

Acknowledgments

In working toward publication of this book, we had our own "ultimate strategic assets"—individuals who contributed in a variety of ways—whom we would like to acknowledge.

We would like first to thank our editor, Margo Beth Crouppen, who was with us every step of the way, from the very inception of the book to the final manuscript. Her comments and feedback on the overall concept of the book, as well as on the content of each chapter, helped us tremendously. She was a great editorial partner!

In preparing the case studies presented throughout this book, we used both published information on well-known companies and our experience as consultants. We would like to acknowledge the contribution made to this book by all of the companies that invited us to serve as consultants and advisors. We would also like to specifically recognize those companies that allowed us to share their stories in depth and by name.

At Emergent BioSolutions, the Executive Management Committee is highly focused on making their culture real for all employees. We would like to thank Emergent's CEO, Fuad El-Hibri; COO, Dan Abdun Nabi; CFO, Don Elsey; and vice president of human resources, Paula Lazarich, for allowing us to share the company's progress in developing and implementing culture management plans—including the statement of company values.

At Smartmatic, CEO Antonio Mugica, senior vice president of human resources Victor Ramirez, and Samira Saba, marketing communications manager, took the time to be interviewed—in depth—about specific aspects of their company's culture. We thank them for this time, as well as for the time spent reviewing and providing feedback on their company's case studies, which appear in Chapters 6 and 7.

The case studies of Infogix's performance optimization process and approach to planning reflect significant input from Company Leader Madhavan Nayar. We greatly appreciate the time he took to read and offer feedback on these cases.

We would like to thank Zhenmei Hou, the founder of Talent International College in Guangxi, China, for sharing the story of her company's culture with us. She also supplied input on the written case study.

Delta Dental of Missouri's April 2010 planning meeting, which created a "wow"—not just for the management team but for one of the authors—led to a late addition to this book. We would like to thank the entire management team and CEO David Haynes in particular for allowing us to tell their story.

Bob Befus, the CEO of Interactive Holdings, and his team are strongly committed to "more than business" (as described in Chapter 8). We want to thank Bob for taking the time to share the background on and results of this effort with us.

Yixiao "Kenny" Zhang, CEO of Haohe Construction, located in Guangzhou, China, gave us extensive input on the case study that appears in Chapter 10. We greatly appreciate the time he took in imparting a great deal of information on his company's culture management and organizational development efforts.

We also wish to acknowledge Rangapriya (Priya) Kannan-Narasimhan, a doctoral candidate at UCLA's Anderson School of Management; and Peter Schwarz, vice president and manager of organizational analytics at Management Systems Consulting, for their assistance in preparing the Haohe construction case that appears in Chapter 10. Priya also assisted us with our research on existing culture literature.

Although we acknowledge with gratitude the contribution of all those cited, we remain responsible for the book and its imperfections.

Eric G. Flamholtz
Yvonne Randle
Los Angeles
June 2010

Corporate Culture

Part I

The Role of Corporate Culture and Culture Management in Organizational Success

1 Corporate Culture
The Invisible Asset

Scholars, students, and practitioners of organizational studies are faced with a variety of "corporate enigmas"—strange organizational phenomena that, at least on the surface, require some special explanation. Specifically:

- How does a little company headquartered in Bentonville, Arkansas, become one of the largest retailers in the world, with more than $400 billion in sales?
- How does a company selling a commodity product that has existed for centuries grow from $122 million in sales to more than $5 billion in slightly more than a decade, and more than $12 billion in two decades?
- How does a small company in Texas with all the cards stacked against it—whose business plan was created on a napkin—grow into one of the largest and most profitable players in its market?
- How does a company with an odd, unbusinesslike name come out of nowhere in the competitive environment of Silicon Valley to challenge the behemoth Microsoft and replace it as the leader in the Internet space?
- How does a company retain its vitality for more than one hundred years when virtually all of its peers of a century ago have disappeared?
- How does a company with a dominant market position (more than 42 percent market share) fall from grace over a period of twenty years and face the abyss of failure?

- How does a company that has developed a carefully nurtured reputation for quality over a period of more than fifty years suddenly have it tarnished by serious product defects that were known to management but concealed from customers?[1]

Corporate Culture: An Invisible Strategic Asset

The answer in all these cases, we believe, is attributable to something that is very real but invisible to the naked eye. It is not magic but something that, under the best of circumstances, works much like organizational magic. The answer is the invisible asset (or liability!) of corporate culture.[2]

In the case of the little company from Bentonville, Walmart has grown to be a retailing colossus. In his book *The Wal-Mart Way*, Don Soderquist, former vice chairman and chief operating officer, of Walmart, now retired, attributes its success to the company's culture.[3] Similarly, both Howard Schultz, founder and chairman of Starbucks Coffee Company; and Howard Behar, former president of Starbucks International, have attributed their company's astounding success to its culture rather than its coffee.[4] Southwest Airlines recognizes that corporate culture has been a key ingredient to success and the ability to remain profitable, even in the face of significant challenges. As stated in their 2008 report "Southwest Cares: Doing the Right Thing," "It is the Southwest Culture that sets us apart."[5] Other airlines went bankrupt in the aftermath of September 11, 2001, or as a result of the financial crisis that began in the fall of 2008, but Southwest remained profitable[6] and consistently ranked in the top ten on *Fortune* magazine's "Most Admired Companies" lists.

The company from Silicon Valley with the odd, unbusinesslike name of Google has become the leader in the Internet space through its search engine technology. However, a key to the continuous development of that technology is the talent and creativity of its people. As one article aptly stated, "The secret of Google's success is its way of turning talented engineers into an extraordinarily creative team."[7] Google attracts its talent because of its culture. As a result of its special culture, Google is recognized as one of the best companies to work for.[8]

Almost unbelievably, GE is one of only two companies that were among the most successful at the beginning of the twentieth century that are still highly successful today. The company's success has also been attributed to corporate culture.[9] GE's cultural values emphasize creating a clear, simple, reality-based, customer-focused vision; a passion for excellence; and not just acceptance of change but initiation of it.

General Motors, which was once the undisputed leader and apotheosis of business greatness, has fallen from grace and is now in a battle for its very survival. Many people attribute this to the insularity of the GM culture, and its unwillingness to look beyond the boundaries of Grosse Pointe, Michigan. While GM was in decline, one of the chief beneficiaries was Toyota. For more than fifty years, Toyota burnished its image and reputation as a manufacturer of high-quality automobiles and strived to surpass GM and become the biggest automaker in the world. However, beginning around 2008 some of Toyota's automobiles experienced a "sudden acceleration problem" that led to a significant decline in the company's exquisite reputation and its sales as well. In a public apology, the president of Toyota explained that the company's managers were distracted from adhering to "the Toyota Way"—the cultural values and principles instilled by the company's founders—by the drive to become the biggest automaker in the world and by the push to increase manufacturing in North America.[10]

Like bacteria or X-rays or other invisible phenomena, corporate culture is real but difficult to observe. In spite of this invisibility, it has a profound impact on organizational success and failure;[11] it can be a true strategic asset and sometimes a toxic liability.[12] Throughout the remainder of this book, we describe in more depth how the culture of the companies identified here (and others) had a significant positive or not-so-positive impact on organizational success.

Corporate Culture: An Introduction

During the past few decades, the term *corporate culture* has become widely used in business. It is now well recognized that corporate culture is a significant aspect of organizational health and performance.[13] Explicitly or implicitly, it is presumed that corporate culture affects a company's overall financial performance.

Although its significance is recognized, the concept of corporate culture as well as how to manage it in a practical way in organizations have remained tantalizingly elusive. As a result, several important questions arise:

- What is corporate culture?
- How is it manifested (how can we see it) in organizations?
- Why is it important?
- What are the key aspects of corporate culture?
- How can it be managed?
- What tools are available to help manage corporate culture?

All of these questions and others related to this topic are addressed in this book in the following chapters. In Chapter 1, we begin by addressing the first three of these issues: What is culture? How is it manifested? Why is it important?

What Is Corporate Culture?

The concept of corporate culture has become embedded in management vocabulary and thought.[14] Although there are many definitions of the concept, the central notion is that culture relates to core organizational values.[15] In a very real sense, corporate culture can be thought of as a company's "personality." Every organization—regardless of size—has a culture that influences how people behave, in a variety of areas, such as treatment of customers, standards of performance, innovation, etc.

How Is Culture Manifested in Organizations?

Culture is manifested almost everywhere in an organization, if we know where to look for it. It is reflected in the words and language people use in communicating with one another. For example, a company with a language rich in acronyms can communicate that the company values efficiency. At the same time, though, it can signal that there are barriers to cultural entry; one needs to know the language to understand what is being discussed.

Culture is also manifested in the artifacts that are in (and on display in) the company's facilities. Everything in an organization—from coffee cups to artwork—contains a cultural message, whether explicitly intended or not. A simple coffee cup can be quite valuable to the person who owns it, if it was given for a reason that has meaning and purpose to the individual and to everyone in the company.

In brief, culture is manifested in everything from the cultural statements on posters to the furnishing of the office and to the art that adorns the walls. Sometimes, the culture of a company is obvious and clearly visible, as in the treatment we receive as customers and the artifacts we see that support this focus on customer service. Sometimes, a company's culture is subtler and needs to be "read."

Clear and Explicit Cultural Messages

Cultural messages may be clear and explicit, as in formal statements of culture. The Johnson & Johnson Credo is posted on the walls of subsidiaries such as Neutrogena and LifeScan; it is clearly meant to be absorbed by employees as well as observed by visitors.

Another clear but very different type of message about the importance of culture is found at Google, the quirky Silicon Valley company that has become a powerhouse in Internet search and caused mighty Microsoft to try to purchase its rival Yahoo! In 2006, Google's co-founders, Larry Page and Sergey Brin, decided to establish the position of "chief culture officer," currently held by Stacy Savides Sullivan, who is also director of human resources. The very existence of this position is a clear statement about the importance of corporate culture at Google. Sullivan's mission is to retain the company's culture as it grows, and keep the "Googlers" (the term used by the company to refer to its employees) happy.

At Southwest Airlines, a number of mechanisms are used to help reinforce and make the company's values real to all employees. There is a Culture Committee with 120 members and a number of alumni. Each cultural ambassador (team member) serves a three-year term and works as a member of the team to communicate and find ways to reinforce the company's culture. The company's blog frequently presents a description of this committee's activities. In addition, the company's website, written publications, and facilities (including the airplanes) all include statements of the company's values, whether presentation of the written values statement, recognition of the "Star of the Month" (in the company's *Spirit* magazine), or the heart that is present on every employee's shirt.

Implicit Cultural Messages

Sometimes you are literally surrounded by cultural symbols or icons of the organization, reflecting the company's identity but not containing an explicit message. For example, walking the halls at the Disney offices in Burbank or Glendale, California, you see the Disney characters (Mickey and Minnie, Goofy, Donald Duck, and all their compatriots) everywhere—as stuffed animals, in glass and plastic replicas, in pictures, and on posters. Similarly, the hallways of *Architectural Digest* are lined with framed covers from issues of the magazine. The halls of Pardee Homes, headquartered in Los Angles, are adorned with pictures of the houses and communities developed by the company. The offices of many investment bankers or venture capital firms in Silicon Valley contain various symbols of companies that were taken public. The boardroom of Citation Corporation, headquartered in Birmingham, Alabama, has framed pictures of people working in the foundries located throughout the United States. All of these are reminders of a company's business identity.

Cryptic Cultural Messages

Cultural messages may also be clearly visible, but subtler in meaning. Many U.S. company boardrooms boast art or statuary—expensive symbols of the stature of the company. However, in the boardroom of Melvin Simon & Associates (now Simon Properties), the largest shopping center (mall) developer in the country, there was displayed a picture of an old man and an old woman.[16] It was not artwork, but more like a family portrait, something one would see in a home rather than a boardroom. In fact, it was a picture of the parents of the founders and leaders of the company (Mel, Herb, and Fred Simon). The message, if somewhat cryptic, was a strong, implicit culture (values) statement: We are the Simons. We know who we are; and we assume you know who we are. We value family and where we came from; and we do not need to try to impress you. Needless to say, we were impressed by this message.

A "Cultureless Culture"

Although culture is everywhere and in everything, in some companies there are few clues about what the culture is: no culture statement, no pictures pertaining to the history of the business, no hint of what line of business the company is in. This is characteristic of a company whose culture is ill-defined (almost a "nonculture culture"), one devoid of obvious cultural symbols. This usually occurs by happenstance, rather than design. It is a marker of a company that does not recognize the importance of culture to people, whether to members of the organization or to those with whom they do business.

But the notion of a "cultureless" company is an illusion. Just as an individual must have a personality, a company must have a culture, even though it *appears not to exist. A company that appears cultureless is actually a company with a weak or ill-defined culture.* Nevertheless, we are using the term *cultureless* to characterize a special kind of organization that *seems* devoid of culture.

A Typology of Culture

All companies can be viewed as belonging to a few classic cultural types. Some have murky cultures, which are ill-defined and not clear to observers or employees. Others have well-defined cultures with specific statements of core values that all employees embrace and live by. This section provides a brief typology based on two key variables that can be used to classify culture: *cultural strength* and *cultural functionality.* Cultural strength refers to whether a culture is strong or weak (as explained below). Cultural functionality refers to whether a culture is functional or dysfunctional.

Strong and Weak Cultures

Companies differ in the extent to which they are effective in defining, communicating, and managing their culture. Companies where there is a clearly defined culture, where time is invested in communicating and reinforcing this culture, and where all employees are behaving in ways consistent with this culture are defined as having a strong culture.[17] Simply having a values statement is not enough to have a strong culture; the values need to be communicated in both words and actions, and they need to be reinforced. A strong culture is one that people clearly understand and can articulate.[18] A weak culture is one that employees have difficulty defining, understanding, or explaining. The culture may not have been defined, or it is not being actively managed. As a result, employees are left to interpret the company's values for themselves, which sometimes results in the company having not one but many cultures.

Cultural Functionality

Strong company cultures can be positive (an asset) or negative (a liability). If the company's values are constructive and support its goals, then having a strong culture is an asset. We define this as a functional culture. If the company's values are negative or dysfunctional, then having a strong culture will be a liability.

The culture at Ford Motor Company in the late 1960s and 1970s is a good illustration of a dysfunctional culture. The informal culture at Ford during the late 1960s and early 1970s was captured in a statement often made among employees: "If you can get it to drive out the door, we can sell it!" This was not a formal corporate pronouncement, of course, but a statement prevalent in conversations around the company. It contained an implicit disrespect for the customer and suggested that working to achieve high quality products was not important. The lack of focus on quality and reliability was also reflected in how customers talked about the company. Many customers said Ford stands for "Fix or Repair Daily." Ford later made the pronouncement that "Quality is Job One"—a clear response to the damage that had been done to its brand. Unfortunately, it took some time to overcome the perception of poor quality in customers' minds. This is an example of a strong dysfunctional culture in action.

In contrast, the Four Seasons Hotel chain is a good example of a strong, functional culture with respect to customer service. The Four Seasons trains its employees to stop what they are doing and escort "guests" to their desired destination whenever the latter ask for directions to someplace in the hotel, such as a ballroom, meeting room, or restaurant. Employees live the culture of customer service, and customers see it in action.

A culture can also be weak and functional, or weak and dysfunctional. In companies with weak functional cultures, employees behave in a way that supports achievement of company goals, but there is no overall understanding of the company's true personality because the culture is not being actively managed. Employees may understand that the customer is important, but they may have quite different interpretations of how to treat the customer. To overcome this problem, people must be trained or told how to treat customers under various situations. Dave Gold, the founder and now chairman of 99 Cents Only Stores (a NYSE-listed company with more than 250 stores and $1.5 billion in revenues), emphasizes to "99ers" that when they need to give a refund to a customer "it should be done with a smile and not a frown."

In companies with weak dysfunctional cultures, there is no consistent understanding of what the culture is, and employees' behavior significantly detracts from the company's overall effectiveness and ability to achieve its goals. Even though U.S. automakers such as Ford are trying to reestablish their reputation for quality, one of the authors who owned a Jaguar automobile at the time heard a service person at the car dealership refer to the car with a smirk as a "Jagataurus," a reference to the fact that the Jaguar was built on the platform for a Ford Taurus. This was an expensive car, and it was being demeaned (degraded) by an employee of the dealership that sold it. We are sure that neither the Jaguar dealership in Los Angeles nor Ford Motor would be pleased at this employee's comment, which denoted disrespect for the car, and probably also for the buyer.[19] We also believe that it is unlikely that either Ford or the dealership had engaged in culture management training to ensure that employees would avoid making such damaging comments.

Culture Typology Matrix

The two factors of strength and functionality can be brought together to create a culture typology matrix. This tool can be used to identify the type of culture present in a company, with the "best" type of culture being strong and functional. A sample culture typology matrix, with companies of each type, is shown in Exhibit 1.1.

	Functional	Disfunctional
Strong	Starbucks GE Southwest Airlines	Ford GM PowerBar
Weak	Amgen Toyota	A19 Kodak

Exhibit 1.1. Culture typology matrix.

Real vs. "Nominal" Cultures

What is presented in a values or culture statement is not necessarily what the real culture is within a company. We refer to formal statements of a company's culture as the "nominal" or "stated" culture. This is, in brief, what a company wants its culture to be. The real culture, by contrast, consists of the values, beliefs, and norms that actually influence employee behavior. A company can state that it values treating all employees as "assets" but then fail to invest in their development. Similarly, a company can talk about its most important assets as being its people, but then treat them poorly. These are examples of lack of alignment between the nominal (stated) and real cultures. Another company—like Southwest Airlines—might have an explicit statement of the value placed on meeting customer needs that is very much a reality for all of its employees. This value is reinforced through, among other things, constant communication with and feedback to employees, standards of performance relative to customer service, and recognition of those employees who achieve outstanding results in terms of meeting customer needs.

Why Is Culture Important?

As we shall explain in detail below, culture is not only manifested throughout virtually everything in an organization; it is of critical importance to all organizations. We believe that, if managed correctly, *culture might well be the ultimate strategic asset and competitive weapon for most companies.*

At the most fundamental level, culture is thought to be important because it is hypothesized to have an impact on organizational performance. The basic paradigm underlying the notion that culture affects performance is based on a few key ideas. The first is that culture affects goal attainment. More specifically, companies with strong cultures are more likely to achieve their goals than those with relatively weak cultures. So-called strong-culture organizations are thought to have a higher degree of organizational success (measured in market value or other financial measures of performance) because of a believed link to motivation. As stated by John Kotter and James Heskett, strong cultures are often said to help business performance because they create an unusual level of motivation in employees.[20]

There are, in fact, several specific reasons corporate culture is of vital importance in an organization:

- Culture does influence organizational success.
- Culture is a strategic asset (a source of competitive advantage), and it can even be the ultimate source of sustainable competitive advantage.
- Culture functions as "organizational glue," especially in siloed organizations.
- Culture affects financial performance.
- Culture is a driver or strategic building block of organizational success.
- Culture influences the success of people in organizations.
- Culture is a more important factor than "strategic fit" in mergers and acquisitions.

We shall examine each of these aspects of the importance of culture in turn, below.

Culture and Organizational Success

An increasing number of highly successful organizations have, at least in part, attributed their success to effective culture management. Among them are Starbucks Coffee, Google, and Walmart, to cite just three.[21]

Starbucks Coffee Company

Starbucks Coffee has grown from just two retail stores in Seattle to more than twenty-five hundred stores worldwide. Starbucks has accomplished this with a commodity product that has been around for quite some time: coffee.

Starbucks views culture as a critical factor in the organization's success.[22] Specifically, the company's paradigm is that "the way we treat our people affects the way our people treat our customers, and, in turn, our success, which includes financial performance." This belief has led the company to a number of human resource practices that are designed to enhance people's feeling of being valued by the company. Two examples are widespread use of stock options and the practice of offering full benefits to all employees who work more than twenty hours per week.

Howard Behar, former executive vice president of operations for Starbucks and president of Starbucks International, has stated very clearly in his book about the company that its success is not about the coffee![23] According to Behar (whose book is, in fact, entitled *It's Not the Coffee!*), the company's success is based on the leadership and culture of Starbucks. Similarly, Howard Schultz, the founder, chairman, and CEO of Starbucks, has stated that much of the company's success is attributable to culture. When asked about the secret to Starbucks' success, Schultz has said: "When people ask me about the reasons for Starbucks success, I tell them not what they expect to hear. I tell them that it was the people at Starbucks and the way we managed them that was the true differentiating factor."[24]

Google

Google has become the undisputed leader in the Internet space through its search engine technology. However, a key to the continuous development of that technology is the talent and creativity of its people, which in turn is influenced by the company's culture. As a result of its special culture, Google has become recognized as one of the best companies to work for, and this attracts talent—a truly virtuous circle.

Early in Google's history, Brin and Page recognized the importance of corporate culture. They instilled a trio of distinctive core values:

1. Don't be evil.
2. Technology matters.
3. We make our own rules.

Though stated provocatively, the first value refers to integrity and fair treatment of customers. As "Google's Statement of Philosophy" indicates, "We never manipulate rankings to put our (advertising or content) partners higher in our search results. No one can buy better PageRank. Our users trust Google's objectivity, and no short-term gain could ever justify breaking that trust."[25] The second value, concerning technology, is self-explanatory. The third value, about Google making its own rules, refers to various unorthodox practices. For example, Google auctioned its IPO shares rather than the traditional approach of allocating them on the basis of an underwriter's discretion. The company also refused to furnish earnings guidance to Wall Street, which, though not a unique practice, was not common.

In part, these values seemed to be related to the personalities of the founders, Page and Brin, who were not traditional corporate types but rather more like Silicon Valley entrepreneurial types in the tradition of Jerry Yang of Yahoo! and Pierre Omidyar of eBay. In part, Google's stated values also seemed to be an attempt to create the antithesis of the then-dominant player in software, Microsoft, which some wags termed "the evil empire" and which (in spite of its dominant market position) was not known for excellence in its technology. Page and Brin seemed to be creating the culture of a company that might be termed the "anti-Microsoft." In fact, Google has been able to attract talent because of its culture and some of this talent has come from former members of Microsoft.

To reinforce their commitment to culture, Page and Brin (as noted above) created the position of chief culture officer at Google. The mission of this position is to retain the company's culture as it grows and to keep the Googlers happy. The intent of this is to increase the likelihood that the company's culture remains a strategic advantage for Google.

Walmart

In his book *The Wal-Mart Way*, Soderquist attributes the company's success to its culture, which is labeled "the Wal-Mart Way."[26] As he states it, "The Wal-Mart Way is not about stores, clubs, distribution centers, trucks, or computers. These tangible assets are all crucial ingredients in the company's business plan, but the real story of success is about people." It is about how Walmart treats its people and customers. This is what makes up the culture or core values of Walmart.

The culture of Walmart consists of three key values, captured in these statements:

- We treat everyone with respect and dignity.
- We are in business to satisfy our customers.
- We strive for excellence in all that we do.[27]

These values are the cultural foundation of Walmart.[28] On the surface, they are relatively simple concepts or precepts. They are things that could have been (and sometimes are) stated by other companies as well. However, they have been the springboard for an unbelievable success story: in 2009, Walmart became the largest company in the world, with $408 billion in revenue.

Walmart vs. K-Mart: Financial Performance

To demonstrate the power of culture as a factor in success, compare the performance of Walmart with the company that (at least on the surface) is its "identical" competitor, K-Mart. There is virtually no product that Walmart has that K-Mart does not have. They sell the same things: Johnson's Baby Powder, Allegan lens solution, Colgate toothpaste, etc. They both have the same kinds of stores, and they operate in similar locations. They market to the same customers. They recruit employees from the same pool of people. Yet in spite of these similarities, one of them (Walmart) has produced vastly different financial results for investors from the other.

As seen in Exhibits 1.2 and 1.3, if we examine the financial return to investors measured in terms of stock price, Walmart and K-Mart have highly contrasting results. For the decade of the 1990s, the stock price of K-Mart almost doubled. An original investment of $10,000 would have been worth almost $20,000 by 1999. Not a bad return, but less than what might be expected. During the same period, an investment in Walmart of $10,000 in 1990 would have grown, by the end of the decade, to approximately $280,000! This is an astounding difference, especially because these companies are not like Microsoft or Amgen, with their proprietary intellectual property. Walmart and K-Mart are selling essentially the same commodities, but with vastly divergent results.

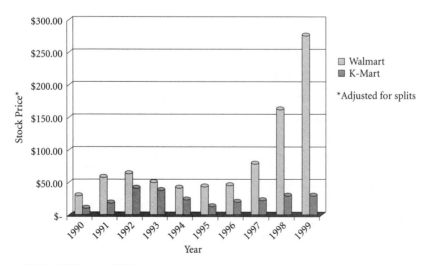

Exhibit 1.2. Walmart vs. K-Mart, 1990s.

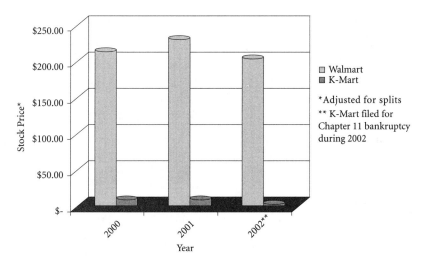

Exhibit 1.3. Walmart vs. K-Mart, 2000–2003.

If we carry our analysis a little further, the results are even more dramatic. By the end of 2003, K-Mart had gone bankrupt. An investor would have lost the entire investment. Walmart's stock price did decline as a result of the market collapse from 1999 to 2003, but the original investment of $10,000 would still have been worth just under $200,000.

What accounts for these differences? We believe, as suggested by Soderquist, that they are attributable to the two companies' corporate cultures. This is not to suggest that Walmart is a perfect company, or even a model one. There have been numerous criticisms and lawsuits against Walmart.[29] Nevertheless, from an economic standpoint of organizational success, Walmart is clearly the superior organization, the victor versus K-Mart, and the dominant player in its market space.

Culture as a Strategic Asset

Another implication of this analysis of Walmart and K-Mart is that culture is a true strategic asset, a source of competitive advantage.[30] Most of the areas in which organizations compete can be copied or neutralized by competition. Products can be imitated or improved on. Financial resources are fungible, and most companies have capable people. However, corporate culture is not easily replicated. Even when one company knows the culture of another, it is virtually impossible to copy or replicate it.

A company's culture—if well managed—is transmitted to generations of employees through the company's "DNA," thus perpetuating this source of competitive advantage. Although it is possible to clone sheep, it is not simple to do. Similarly, it is not simple to clone companies—especially with respect to culture. Corporate culture is, then, not just a source of competitive advantage; it might actually be the *ultimate* source of true, sustainable competitive advantage. This is because of the extreme difficulties of replicating culture across organizations. In addition, the fact that it is relatively invisible to observers makes it function as a stealth competitive weapon.

All of this makes culture a powerful and invaluable strategic asset. This has led some companies, such as Starbucks, Southwest Airlines, and Walmart, to view culture as a core component of their overall business strategy.

Cultural DNA

The culture of a company is derived from its founder or founders. The personal and professional values of the founder(s) are the DNA of the culture of the company during its initial stages. If the founder is a perfectionist, then the performance standards for the company will be all about perfection. If the founder is hypercritical, then the culture will take on a critical character. If the founder is all about customer service or frugality, then the culture will be all about those same things. If the founder has a sense of humor and wants to have fun, then the culture will reflect this—as is the case at Southwest Airlines, where fun is still very much a part of the company's culture, even though one of the founders who gave life to this aspect of culture is now retired.

This culture will be transmitted by the personal, day-to-day interaction of people with the entrepreneur or founding group. As the entrepreneur makes decisions and takes actions, his or her values are communicated in behavioral terms. People will simply tend to mimic the founder(s). During the early stages of growth, culture can be, and typically is, managed by informal methods, principally personal leadership.

The management of corporate culture at Talent International College by Ms. Zhenmei Hou is a good illustration of this approach. Talent International College was founded by Hou in 2005. The company's headquarters are located in Guangxi, China. It also operates other auxiliary privately run high schools and employment centers in cities such as Nanjing, Shanghai, and Weifang. Talent International College is one of the fastest-growing and most successful higher education institutions in the Guangxi region, offering students a range of diploma majors that suit their needs. It is one of a new breed of dynamic international institutions in China focused on offering specialist diploma courses to meet the demands of employers in the twenty-first century.

For a number of years, the college has been undergoing changes that include improving the campus and construction of well-designed accommodations and classrooms, transforming it into a lively and harmonious learning institution. The company has around 6,500 students living on campus and employs more than 350 teachers and staff. During 2009, total revenues exceeded 65 million RMB. Hou is acutely aware of the importance of culture and places college culture at the top of the list of priorities for daily running of the institution.

At this stage of its development, Talent International College has no defined formal statement of corporate culture. Hou describes the college culture as awareness on the part of teachers of what the college's mission and goals are. She also describes it as a "family-oriented culture." Hou is aware of the importance of traditional Chinese culture in educational institutes. However, she believes that gearing her company toward a more family-oriented relationship with students and staff gives rise to new types of key decision making and management practices that increase production of well-trained and well-motivated students. Hou wants the culture to be very participative, with her senior managers involved in all key decisions.

Hou manages the culture of the company by example, and she communicates this method to her teachers as well. She believes teachers should act as role models for the students by setting examples of how to be good citizens, passing on not only teaching knowledge but also life skills by way of manners, values, attitudes, and skills, with a particular emphasis on those skills that relate to critical thinking and problem solving, self-management, and communication. Teachers are obliged to prepare and deliver good lessons daily, thus maintaining high motivation among the students and aiding their continued development. In addition to this approach, teachers should also be actively engaged with students in a range of extracurricular activities on and off campus, serving the community. Hou believes that a family-oriented relationship is generated in the college for all teachers and students using this cultural management method.

For the moment and at the present stage of growth and size of the college, Hou's current methods for managing culture are working well. But she is aware that as the company grows she will need to take additional steps to further define and manage the company's culture. This need to focus on culture management will be faced by all companies.

As a company grows and adds more people, most employees will no longer have daily direct contact with the founder or other members of senior leadership. In fact, direct contact with senior leadership will probably become rare. This means the company will have to develop new methods to transmit and reinforce its culture as a way of retaining the competitive advantage that it provides.

Culture as Organizational Glue

Another key reason culture is important is that it functions as "organizational glue"; it helps people come together with common purpose and values. This is particularly important in siloed organizations, where people tend to work in their own functional or divisional areas without significant interaction with others. It is also especially important in large and geographically dispersed organizations. A strong, well-managed culture helps create a sense of team throughout a company—a feeling that "we are all in this together, that we are all a part of something special, and that each of us is a contributor to the company's success."

Culture as a Driver of Financial Performance (the Bottom Line)

Culture is vitally important to a company because it has been shown to have a direct, statistically significant impact on the bottom line of corporate financial performance.

Research by Kotter and Heskett

John Kotter and James Heskett produced some of the first empirical evidence of a statistically significant relationship between culture and financial performance.[31] Their intent was to test the prevailing assumption of a link between strong cultures and superior financial performance. In their cross-sectional research study, they selected 207 firms from 22 U.S. industries.[32] Using a survey, they constructed "culture strengths" indices. They then calculated measures of economic performance for their sample of companies: average yearly increase in (1) net income, (2) return on investment, and (3) stock price. Then they examined the relationship between the performance measures and the culture strength measure. They found a positive correlation between corporate culture strength and long-term economic performance: "Within the limits of methodology, we conclude from this study that there is a positive relationship between strength of corporate culture and long-term economic performance."[33]

Research by Flamholtz

In another empirical research study, Flamholtz found that culture can account for as much as 46 percent of EBIT (earnings before interest and taxes).[34] The intent of his study was to determine whether corporate culture has a significant impact on financial performance.[35] The study by Flamholtz differed from the prior research by Kotter and Heskett in that it used data from a *single* company with eighteen operating divisions, as opposed to cross-sectional data. This research is described in a technical appendix to Chapter 2.[36]

Culture as a Strategic Building Block of Organizations

In addition to the relationship between culture and financial performance, culture also has come to be viewed as a component of organizational effectiveness or success models. It is theorized that the role of culture, as part of a six-factor framework, explains organizational effectiveness and, as a consequence, financial performance.[37] This is shown schematically in Exhibit 1.4.

Specifically, culture is viewed as a critical organizational development area, or key strategic building block, of successful organizations. This framework is well supported by empirical research.[38]

Culture and the Success of People in Organizations

Even if an individual possesses the capabilities needed to fill a specific position within a company, he or she may be a better fit in one type of organization than in another, as a result of culture. It is not uncommon for people to be successful or unsuccessful in an organization simply as a result of its culture. For example, Carly Fiorina did not fit with the culture at Hewlett-

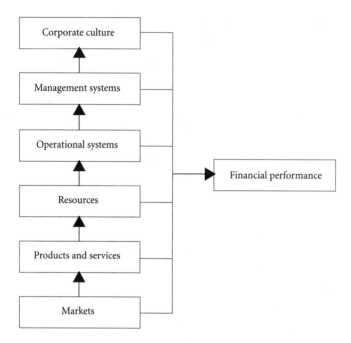

Exhibit 1.4. Strategic building blocks of organizations and drivers of financial performance.

Packard. She was the CEO and tried to change the culture, but the company ultimately rejected her and she lost her job. Similarly, Richard Belluzzo, a veteran of Silicon Valley stalwarts Silicon Graphics and Hewlett-Packard, had a relatively short tenure at Microsoft. As it is explained by insiders, he failed to embrace the distinctive culture at Microsoft—a "shortcoming" that ultimately led to his ouster.

Culture as a Determinant of Success in Mergers and Acquisitions

Culture is increasingly recognized as a more important factor in the success of mergers and acquisitions than "strategic fit." Unfortunately, the organizational landscape is littered with unsuccessful mergers and acquisitions caused by lack of cultural fit. Some are merely less successful than original expectations, while others are deemed failures. For example, the mega merger between America Online and Time Warner (now Time Warner) was seen as a colossal failure attributable to the difference in culture between a Silicon Valley company and a traditional entertainment and publishing company to be found in New York or Hollywood.

It is speculated that culture clash is the reason Jerry Yang and the board of Yahoo! resisted acquisition by Microsoft in 2008. Merging with the enemy is almost unthinkable, a fate worse than organizational death for some in Silicon Valley.

Culture as a Liability

Although in the technical accounting sense corporate culture cannot be a *liability*, we are using the term in its colloquial sense of a limitation or handicap. In this sense, culture can indeed be a true liability. Just as some companies have strong positive cultures, others have weak or dysfunctional cultures.

Eastman Kodak—once a proud and highly successful company—had serious cultural problems that contributed to its economic decline. Specifically, there was a culture of "avoiding hasty action." This led to inability to move quickly and innovate. Kodak watched as competitors developed instant photography, the 35mm camera, and VCRs. Ultimately, this very conservative and risk-averse culture caused Kodak to need to downsize significantly, after decades of never having layoffs.

Another example of how culture can be a liability is IBM. At its peak, it was a very rich and powerful company. Throughout its history, IBM was willing to bet the company on anticipated changes in the market. But in the mid-1980s this cultural trait was lost. Even though IBM had done environmental scans and understood that companies were moving away from mainframes to distributed computing requiring mini and micro computers, it was unable to make the transition organizationally. It required that an outsider, Louis Gerstner—whose background in chips was at Nabisco, with potato chips and not silicon wafers—come in and shake up IBM to force the needed changes.[39]

The 1 Percent Difference Principle of Culture Management

Another aspect of the problem of corporate culture management is that small differences in culture often result in significant differences in results and performance. Although it often seems that many companies have essentially the same culture, as represented in formal statements of company values, there are sometimes vast differences in the financial performance of culturally similar companies, even when everything else appears to be the same. For example, Starbucks Coffee and the Coffee Bean and Tea Leaf have relatively similar statements of cultural principles about the importance of treating people well, but they have vastly different economic performance. The explanation can sometimes be found in minute differences in cultural DNA.

Genetic research has determined that humans and chimpanzees share about 99 percent of their DNA.[40] Although 1 percent might seem to be a miniscule difference, it is actually quite significant in terms of the abilities of the species. For example, the late Brian Maxwell, founder of PowerBar, was a world-class marathon runner. He told the authors (who were working with him at PowerBar as consultants) that he used to spend a year in training in order to improve his performance by 1 percent. When he found that additional training would not enhance his performance further, he turned to nutrition as a source of competitive advantage. This ultimately led to his development of PowerBar, a nutritional food bar.

The 1 Percent Difference in Cultural DNA

This concept, in turn, led us to formulate the "1 percent difference principle" of culture management. Specifically, small differences in cultural DNA in organizations can actually lead to significant differences in corporate performance. Thus, even though two companies might state in their cultural principles that "people are our most important asset," there can be subtle but significant differences in how this is operationalized, which leads to significantly different results in how people feel about membership in an organization and their performance in it.

Conclusion

This chapter has examined the nature and importance of the elusive concept of corporate culture. We have shown that culture is a critical, if invisible, variable in many aspects of organizational performance, ranging from competitive success to mergers and acquisitions.

The difference in cultural DNA found in organizations can be attributed to small but significant differences in the culture management process—that is, the processes of managing an organization's culture. In the next two chapters, we offer a framework for the management of corporate culture. We show how culture management can be a critical component of creating competitive advantage.

2 Culture Management Foundations

Many companies talk about their culture and might even emphasize its importance, but they do not actually manage it in a systematic way. In some cases, there may not even be a statement about the actual or ideal core values of their culture. To convert the notion of culture from an interesting but somewhat abstract construct, we need a theoretically sound yet practical framework to guide managerial action. This chapter is the first of two designed to present such a framework.

In Chapter 2, we (1) define corporate culture operationally (so that it is susceptible to management rather than just an abstract concept), (2) identify the key dimensions of corporate culture, (3) examine how to identify a culture, and (4) present a method to measure corporate culture. A case study illustrates how organizations can use these culture measurement methods as practical tools. A technical appendix summarizes research using the measurement methods described and shows that culture has an impact on financial performance.

A Formal (Operational) Definition of "Corporate Culture"

In Chapter 1, we stated that the central notion of the concept of corporate culture relates to core organizational values.[1] This is correct, but somewhat vague. A more formal operational definition is needed to serve as the basis for understanding the concept and developing strategies for managing it.

Corporate culture consists of values, beliefs and norms that influence the thoughts and actions (behavior) of people in organizations. Values identify what an organization considers to be most important with respect to its operations, employees and customers. They define what an organization holds most dear—the things it strives for and wants to protect at all costs. As described in the first chapter, for example, a value at Google is that "technology matters."

Beliefs are assumptions individuals hold about themselves, their customers, and their organization. Starbucks believes that how the company treats employees will influence how employees treat customers.

Norms are behavioral practices—typically unwritten rules of behavior—that address issues such as how employees dress and interact. Norms help operationalize actions consistent with values and beliefs. At some companies, a norm is to address everyone by his or her first name, regardless of position. At other companies, the norm might be that those in senior management positions are addressed more formally (Mr., Ms., Dr., etc.). Although there are alternative conceptions of culture, we have found this typology to be useful in working with organizations.[2]

Corporate culture is, in essence, a guide to behavior as well as a mechanism for creating expectations with respect to rewards and action. We clarify this definition of culture through specific examples.

Illustration of Values, Beliefs and Norms: Ritz-Carlton Hotels

The Ritz-Carlton hotel chain offers a good illustration of values, beliefs, and norms (see Exhibit 2.1). The Values Statement focuses on the customer and the customer experience.[3] The Beliefs Statement prescribes a way of thinking about the people interacting with the customer.[4] The Norms Statement suggests specific modes of behavior that are based on the values and beliefs statements.[5]

Ritz-Carlton has clearly articulated its values and beliefs and translated them into specific norms of behavior. This example illustrates the nature of our definition of culture in concrete terms.

Core Values of Li Ning

Li Ning, a company headquartered in Beijing, offers another example of culture values. The company is named for Li Ning, the well-known gym-

---

Ritz-Carlton Values

- The Ritz-Carlton Hotel is a place where the genuine care and comfort of our guests is our highest mission.

- We pledge to provide the finest personal service and facilities for our guests, who will always enjoy a warm, relaxed, yet refined ambience.

- The Ritz-Carlton experience enlivens the senses, instills well-being, and fulfills even the unexpressed wishes and needs of our guests.

Ritz-Carlton Beliefs

We are Ladies and Gentlemen

Serving

Ladies and Gentlemen

Ritz-Carlton Norms

- A warm and sincere greeting. Use the guest's name, if and when possible.

- Anticipation of and compliance with guest needs.

- Fond farewell. Give them a warm good-bye, and use their names, if and when possible.

Exhibit 2.1. Ritz-Carlton values, beliefs, and norms.

nast and entrepreneur who won six medals (three gold, two silver, and a bronze) in the 1984 Summer Olympics held in Los Angeles. Known in China as "the Prince of Gymnastics," Li Ning ignited the cauldron with the Olympic flame at the opening ceremonies of the 2008 Summer Olympics.

Li retired from sporting competition in 1988 and in 1990 founded Li-Ning, a company selling footwear and sporting apparel in China. He remains chairman of the company's board of directors.

The core values, according to the company's website,[6] are:

Live for Dream

Integrity and Commitment

We Culture

Achieving Excellence

Consumer-Oriented

Breakthrough

The Key Dimensions of Corporate Culture

When most companies create a statement of cultural values, they consider what is important to them. On the surface, this approach seems reasonable, but it doesn't ensure that the company is dealing with all key aspects of culture needing to be addressed for optimal organizational performance. For example, the core values of the Walt Disney Company (as seen on its website) are "innovation, quality, community, storytelling, optimism, and decency."[7] These are clearly what was important to the founder, Walt Disney. They include some elements that are idiosyncratic and of particular importance to the Walt Disney Company but are not of general importance to all organizations (such as storytelling and optimism).[8]

From our original research and experience in working with companies, we have identified certain key aspects of culture that have a statistically significant relationship to financial performance.[9] We believe that although many aspects are important, there are *five key or critical dimensions of corporate culture that must be defined* in order to have a strong positive impact on organizational effectiveness and performance. Failure to explicitly include all of them could lead to something being overlooked or neglected. If something is not in people's mind-set, they are likely not to pay attention to it.

The five critical areas or key dimensions of culture identified by our empirical research are (1) customer orientation, (2) orientation toward employees, (3) standards of performance and accountability, (4) innovation and commitment to change, and (5) company process orientation.[10] Each dimension—included in what we term the "five-factor approach to cultural definition"—is described briefly below.[11]

Customer-Client Orientation

The first key aspect of corporate culture is how a company views its customers or clients. Some companies view customers as a valued asset, while others view them as a nuisance, or worse.

How the company views customers or clients will influence how its people (employees) treat customers and clients, and this in turn can have a profound impact on its success.

Some companies are effective in developing and communicating to their employees their values with respect to customers. The Walt Disney Company is a master at this practice. For example, employees at Disney Theme Parks refer to customers as "guests." The word was chosen carefully to send a message to Disney employees about the company's customer orientation. It is intended to influence how employees interact with customers, and in fact employees are trained to make customers feel "at home." The ultimate goal is customer satisfaction, with the hope of encouraging customers to return to the park in the future.

Southwest Airlines is another company that has, throughout its history, effectively managed its culture with respect to treatment of customers. The culture promotes having fun and was built on "Luv" (a play on the name of the airfield where the company was born). Customers who fly this airline, which offers no-frills, low-cost travel, experience the caring firsthand, from check-in to baggage claim. Flight attendants have been known to play games in flight (such as finding out who has the most pennies) and to sing songs. Southwest has also won the airline industry's highest award for customer satisfaction many times and was, until late 2009, consistently and highly profitable.

It is unlikely that *any* company would explicitly state that customers are not valued, but there are companies in which the real culture is exactly that way. In one large multibillion-dollar manufacturing company, customers had, for a number of years, expressed dissatisfaction with the product and offered a great deal of input on what could be done to better meet their needs. When presented with this information, the product development and manufacturing functions basically responded (more through action than through words): "We don't care what they say. We know what they need. If we build it, they will buy it." Customers were frustrated by the lack of response to their needs and began purchasing from the competition. It was only after the company lost significant market share (and declined in revenue and profit) that it began to change its culture.

People (Employee) Orientation

The second critical cultural dimension is how people (employees) are viewed. Companies can view people as assets or as expenses, as the key to their success or as warm bodies that are easily replaceable. A key aspect of a company's orientation to people is the extent to which its employees feel important and valued. The basic notion is that if people feel valued and appreciated, they will be motivated and committed to the company and its objectives. Some companies devote a great deal of effort to satisfying employee needs and making them feel valued. In Chapter 1, we discussed the focus on employees at Starbucks.

Another example is Southwest Airlines, a company that has very low turnover and high employee satisfaction compared to the competition (and to many companies in other industries). These results are achieved, at least in part, through effective management of the people orientation dimension of culture. Southwest has sophisticated hiring practices intended to attract people who will fit in and help promote the Southwest culture. There are many mechanisms through which employees can voice their concerns, and they know that these concerns will be listened and responded to promptly. Finally, Southwest employees have a stake in the company's success because they are in fact shareholders.

It is easy to identify companies such as Southwest where people are valued, but it is just as easy to identify organizations having problems with their orientation toward employees because they usually experience high turnover. Conversely, organizations successful at making employees feel valued (by whatever means) tend to experience relatively low turnover. (We do not wish to imply that employee orientation is the *only* cause of turnover, but it is often a significant one.) In one $100 million company, employees expressed a high level of fear about the future and felt that anyone below senior management was a second-class citizen. Turnover was rampant, not only among the lower levels of the company but also among the executive team.

Performance Standards and Accountability

The third dimension of culture contains two related aspects: performance standards and accountability.

Performance Standards

Performance standards include what and how much employees are held accountable for, the level of quality expected in products, and the expected level of customer satisfaction. If an organization has high performance standards embedded in its culture, there can be a profound impact on people's behavior. For example, one of the authors had a recent experience with the service department of his Lexus dealership. Bringing his car in to be serviced, he gave the service representative a warranty notice from Toyota Motor and asked whether it was a serious issue. The service representative replied, "No, it's not serious; but you know the Japanese. They want everything to be perfect." That communicated the ultimate in performance standards! Contrast this with the attitude reflected in the example of the culture at Ford in the late 1960s and early 1970s, cited in Chapter 1: "If you can get it to drive out the door, we can sell it!" Unfortunately, this attitude was prevalent not just at Ford but at all of the U.S. car manufacturers.[12]

Accountability

In some companies, employees believe they are held accountable only for coming to work on time. In others, they are accountable for achieving goals that assist the organization in meeting its mission. Sometimes the definition of accountability can be distorted, as was the case in one $35 million high-technology manufacturer that traditionally had placed high value on "commitment." Over time, employees came to believe that commitment meant spending eight or nine hours a day at work, regardless of what they were actually doing during that period. The norm was to come to work early and never leave the office before 5:00 (if possible staying until 5:30) as a way of showing commitment. Although the company had many employees "working," it was having difficulty meeting goals because employees were focused on an inappropriate standard of performance.

At some companies, all managers are held accountable not only for achieving goals but also for behaving consistently with the company's values. One firm created "mirror" meetings to give managers feedback on the extent to which they are behaving consistently with stated values. In Chapter 6, we describe how another company, Smartmatic, embeds its values in the performance evaluation process for *all* employees.

Commitment to Change and Innovation

The fourth major cultural element relates to how a company views, embraces, and reacts to change and innovation. Briefly, change relates to the notion of making something different in some particular way. The "something" can be virtually anything in the organization. Innovation is a special type of change. As used here, innovation refers to the act of creating differences in products or operations in an attempt to foster competitive advantage.

Some organizations embrace innovation as a core strategy. In Chapter 7, we describe how Smartmatic embraces innovation as a core strategy and way of life. Employees are constantly looking for ways to improve products, services, and overall operations. In addition, they are recognized and rewarded for their efforts. In other companies, innovation is at best an afterthought. They tend to want to be followers, rather than innovators, and in some cases their culture is marked by the notion that the "pioneers are people with arrows in their back."

There can be a tremendous financial payoff to a company using innovation as a core strategy and key cultural component. For example, on May 27, 2010, one-time underdog Apple surpassed Microsoft to become the world's most valuable technology company as measured by stock market value.[13] Clearly stock market values fluctuate, but this event was trumpeted as evidence that Apple's culture of innovation was superior to Microsoft's culture of copying their competitors.[14]

Similarly, some organizations embrace change. Toyota, as we shall see in Chapter 7, views change as part of the "Toyota Way." In other companies, there is resistance to change to the point where people suggesting change are viewed as a threat. There is also this perception (sometimes actually verbalized): "Why should we change? We've always done it this way, and it's worked." Unfortunately, unwillingness to change can lead to decline. As described in Chapter 9, this is what happened at IBM in the 1980s.

Our research suggests that change and innovation are explicit dimensions of a culture. Companies embracing these aspects of culture are more likely to be successful both in the short run and the long run.

Company Process Orientation

The final dimension of culture focuses on the view people hold of specific aspects regarding how the company operates. Some of the processes around which culture needs to be defined are planning, decision making, communication, and corporate citizenship (or social responsibility). How the culture is defined with respect to these processes directly affects how these systems actually work.

How this dimension of culture is and should be defined depends on the company's size, structure, growth strategy, and other factors. For example, with respect to the planning process the culture will (and should) differ in a small, entrepreneurial company from what it is for a member of the Fortune 500. The belief that "the CEO will make most significant decisions" in a small company seems to make sense, but adopting this same belief in a large company can result in untimely and ineffective decisions. Regardless of how the formal communication system is supposed to operate, if the belief is that information is power then people will tend to hoard, as opposed to share important information; and the overall performance of the company will likely suffer.

If a company is large or high-profile (Walmart, Microsoft, Starbucks), then the culture must also define what *corporate citizenship* or *social responsibility* means. This aspect of the process orientation dimension can also be an important part of some smaller, entrepreneurial companies, as is described in Chapter 8.

The Five Key Corporate Culture Dimensions at Emergent BioSolutions

Emergent BioSolutions has a formal statement of company values that illustrates use of the five key factors approach to culture definition in action. Emergent is a biopharmaceutical company focused on developing, manufacturing and commercializing vaccines and therapeutics that assist the body's immune system in preventing or treating disease. The company's marketed product BioThrax (Anthrax Vaccine Adsorbed), is the only anti-anthrax vaccine licensed by the U.S. government.

Emergent is headquartered in Rockville, Maryland, and has operations in Gaithersburg, Maryland; Lansing, Michigan; Munich, Germany; and Reading in the United Kingdom. The company was assembled by means of acquisitions, such that each business unit and location presented its own challenges to creating a single unified company culture.

In 2009, Emergent launched a culture management initiative and engaged the authors' consulting firm to work with them. As part of this initiative, the company's Culture Project Team and Executive Management Committee applied the five-factor approach to develop a culture statement for Emergent. This statement, which illustrates application of this framework, is described below and summarized in Exhibit 2.2.

Emergent has five culture value statements, and each is identified by one word followed by a single-sentence definition. Each value statement includes a detailed definition—four or five bullets—intended to help all employees understand it. The company identifies the link between each of its value statements and the five dimensions of culture described above.

The Emergent Culture Value Statements are an excellent illustration of applying the five-factor approach to culture definition. The method of presentation is also an effective template for communicating the company's culture.

The Corporate Culture Map

We have developed a tool for defining and evaluating a company's culture in terms of the key components of culture (values, beliefs, and norms) and the five key cultural dimensions (customer orientation and so on). The "corporate culture map," shown schematically in Exhibit 2.3, can be used to summarize an organization's corporate culture and identify any gaps. Specifically, it shows whether the culture embraces all of the key dimensions: customer orientation, people orientation, and so forth. It can also help identify whether all of the components of culture (values, beliefs, norms) have been articulated.

To illustrate the culture map, we return to the Ritz-Carlton example presented earlier (see Exhibit 2.1). Using the culture map as a template, we see that the values statement and norms focus on the customer. This is one of the five key dimensions of culture. The Ritz-Carlton statement of beliefs, that "We are ladies and gentlemen serving ladies and gentlemen," is also

DEFINING WORD & CULTURAL DIMENSIONS	VALUE STATEMENTS	CLARIFYING COMMENTS
Respect Employee Orientation	**We respect each other.**	• We treat others as we want to be treated. • The knowledge, commitment and talents of our employees sets us apart. • Diversity is essential. • Consideration is shown for employee's time, commitments and work life balance
Commitment Customer-Client Orientation; Performance; Planning	**We deliver on our commitments.**	• Quality is a top priority. • We strive for excellence. • Commitments to our shareholders, partners, customers, employees and communities are fundamental to our success. • We achieve shared goals through collaboration and teamwork. • Sufficient time and resources are allocated for proactive planning and execution.
Empowerment Decision Making; Employee Orientation; Performance; Planning	**We empower our employees.**	• We delegate effectively. • Analysis, planning and collaboration inform decision making at all levels. • Employee's talents and subject matter expertise are sought out and trusted. • We are accountable for and learn from our mistakes. • We encourage and support employee development.
Communication Communication	**We communicate openly.**	• Communication is everyone's responsibility. • Communication flows in all directions. • Communication occurs in a timely manner and provides the appropriate context. • Divergent perspectives add value.
Performance Business Management; Openness to Change/ Innovation	**We pursue innovation.**	• Our growth depends on well-considered change. • Adaptability and flexibility are key to long-term success. • Creative thinking is encouraged. • We pursue continuous improvement.

Exhibit 2.2. Emergent BioSolutions culture value statements.

Cultural Dimension	Values	Beliefs	Norms
Customer/client orientation			
People orientation			
Performance standards and accountability			
Openness to change and innovation			
Company process orientation			

Exhibit 2.3. Corporate culture map.

oriented to customer service. Two components of the values statement—"the genuine care and comfort of our guests is our highest mission" and "we pledge to provide the finest personal service and facilities for our guests"—can be viewed as implicit aspects of performance standards. By contrast, the Ritz-Carlton culture statements are silent about the other dimensions of culture: treatment of Ritz-Carlton employees, openness to innovation and change, and company process orientation.

Our view is that even though Ritz-Carlton is a successful organization—one in which there is a strong focus on the customer experience—it might be even more successful if it also emphasized the other key dimensions of culture. This conclusion results from use of the culture map as a template for analyzing the comprehensiveness of the culture at Ritz-Carlton.

How to Measure Corporate Culture: The Culture Survey

One precept of management states that if you cannot measure something, you cannot manage it. Through our research and experience, we have developed a "culture survey" that measures the effectiveness of a company's culture and its management. The culture survey measures:

- Cultural alignment: agreement with the stated or desired culture
- Behavioral consistency: the extent to which behavior is consistent with the desired (stated) culture

- Cultural gaps: the difference between the stated or desired culture for a given value and the actual or observed culture in practice

The first step in developing a culture survey is to identify the elements of a company's culture. A written (formal) values statement can serve as a starting point. If no values statement exists, then this step will involve identifying what the company wants its values, beliefs and norms to be (that is, the desired culture) with respect to each of the five dimensions of culture: customer/client orientation, people orientation, performance standards and accountability, innovation and change, and company process orientation.

The next step is to convert the elements of a company's desired culture into a set of survey items that reflect or capture the values, beliefs, and norms. The number of survey items will vary, but it is typically best to limit the total to no more than fifty. Each survey item should "load" onto one of the five dimensions and, in turn, one of the elements of the company's culture. (Note that developing technically sound survey items is a science that may require the input of an outside expert.)

Once the survey items have been developed and selected, they should be organized randomly in the culture survey document. In our approach to culture surveys, respondents are asked about the extent to which they agree that the statement, as written, should be part of the ideal or desired culture. They are also asked to what extent they see the value, belief or norm represented by each statement being practiced in the current or existing culture. A five-point Likert scale is used to collect responses.[15] This is a five-item response scale where the respondent can calibrate his or her level of agreement with each survey item: 5 = to a very great extent, 4 = to a great extent, 3 = to some extent, 2 = to a slight extent, and 1 = to a very slight extent. A numeral (1–5) is assigned to each response.[16] This method achieves an "interval level of measurement," which is significant in that classic parametric statistics can be employed to analyze the data. An excerpt from a sample culture survey using this methodology is presented in Exhibit 2.4.

Survey results can be analyzed to identify the degree to which employees throughout the company agree with the desired culture (as defined in the survey) and perceive that the culture (as defined in the survey) is currently a reality. In addition, survey results can be used to identify culture gaps—that is, the difference between the proposed (desired) and actual cultures. The

Current Statement	Current Culture					Desired Culture				
	To a very slight extent	To a slight extent	To some extent	To a great extent	To a very great extent	To a very slight extent	To a slight extent	To some extent	To a great extent	To a very great extent
1. We keep our commitments to our customers/business partners.	☐	☐	☐	☐	☐	☐	☐	☐	☐	☐
2. Our people are the company's most valuable asset.	☐	☐	☐	☐	☐	☐	☐	☐	☐	☐
3. Our company reacts quickly to changes in the marketplace	☐	☐	☐	☐	☐	☐	☐	☐	☐	☐
4. Our leaders act and communicate with integrity	☐	☐	☐	☐	☐	☐	☐	☐	☐	☐
5. People are rewarded on the basis of their performance.	☐	☐	☐	☐	☐	☐	☐	☐	☐	☐
6. Good planning is rewarded.	☐	☐	☐	☐	☐	☐	☐	☐	☐	☐
7. Company policies are applied consistently.	☐	☐	☐	☐	☐	☐	☐	☐	☐	☐
8. Changes that affect employees are communicated quickly and effectively.	☐	☐	☐	☐	☐	☐	☐	☐	☐	☐

Exhibit 2.4. Sample culture survey excerpt.

culture gap is a measure of how successful the company has been in helping people embrace and practice its stated culture. In brief, it is a measurement of the effectiveness of the company's culture management processes.

The Difference Between Culture and Attitude Surveys

In some companies, there is a belief that standard off-the-shelf attitude surveys can be used to assess the effectiveness of the company's culture and its management. This belief is misguided, at best, because culture and attitude surveys *are not* the same. Standard attitude surveys focus on identifying how "satisfied" people are with various aspects of employment (job, pay, benefits, supervision, and so on). The purpose of attitude surveys is to measure attitudes toward aspects of employment.

Culture surveys, by contrast, are designed to assess the extent to which employees understand and embrace the core values of an organization and practice them (that is, behave consistently with these values). Culture surveys, as described above, should be built around the unique values, beliefs, and norms of a particular company. This means that each company's culture survey will be unique—reflecting not only its own culture but also its way of talking about or communicating about culture (that is, the company's language). For example, even though Disney and Southwest Airlines are both focused on the customer and on providing excellent customer service, culture surveys at these two companies will include items worded in specific ways that reflect how each company defines this dimension of culture.

There can be some overlap between attitude and culture surveys with respect to their focus on one or two culture dimensions (treatment of employees, for instance, and performance standards), but the surveys have fundamentally different purposes.

Culture Measurement: An Illustrative Case

To assist managers in seeing the practicality of the method for measuring culture presented above, this section presents an example of how a company actually measured culture as part of an overall organizational development program. The discussion is necessarily somewhat technical in nature. The measurement of culture was conducted as part of a program of action research in a medium-sized industrial enterprise. The company was engaged in an organizational development program designed to enhance overall organizational effectiveness, and consequently financial performance. During the program, it became apparent that culture management (discussed later) was a critical area for the company's organizational development.

The Organization: "Banner Corporation"

The company (for which we shall use the pseudonym "Banner Corporation") is a U.S.-based, medium-sized industrial enterprise. Banner represents the classic old economy and manufactures parts for industrial, truck, and other automotive businesses. It supplies parts for companies such Ford, Navistar, and Dana.

Banner was formed primarily in a classic roll-up strategy of industry consolidation through acquisitions. It consisted of several divisions, each of which was once a stand-alone entrepreneurial company, with annual revenues ranging from about $25 million to $100 million. At the time of this study, the twenty divisions totaled about $800 million in annual revenue. These divisions consisted of a set of reasonably related technologies, such as foundries and forges. The foundries ranged from processing capacity for grey iron to ductile iron to lost foam and other similar technologies. Job order manufacturing is the nature of the business of these entities.

The similarities between the divisions presented a unique opportunity for comparison. Because the company had been formed from a set of stand-alone companies, there was no common corporate culture at Banner. Each individual company or division operated in a specific part of the United States. Many kept their own name and logo after Banner acquired them. An organizational assessment determined that some employees of Banner did not know who the parent company was, and others seemed not even to care.

Developing Measurements of Corporate Culture: Specific Steps

This process of measuring corporate culture at Banner consisted of four steps: (1) formulating the desired culture values, (2) developing a set of culture value statements, (3) creating the culture survey instrument, and (4) administration of the survey to a sample of organizational members.

Step One: Formulating the Desired Culture
The first task in the process was to formulate the desired corporate culture, or a statement of core values designed to guide development and functioning of the organization. Although some organizations have a formal (written) statement of values, others have an implicit or implied culture but no formal statement. In this instance, because it was created as part of a roll-up strategy, the company did not have an explicit cultural statement.

The first action step in this phase was to provide training to the senior management team (including the CEO, CFO, senior group VPs, VP of human resources, and selected others) on the nature of culture and culture management. The next step was to develop an explicit statement of cultural values.

To facilitate this process, a set of key categories for defining cultural values were used: (1) how people are treated by the organization, as well as the implicit or explicit view of people; (2) how customers are treated by the organization; (3) standards of performance and accountability; (4) teamwork among people in the organization; and (5) corporate "citizenship" (or the way in which the organization operates as a member of its communities). These areas corresponded to four of the key dimensions of culture proposed earlier in this chapter. The category of innovation and change was not included, and teamwork was added. (It should be noted that in some companies, teamwork is treated as a subcategory under either the people orientation or the performance standards cultural dimension).

Step Two: Developing Culture Statements

The next step was to identify a set of statements that defined the desired culture of the organization in each key area—treatment of people, treatment of customers, etc. The intent was to develop a statement of the ideal way in which the company should function culturally in all of these areas. This was done through facilitated discussion of how the organization wanted to work and what it wanted the culture to be with respect to each key dimension. For example, the senior management team discussed the ideal way people would be treated at Banner and then converted this discussion into a set of cultural statements.

Step Three: The Culture Survey

Once these cultural statements were formulated, the next step was to determine whether there was agreement or buy-in throughout the organization. Specifically, the statements developed in step two were incorporated into a cultural assessment survey using a Likert scale to determine agreement by members of the organization, as described in the previous section.

Step Four: Administration of the Survey

The survey was administered to all 950 salaried employees of the organization. The response rate was 78 percent, which was deemed excellent.

Results of the Measurement of Culture

The survey was designed with two objectives: to determine the extent to which people throughout Banner (1) agreed with the stated or desired culture and (2) perceived that each division, as well as the corporate office (headquarters), was behaving consistently with the desired or ideal corporate culture.

Extent of Agreement with the Proposed Culture

The data generated by the culture survey measurement showed there was acceptance of the proposed culture. What was truly astounding was that more than 96 percent of those responding agreed with the stated or ideal culture of Banner. This meant the senior executive team had tapped into the way people throughout the corporation wanted the company to be managed.

Extent to Which Behavior Is Consistent with Proposed Culture

The culture survey also showed, however, that there were significant differences in the extent to which people were behaving consistently with the proposed culture. In most of the divisions, gaps existed between the proposed desired culture and the way respondents viewed people actually behaving. There were also differences in behavior *among the divisions*, with respect to "walking the talk" or behaving consistently with the proposed culture. In particular, it was observed that the higher-performing divisions were behaving most in alignment with (acceptance of) the proposed culture. Behavior in the lower-performing divisions was less in alignment. (As described in the Appendix to this chapter, the difference in cultural alignment between high- and low-performing divisions was statistically significant.)

These observed differences were significant to management and led to changes in the performance management and compensation system. Management decided to monitor cultural consistency between a division's culture and the overall corporate culture and reflect this in the compensation of divisional managers.

Conclusion

This chapter presents the first part of a framework for management of corporate culture. We have defined corporate culture operationally, named the key dimensions of corporate culture (the five key cultural factors approach), and presented a method of measuring corporate culture to assess agreement with the desired culture as well as to identify gaps between the desired and actual current cultures. The chapter also includes a case study illustrating how the culture measurement methods presented here can be used as a practical tool by organizations. In addition, we illustrate application of the five key cultural factors approach in an actual organization.

In Chapter 3, we continue our development of a culture management framework by focusing on the process and tools for managing the five specific dimensions of corporate culture described here.

Appendix:
Research on Cultural Impact on Financial Performance[17]

As a byproduct of the Banner case described in this chapter, it was possible to assess the impact of a company's culture on its financial performance. This aspect of the case is described in this technical appendix.

The general research question addressed was, Is there a relationship between corporate culture and the financial performance of an organization? We were also interested in determining the relationship between (1) the extent to which people in the divisions accepted the stated culture of the company and (2) the company's financial performance. More specifically, as a result of the nature of the formation of this company there was no common or unified "Banner Corporation" culture, so we were able to observe the full effects of culture on Banner's financial performance.

To address the question concerning the impact of corporate culture on financial performance or the bottom line, the study compared divisional data with divisional EBIT (earnings before interest and taxes), a classic measure of financial performance and the one that Banner also uses to assess its own divisional performance. Specifically, a regression was run between (1) the degree to which each division was perceived by its own personnel to be living the desired corporate culture, and (2) EBIT.

The data derived and used in this comparison are shown graphically in Exhibit 2.5. The x-axis shows "divisional agreement with corporate culture score"; this is a measure of the degree of similarity between the desired corporate culture and the culture perceived to exist in each division. It can be viewed as a measure of cultural buy-in on the part of the divisions. This is how much people perceive that their division is behaving consistently with the company's desired culture. Operationally, agreement was measured by the percentage of favorable responses to value statements, where *percent favorable* was defined as the sum of responses that were "to a very great extent" and "to a great extent" (on a Likert scale) divided by the total number of respondents. The y-axis presents EBIT values for the various

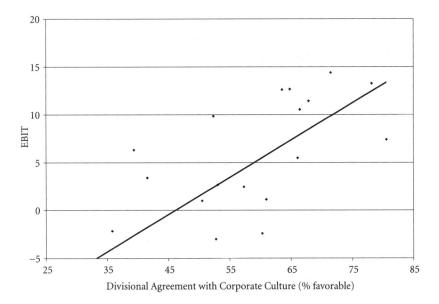

Exhibit 2.5. Divisional culture buy-in vs. EBIT at Banner Corporation.

divisions. Accordingly, Exhibit 2.5 shows the relation between the degree of cultural agreement between the division and the corporate culture and EBIT for all divisions.

The regression equation describing the relationship among variables was statistically significant at the 0.05 level.[18] The results indicated that approximately 46 percent of EBIT is explained by the variable of corporate culture, or cultural buy-in.

3 Culture Management Process and Tools

Building on Chapter 2, we continue discussing the management of corporate culture. First we present a systematic six-step process. Next, we identify and describe tools for managing corporate culture. Finally, we examine the need for culture management at different stages of organizational growth.

A Process for Managing Corporate Culture

Our experience in working with companies suggests that the process of managing corporate culture can be as important as the content of the culture per se. Our approach is shown in Exhibit 3.1 and explained below. (Note: This is the process that was used by "Banner Corporation," described in Chapter 2.)

Describe the Current Culture

As seen in the exhibit, the culture management process begins with identifying the current corporate culture. This is the culture actually influencing employee behavior—the culture that employees are living and breathing. The current culture may or may not be consistent with the company's formal written values or culture statement (if one exists). In this step, it is important to identify how each of the five dimensions of culture—treatment of employees, treatment of customers, performance standards and accountability, openness to change and innovation, and company process orientation—is being currently defined within the company.

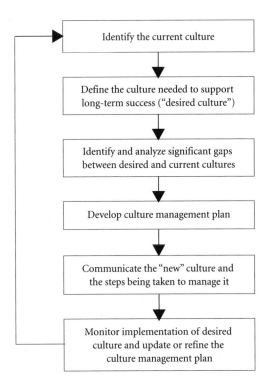

Exhibit 3.1. The culture management process.

Define the Desired Culture

The desired culture is what the organization wants its culture to actually be or become. The desired culture can be viewed as the organization's strategic culture because it is intended to support the overall strategic development of the enterprise. The output of this step will ultimately be reflected in a formal statement of culture, such as that of Emergent BioSolutions shown in Chapter 2, or that of Starbucks presented later in this chapter.

It should be noted that steps 1 and 2 can be reversed, with identification of the desired culture being completed before identification of the current culture. This might be necessary in situations where there is no strong pre-existing culture, as was the case at Banner.

Identify Cultural Gaps

A cultural gap, as defined in Chapter 2, is any significant difference between the current and desired cultures. In brief, this is the difference between what a company wants its culture to be and the culture that actually influences employee behavior day to day. As described in the previous chapter, a culture survey can identify culture gaps.

Develop a Culture Management Plan

This is a formal (written) document that identifies objectives, goals, and action steps for managing the five dimensions of a company's culture. The content of the plan will depend on the specific culture issues facing the company, such as lack of a clearly defined culture, ineffective communication of the company's desired culture, gaps between the company's desired and current cultures, the need to change the desired culture, and so on. In developing this plan, management will draw on the culture management tools described in the next section. This plan is an important tool for communicating the current and future focus of culture management throughout the company.

Monitor Performance Against the Culture Management Plan

This final step in the culture management process involves assessing the progress being made against the plan developed in step 4. The leadership of the company's culture management efforts—whether senior management, the human resource function, or a culture committee—should meet at least quarterly to discuss:

- Progress being made against culture management goals
- Problems being encountered in meeting goals and steps to overcome these problems
- Any "new" culture management issues and steps to address them

The output of the plan review will be an updated formal (written) culture management plan that documents progress being made against existing goals, any new goals developed as a result of the meeting, and perhaps new action steps that need to be taken to achieve goals.

Culture Management: An Iterative Process and a Way of Life

Effective culture management is not a "six steps and done" process. To be optimally effective, it must become a way of life in an organization. As described above, culture management needs to be done as an annual cycle— just like budgeting or strategic planning. In addition, a company should periodically (every year or two) conduct a more formal assessment of the extent to which its desired culture is a reality for all employees. This will involve re-administering and analyzing the results of the culture survey.

The Primary Tools of Culture Management

This section examines the ten major tools, listed below, that can be used singly or in combination to develop a comprehensive culture management plan.

- Develop a clear statement of the company's culture and values.
- Use communication to reinforce corporate values.
- Use symbols to reinforce corporate values.
- Recruit and select people for cultural fit.
- Manage culture through orientation and training.
- Retain people who fit with the culture.
- Use the reward system to recognize and reward those who exemplify the values.
- Embed core values in performance standards and procedures.
- Change leadership practices.
- Align the structure to support core values.

Each tool is described in more detail below.

Develop a Clear Statement of the Company's Culture

One of the most basic tools for managing corporate culture is a culture values statement, a written statement of the organization's core values. The culture values statement used at Ritz-Carlton was shown in Exhibit 2.1.

Although there are many ways to present these values—in sentences, as sound bites, in document form, or even in pictures—the key to preparing the values statements is to use terms and language that have meaning for those who are or will become members of the company. It is also important that the culture values statements clearly identify what is most important to the company. For example, Southwest's statement of company values appears as two very short paragraphs. Within each, certain terms (People and Customer, in particular) are capitalized, as a way of communicating the importance of these factors to the company's success.

Developing a formal values statement is not as easy as "just writing down what is important to us." It typically requires some time and effort to ensure that the statement truly reflects the company's unique personality. The bottom line: for people to embrace the corporate culture, they must know what it is. This is the purpose of the formal statement of values.

Starbucks Coffee Values Statement

An example of a culture values statement is the set of six guiding principles used at Starbucks Coffee Company:

- Provide a great work environment and treat each other with respect and dignity.
- Apply the highest standards of excellence to the purchasing, roasting, and fresh delivery of our coffee.
- Develop enthusiastically satisfied customers all of the time.
- Contribute positively to our communities and our environment.
- Recognize that profitability is essential to our future success.
- Embrace diversity as an essential component in the way we do business.[1]

These principles deal with the product, treatment of people, customers, the company's role in relation to the environment, and profitability.

Howard Schultz, founder and CEO of Starbucks, initially articulated five guiding principles, intended to serve as the basis of the Starbucks culture. Subsequently, a sixth principle was added (the last one in the list). This was done at the suggestion of Sharon Elliott, who was then senior vice president of human resources. Schultz believed that the kind of organization Starbucks was, and how it did business, would become a source of sustainable competitive advantage. In his words, "The values of the company and the guiding principles became a unique sustainable competitive advantage."[2]

Emergent BioSolutions Cultural Values Statement

Another example of a culture values statement is the set of points from Emergent BioSolutions, seen previously in Exhibit 2.2. The significance of this culture values statement is that it adheres to the approach described in Chapter 2, in which the values statements reflect all five key dimensions of culture.

Although a formal culture statement is an important tool, it is not enough to ensure that people will fully understand and embrace a company's culture. It is, however, a useful starting point.

Use Communication to Reinforce Corporate Values

Communication is an indispensable tool of culture management. Communication is about not only the content of the message but also how this message is conveyed, and the frequency with which it is sent. The three rules for communication of culture are Communicate! Communicate! Communicate! Tell them what you are going to tell them, tell them, and then tell them what you've told them. It should be noted that there are also values, beliefs, and norms helping to define what effective communication is within a company. This aspect of communication will be discussed in Chapter 8.

The goal of communication as a culture management tool is to help people understand and embrace the desired culture. As described in Chapter 8, Southwest Airlines developed sophisticated communication systems not only to regularly communicate the company's culture but also to reinforce key aspects of it, including empowering employees to make decisions, valuing employees, and emphasizing customer service.

There are a variety of culture communication methods. Some companies use videos; others use all company meetings like a "company summit" or "town hall"; still others use written materials or company intranets. Most companies use a variety of methods. More important than the method used is the content of the messages. Every communication and response to employees represents an opportunity to convey and reinforce company values. Recognizing this, some companies develop specific corporate culture communication strategies and tactics, involving everything from website content to the structure and content of all company events, to the formal speeches that are given by senior executives, and the list goes on.

An example of successful communication is how DeBeers communicates company values at its Cullinan Diamond Mine in South Africa. As you walk through the diamond mine, you see posters reminding employees of the company's values: "Be passionate, show we care, pull together, build trust, and shape the future." These values are reinforced through daily communication with employees on performance against goals—including performance against safety standards and production targets. There are large "scoreboards" throughout the facility presenting information about how the company is performing relative to its goals.

Other examples of companies that effectively use communication as a culture management tool and that embed this communication within their company cultures are described in Chapter 8.

Use Symbols to Reinforce the Company Culture

A symbol is anything that has meaning to an employee. We also sometimes refer to these as "company artifacts." Anything can be or become a positive (or not-so-positive) symbol of a company's culture. For example, a number of years ago a paralegal in a rapidly growing company that had just moved its offices shared with us her view of how the company was treating employees: "I know that I am not as valued as other members of the team because I did not receive a speaker phone when we moved." The fact that she was working in an open cubicle, where a speaker phone would have been impractical, did not matter to her. The type of phone that an employee received had become a symbol of his or her value. As this example suggests, it is important that companies manage symbols as part of their overall corporate culture management process.

The key in using this culture management tool is to find the right symbols of the desired culture and then effectively manage how they are used. Employees of Southwest Airlines wear a heart on their shirts, symbolizing the "Luv" dimension of the company culture (a play on the airfield where the company was founded, but also symbolic of the focus Southwest places on caring for its customers and employees). IBM, in former days, was known for the white shirts worn by its managers—a symbol of "professionalism." The white shirt was a de facto IBM uniform. One of the authors witnessed an exchange between an employee of IBM and an employee of

Apple concerning the symbolism of their attire. With tongue in cheek, the IBM employee said to the disbelieving Apple employee: "We both have dress codes! We must wear white shirts, and you can't do that." Similarly, but with a different twist, the servers at Charthouse Restaurants as well as corporate management—all "crew members" (employees)—wear Hawaiian shirts, symbolizing the informality of their culture as well as the company's commitment to the "Aloha spirit" found in the Hawaiian Islands.

Recruit and Select People for Cultural Fit

Although demographic diversity should be sought, a company needs people who will readily embrace its culture toward customers, treatment of people, performance standards and so on. This seems deceptively simple, but in reality it is a complex problem.

Some companies spend a great deal of time in the recruiting and selection process to ensure that the people they hire will embrace their culture. Examples are Amgen, Apple, Hewlett-Packard, Southwest, and IBM—all leaders in their space. Amgen and Apple use teams of people to interview candidates for their positions. In part, this constitutes a "stress interview" because it is stressful to have several people involved in an interview situation. At the same time, the process offers the opportunity for one person to be questioning or talking with a job candidate while others are observing him or her. Southwest Airlines will sometimes interview candidates in groups as a way of identifying the extent to which potential employees understand the value placed on teamwork and concern for others.

Some organizations have tried to develop questions that can be used in interviews or assessment instruments such as questionnaires. The intent of these questions is to elicit the core values of people in a subtle way and identify whether they would or would not be a good fit with the organization's culture. For instance, the authors' firm did a research study for a large international consumer products organization that was experiencing heavy employee turnover in one division due to lack of fit with the strong culture. The objective was to develop a set of unobtrusive questions that could be used to identify people who were not likely to embrace the distinctive corporate culture.

Finding the right interview questions that can help identify a good fit can sometimes require creativity. At Southwest, candidates are frequently asked to describe how they used humor or fun in the workplace. When Stacy Savides Sullivan of Google was asked if she could give an example of a question someone might pose during an interview to determine whether the candidate is "Googley" enough, she replied: "You know, there are no standard questions that I know of. But we might ask: . . . 'How many bread boxes could you fit in an airplane?' . . . Obviously, there's no right answer, but we are just trying to figure out how people think and the kind of steps they take."[3] Another major company tried a different approach: recognizing that not all people will be comfortable in their culture, interviewers typically tell people about what they might *not* like at the company. The hope is that those who will not fit in the culture will self-select out.

Manage Culture Through Orientation and Training

Once people are selected and join an organization, the next tool for culture management is orientation and training/education programs. All new employee orientation programs should include, in some form, a presentation and discussion of company culture and values. This can be as simple as reviewing the values, or involve creatively communicating what is important from a values perspective. As an example, some orientation programs include skits to illustrate the meaning of values in action.

When a company's culture is being managed well, all employee training includes a focus on culture—even if not explicit. A company that values customer service will devote resources to formal and informal training in how employees should be delivering this service. A company that values continuous development of people will have a fairly comprehensive and systemic employee training process. In every company, leadership development is as much about culture as it is about skills development. First, the very act of having a formal leadership development program (assuming it is effectively designed and delivered) communicates the value the company places on development and on having effective leaders. Second, through the leadership development process, those being promoted to management or leadership positions for the first time and those moving from one level of management to the next can be given the tools they will need to effectively communicate, support, and manage the company's culture.

Cultural Socialization at Disney

The Walt Disney Company is masterful at using training to socialize people into their corporate values and culture in the theme parks. The orientation begins with a course called Disney Traditions, where a variety of games and exercises are used to help people understand and embrace the founder's vision. A Disney trainer asks: "What business are we in? McDonald's makes hamburgers. Toyota makes cars. What does Disney do"? The answer he or she expects to receive (and usually does) is, "Disney makes people happy."

During this initial training, all new employees are told they have been recruited as "cast" in a live stage production (at Disneyland or Disney World). They are all hosts and hostesses.[4] There are no "security people" or "janitorial crew"; everyone is a host or hostess.

Disney also uses on-the-job training with incumbents as role models to further the cultural socialization of people. While they are being trained in roles such as host or hostess, a current holder of the role explains the Disney philosophy of how to treat guests (customers).

Disney is a best-in-class example of how to use training to inculcate corporate culture. The company now offers this training as a product to businesses wanting to use its methods in their own organization.

Retain People Who Fit with the Culture

Even after careful selection and training, not everyone who joins a company will fit or embrace its culture. Another tool for culture management is to retain people who fit the culture, and conversely encourage people to leave if they do not.

Employee Retention and Strategic Turnover at GE

At GE, there is an explicit strategy of what might be termed "strategic turnover." GE wants to retain people who fit or embrace their culture and encourage those who do not to leave the company. The basic assumption is that it is much more difficult to change people's values than to enhance their skills.

GE uses two factors—performance and cultural acceptance—to classify employees for purposes of retention. Putting these two dimensions together results in four categories: (1) "stars," or high performers who accept the culture; (2) "question marks," or low performers who accept the culture; (3) "outsiders," or high performers who do not accept the culture; and (4) "losers," or low performers who do not accept the culture. GE would rather work with question marks to develop their skills than with outsiders to help them embrace the culture. Outsiders are encouraged to leave.

Use the Reward System to Recognize and Reward People Who Represent the Values

Rewards, in an organizational context, are defined as "anything that is given to someone in recognition of appropriate behavior." Rewards can be financial or nonfinancial. Financial rewards include bonuses and incentive compensation; nonfinancial rewards include employee recognition, promotion, and simple acknowledgment of a job well done. By definition, for something to be a reward, it has to be truly valued by the person receiving it.

Organizations and managers can influence the value attached to specific items and can actually create rewards. In one $150 million consumer product company, the vice president of sales would award the "traveling coffee mug" to a team member who "went above and beyond the call of duty." Those who received the reward were quite proud of the recognition. In this example, the vice president had created a valued reward out of a seemingly inexpensive item.

H. Stephen Cranston, who at the time was president and COO of Knapp Communications (which then owned *Architectural Digest, Bon Appétit, Home, GEO,* and Knapp Press, prior to their sale to Condé Nast), offers an excellent illustration of effective use of symbols and their management as a cultural reward. Cranston created a small gold *K* pin that was given to employees who had done something he regarded as a special contribution to the company. His intent (which actually happened) was to have people see the *K*, ask what it was, and, on being told, ask, "How can I get a *K*?" The gold *K* pin became an important cultural icon at Knapp Communications.

Hearing the story of the gold *K* pin at Knapp Communications in a seminar conducted by the authors, the president of a growing construction company purchased hats and leather jackets with the company's name and mantra ("Get Hot!") to use as symbols of achievement in his company. He reported, "You cannot believe the effort and competition among my employees to get a leather jacket!"

Although rewards can be effectively administered ad hoc, as these examples demonstrate, companies typically require a more formal reward system. This consists of identifying the types of rewards available and determining how the organization or individual managers will use them to recognize individual behavior and performance. Reward systems can (and should) be designed to promote and reinforce the company's culture. Compensation systems, for example, can be designed to reward people for their tenure with the organization (an indicator of commitment to the culture). They can also be designed to motivate the kinds of behavior that are consistent with specific aspects of the company's culture. In the case of 3M, a corporation legendary for emphasizing innovation and commercialization of new technology, people are encouraged to "bootleg" up to 15 percent of their time and budget to create new technologies and innovative products.[5] When someone champions a new technology that proves marketable, the person may be rewarded in a variety of ways, possibly by becoming the head of a new division.

Some companies use stock options as a method of creating psychological (and actual) ownership in the company. Starbucks and Southwest Airlines have done this quite effectively. However, if company growth stops, stock options are not always an effective tool to motivate and retain employees. We saw this when many people became millionaires and multimillionaires at Amgen during the period of its rapid growth in the 1990s. Once the growth in its stock price stopped, though, many people left to find "the next Amgen."

Embed Core Values in Performance Standards and Procedures

Transmission and reinforcement of a company's culture can be embedded directly or indirectly in performance standards. In some companies, the extent to which employees are behaving consistently with the culture is included as a part of the formal performance evaluation process. Employees are evaluated, at least in part, on the basis of standards that reflect the company's values. In one $50 million manufacturing company the senior managers' direct reports were asked to complete a twenty-five-item survey every six months on the extent to which their manager was supporting the company's culture. Survey results were tabulated and discussed, and a small portion of the manager's bonus compensation was linked to the score received on this survey. Whenever there was a specific problem, the CEO would work with the individual senior manager to develop a plan for corrective action.

Culture can also be embedded in performance standards and procedures that relate to quality, treatment of customers, and other dimensions. McDonald's wants its burgers and fries in Pacoima to be indistinguishable from those in Poughkeepsie (and possibly in Paris as well)! By having employees adhere to specific standards, they are actually also adhering to the company's culture. Similarly, by enforcing the treatment of norms regarding guests (customers)—a warm greeting, use the guest's name if possible, a fond farewell—Ritz-Carlton is actually enforcing a set of performance standards expected of all employees.

Some companies have been creative in helping people understand and embrace performance standards. During one of the past Olympics, McDonald's set up its own internal "McDonald's Olympics." This involved a competition among employees for preparation of burgers. McDonald's franchisees and managers were the judges. To do the judging, they had to know what the standards were as well.

Align Leadership Practices with the Company's Culture

A great deal of the culture management occurring in companies is through day-to-day management and leadership. As decisions are made and actions taken, culture is communicated in intended and unintended ways, almost as a process of cultural osmosis—transmission of cultural values to people as a by-product of day-to-day operations.[6]

If the founder is still in place, he or she will have the greatest impact on the culture of the organization. This is true whether we are talking about Steve Jobs at Apple or Maxine Clark at Build-a-Bear. If the founder is gone, then the next generation of leaders will be the driving force behind the culture. In large companies, however, every level of management is important from the standpoint of communicating and reinforcing—through words and actions—the company's values.

During the start-up phase of the corporate life cycle, culture is defined and promulgated by the founder or founding core leadership group. Their individual values become the values of the enterprise. Unless there is a major cultural transformation (say, brought about by a merger), many of these values will be retained in some form over the life of the enterprise. This is true in almost every organization and is seen clearly at such diverse companies as Walt Disney, Hewlett-Packard, Google, Walmart, Apple, Starbucks, and Southwest Airlines.

As companies grow, they need to develop strategies for retaining and effectively managing the positive aspects of their culture. In addition, there may be a need to transform some aspects of the culture so that it continues to support the company's strategies and effective operations.[7] There will also be a need to transition from a single or small group of leaders to a cadre of leaders capable of taking the organization to the next level. This can be accomplished by recruiting new leaders from outside or by growing people from within through use of leadership development programs. In companies where the culture is strong, functional, well managed, and a source of competitive advantage, the risk of recruiting from outside is that people will not truly understand or embrace the culture. Starbucks recruited Jim Donald, a seasoned executive, to assume the CEO position when Howard Schultz moved to chairman. In 2008, Donald was "terminated" (not in the Arnold Schwarzenegger sense, but asked to leave the company), and Schultz resumed the position of CEO.[8] In discussing the question of his future replacement as CEO, Schultz said he had learned how important it is for someone to understand the company's distinctive culture and that future candidates for CEO would come from within.[9]

Leadership practices can transmit cultural values in a variety of ways. Hewlett-Packard is credited with using the tactic of "management by walking around," through which Bill Hewlett and Dave Packard, the storied cofounders, were able to talk to people and communicate what was important to them, and thereby establish the culture of the company. At Southwest Airlines, the CEO and other executives make trips to the field—in their annual Message to the Field meetings and in less formal visits throughout the year. The purpose of these interactions is to share company information and address employee questions or concerns. Leaders at Southwest also have an open-door policy; employees at every level have access to all the leadership—not just their immediate supervisor.

Communicating expectations of leaders with respect to their role in managing culture can be done, at least in part, through leadership development programs and processes. In addition, many companies use leadership development programs not just to enhance skills but also to promote their culture. Under Jack Welch, GE used its legendary leadership program as a bully pulpit for him to talk with rising executives and share his philosophy. He was, in fact, disseminating the GE culture.

Managing the Leadership Molecule

An important ingredient to effective design and use of leadership practices as a culture management tool involves a concept that we term the *leadership molecule*. This construct refers to what can be a called a true senior leadership team: a set of leaders who, despite having different roles and capabilities, function as a real team rather than as separate individuals. The classic form of the leadership molecule (shown in Exhibit 3.2) consists of three individuals who together perform five key functions: vision, culture management, systems, operations and management of innovation and change.[10] The first four functions are core because they always exist, while the fifth occurs periodically or intermittently. In the classic form of the leadership molecule, the four core functions of vision, culture, systems, and operations exist as an integrated unit, performed by a set of individuals with overlapping roles working as a true team.

Effective culture management depends on each of the four core functions being owned by a member of senior management and on all members

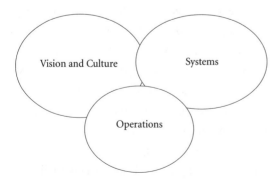

Exhibit 3.2. The classic form of the "leadership molecule."

of senior management working together as a molecule. In brief, to maximize company effectiveness and performance, the culture, vision, systems, and day-to-day operations of the company must be aligned, and this starts with leadership. Starbucks is an excellent example of this concept in action. During the years of rapid growth, the company had a true leadership molecule in place, with:

- Howard Schultz focused on *culture* and *vision*
- Orin Smith, who was first CFO, later COO, and eventually CEO, focused on *systems* and *culture*
- Howard Behar, SVP of retail operations, focused on *operations* and *culture*

The functions of culture management were shared by the team of Schultz, Behar, and Smith. Schultz took the lead in defining Starbucks' culture, as we have previously indicated. As the head of retail operations, Behar's role was subtler but crucial because he influenced virtually everyone at Starbucks day to day. In a sense, he served as an apostle for Schultz to help him implement his philosophy. Similarly, by the nature of his personality and experience, Orin Smith was a true believer committed to the Starbucks strategy and culture.

The Starbucks leadership molecule did not form totally by design or accident. In 1994, the key players were in place, but there was conflict among them and not a clear definition of their respective roles. They were not functioning as an effective team. Over the next few years, their roles became more clearly defined and actually evolved. In addition, through a variety of team-building experiences as well as through the natural course of events, the three developed into a true leadership molecule.

Starbucks did not think explicitly in terms of a leadership molecule (a term we recently coined).[11] Nevertheless, the molecule existed at Starbucks. When Behar left his role and later Smith retired, the molecule "disintegrated" and needed to be recreated. Since Schultz did not think in terms of the molecule, he did not seek to recreate it per se. He merely sought to replace the people who formerly occupied the roles of CEO (Donald) and head of retail stores (Behar). The result, we believe, was a decline in Starbucks' fortunes, which Schultz has sought to reverse (with considerable success) since returning to leadership as CEO in 2008. After returning, he contacted both

Behar and Smith to determine if they would reassume their former jobs, but both chose not to do so.[12] We also believe, however, that if he were to think explicitly in terms of a leadership molecule, the process would be both easier and more successful.

Align the Structure to Support Company Culture

A company's structure has three levels.[13] The first is the macro structure, presented in the company's organization chart. In brief, it is "the boxes on the page." The second is the micro structure, or how the roles of every function and position included in the macro structure are defined. The third level includes all the supporting systems (e.g., performance management, training, communication, planning, etc.) needed to promote effective implementation of the macro and micro structures.

Structure, at any one level or all three, can be used as a tool to support effective communication and management of a company's culture. At the macro level, if there is a strong cultural focus on quality then there may be a specific function whose role is to ensure product quality. At the micro level, if planning is a key value, a key result area (critical success factor) for all managers should be planning. At the supporting systems level, if teamwork is a core value then there should be meetings and other mechanisms to ensure that everyone—within and across units—is able to communicate and effectively coordinate their efforts.

A Final Thought on Culture Management Tools

We have now described a set of tools that can be used, singly or in combination, in creating a culture management plan. These are not the only tools of culture management, but they do make up an important set. It ought to be noted that although these tools have not been organized in a sequence, there is a logic underlying their presentation. They can be viewed as forming a loose progression from the initial statement of the culture to its communication—literally and through symbols—to recruitment, socialization, and retention of people who fit or embrace the culture; and then to the rewards, performance standards and procedures, leadership practices, and structure that reinforce the company's values. In the next section, we present an example of how an actual company uses some of the culture management tools.

Delta Dental of Missouri:
Use of Culture Management Tools in Action

Delta Dental of Missouri (DDMO) is one of several Delta Dental Plans existing throughout the United States. The company sells and manages dental benefits for employers and individuals in the states of Missouri and South Carolina. It also has a subsidiary that manages Medicaid benefits, and another that sells and manages vision benefits. As of 2009, revenues were in excess of $450 million. The company's culture management efforts in 2010 are an example of the culture management tools use in action.

In 2010, DDMO had a formal, written set of core values reflecting what was important to the company: people, customers, quality, leadership, the community, and financial strength. The values statement (a one-page document) contained short definitions, of one to three sentences, of these values. Those who developed the definitions readily admitted they liberally drew on other companies' values statements. As a result, what made DDMO truly unique was not adequately reflected in the definition of the company's core values. This created challenges for management in communicating, managing, and reinforcing the company's desired culture.

Just prior to the April 2010 annual off-site planning meeting of the entire management team (with representatives from all major functions), the new CEO, David Haynes (who was previously the CFO), and the chief marketing officer, Rich Klassen, were discussing what might be done to further enhance the entire company's focus on the customer—not just customer service, but the whole customer. It should be noted the DDMO has a good reputation in its market and is well respected by customers; the issue was what more the company *could* do. As stated by Haynes and Klassen, "Sometimes, it's creating the small changes that can dramatically change the outcome."

Here is the company's current statement of the value related to customers:

> *Customers*—Striving to satisfy our customers better than our competitors do is the focus of all of our business activities. We also realize that service to our customers is our company's reason for being and that failure to do so threatens our survival.

On the first morning of the company's two-day meeting, Haynes posed a question to his team: "What *is* the Delta customer experience—that is, what do we want it to be?" To address this question, participants worked in three small groups of five or six people, randomly assigned. Each group was asked to show the larger group, in any way it deemed appropriate, what the Delta customer experience is or should be, how it is different from the competition, and how to bring it to life. There was a great deal of energy among the members of the full team during the open discussion that occurred before breaking into small groups. A lot of questions were asked of Haynes about what teams were supposed to do and how. These were left unanswered and the groups were told, "It's up to you." This response was, in fact, a statement of the company's culture.

Although not required, all three small groups developed short skits highlighting the elements that differentiate DDMO from its competition. The content of the skits was important, but just as important was the energy and enthusiasm that the exercise created among the management team. One team ended their short presentation with a "Delta cheer" that they created ("Delta, Delta, Delta—We LOVE Delta!") that featured not just the cheer but some pretty animated jumping and kicking, which was quite uncharacteristic of this group. The spirit was becoming evident.

The skits served as the springboard for an animated and lengthy discussion of how the management team could take both the content and the energy around the customer value back to the company. The focus was on how to help all employees reflect the culture in all client interactions, to create a "wow" customer experience. From management's discussion, the methods that would be used to bring the energy and enthusiasm of the offsite back to the company and help all employees understand and embrace the wow included:

- Holding an all-employee event to introduce and explain the value (training and socialization)
- Using symbols (including T-shirts) to promote the value
- Creating some new words (such as "wow") and using the Delta cheer to help communicate the value
- Identifying ways to recognize people who create a wow
- Helping everyone in the company understand that "wowing" the customer is part of his or her job (that is, embed the value in the company's structure as part of each individual's role)

- Using leadership practices to promote the wow. One concept discussed was for the CEO to dress like and be the head cheerleader—which he was receptive to doing!

In addition to these tools, the formal definition of the customer value at DDMO will also change to reflect this focus on taking customer service and satisfaction to the next level and creating a true customer experience in every interaction, with the high-level enthusiasm that is clearly a part of this company's real culture.

Culture Management at Different Stages of Organizational Growth

The types of tools used by a company to communicate, manage, and reinforce its culture will depend, to a certain extent, on its stage of organizational growth or development. This section describes some of the key aspects of culture management at various stages of organizational development. The stages of corporate growth and related cultural issues are summarized in Exhibit 3.3.[14]

Stage	Culture Issues	Culture Management
1	Basic values definition and communication	Informal culture management as a by-product of operations
2	Scale-up: new people	Culture management from the founding (initial) group
3	Transition to professional management	Formal definition of culture (values); developing the culture management system
4	Complete the transition	Formal culture management system in place
5	Transmission of core culture and values across SBUs	Replication of the cycle
6	Balance of centralization and decentralization	Integration of multiple business units
7	Revitalization	Transformation of the corporate culture to fit the new organization

Exhibit 3.3. Culture management at each stage of growth.

Culture Management at Stage 1

A stage 1 company is relatively small, with $1 million or less in revenues and probably about ten people (plus or minus) employed by the firm. As noted in Chapter 1, culture in a company is initially derived from its founder or founders. Therefore the personal and professional values of the founder(s) constitute the DNA of the culture of the company during stage 1.[15]

The culture of most small organizations emphasizes flexibility, ability to respond quickly to the environment, and the notion that the company is a family with the entrepreneur serving as the parental figure. The organization seems to be constantly moving, and even though there is a certain amount of anxiety about the firm's future, there is also a great deal of excitement. In some stage 1 companies, technical wizardry and innovativeness are valued; the technicians are the corporate heroes. In others, the focus is on sales and marketing, and individuals who work in these areas become the heroes.

Many stage 1 companies do not have a formal culture statement because very few entrepreneurs choose to commit their values to paper. Although doing so is not an absolute necessity, it can the basis for communicating values as the firm grows. Whatever is placed on paper, however, should be supported by the daily operations of the firm.

Stage 1 firms use the communication and leadership practices tools as the founder or founding group transmits culture through day-to-day interaction with others. Employees, in fact, look to the entrepreneur for direction. As a result, the entrepreneur is able, almost every day, to define and reinforce the corporate culture as well as monitor and correct it.

At stage 1, the company founder will tend to be involved in all personnel decisions. He or she selects, retains, and rewards those people who fit with the company's culture (which is a reflection of his or her values).

Culture Management at Stage 2

Stage 2 occurs typically from about $1 to $10 million in revenues. The number of employees can vary but will probably be in the range of ten to a hundred. Initially, the corporate culture of the stage 2 firm is very similar to that of stage 1. The firm still values responsiveness, but now, as the organization grows rapidly and increases in size, there is a tendency for this to mean crisis management. The firm still values flexibility, but this means something more like being flexible and creative enough to operate with less-than-adequate resources until personnel interviews are completed or until new facilities are ready. The firm also still values "the family," but now there is an extended family living within the same "house," and one's loyalty seems to depend on the leader to whom one reports. Corporate heroes tend to be those people who are the best "firefighters" (crisis managers) and problem solvers.

The key challenge of stage 2 is to scale up the business, which involves hiring more people and putting day-to-day systems in place to effectively manage the larger enterprise. The corporate culture of most firms starts becoming distorted at this stage of development. Because not all employees can have direct contact with the entrepreneur, they are left to develop their own interpretation of the corporate culture, based on what they have heard. The entrepreneur must depend on other managers to monitor behavior, but these managers may have their own interpretation of the culture. If the company has not yet developed the strategic planning, control, management development, and organizational structure consistent with this stage of development, it may be placed at a further disadvantage because, even if it can develop the appropriate culture, there will be no support for it.

At this stage of development, a company should devote at least part of its planning time to clearly articulating and devising ways to effectively communicate to all employees the culture that will support its goals and long-term growth. If there is an existing culture statement, it may need to be revised to reflect the needs of the current stage of development. In this regard, it should mention a shift toward planning and control, at least implicitly, as well as emphasize meeting responsibilities and goals. Further, the reward system should be reviewed and changed, if necessary, to promote behavior consistent with meeting the company's goals.

During stage 2, there should be a strong focus on developing a formal (written) values statement of some kind and on continued communication and reinforcement (through the reward system) of the company's stated (or implicit) values. There should also be a focus on hiring for cultural fit, to minimize turnover problems as the organization scales up. At this stage, a company should be focused on creating more formal orientation and training programs and processes to develop employees' skills, as well as their understanding of the company's culture.

Culture Management at Stage 3

Stage 3 typically occurs from $10 to $100 million in revenues. Though the number of employees will vary, the range tends to be from one hundred to five hundred people. It is at this stage of development that a company's culture will (or at least ought to) make a fundamental shift toward promoting professional management—while at the same time maintaining the positive aspects of its original entrepreneurial culture. The culture of a stage 3 company should promote planning as a way of life, accountability for meeting departmental and individual goals, commitment to training employees to become professional managers, and other behavior consistent with professionalized management. If the planning, control, management development, and organizational structure systems are inconsistent (not sufficiently developed) with the requirements of this stage of development, then the culture will be inconsistent as well.

At this stage, the culture is, of necessity, still being managed implicitly, and not formally in most cases. To support the needed change to professional management, there should be a focus on redefining the company's culture so that it facilitates this transition. If there is a formal statement of the company's culture, it may need to be revised. If there is no formal statement, then one may have to be created. Management must communicate and constantly reinforce values that are consistent with professionalized management, especially planning versus firefighting, managing versus doing (for those in management or leadership roles), and rewarding performance against goals versus basing rewards on other factors.

Recruiting and training processes may have to be revised to support selection and development of people who fit with the evolving organization and culture. Emphasis should also be placed on using and managing symbols. At this stage companies more formally begin to embed their culture in their structure (e.g., through how individual roles are defined).

Leadership practices are a key culture management tool in stage 3 and beyond. All leaders need to model behavior consistent with the company becoming an entrepreneurially oriented professionally managed firm. It is also at this stage that the leadership molecule, comprising three or four senior managers, should be starting to form.

Culture Management at Stage 4

Stage 4 occurs at about $500 million plus in revenues. The typical company at this stage has at least five hundred people. More important, by this time some of the original people as well as some who came later have left the organization, and the company has now had a minimum of five "waves" of hiring. In this context, a *hiring wave* is defined as recruitment of a cohort of people during a specified time period. Each time a new cohort joins the organization, they will bring with them the values, beliefs, and norms of their generation and their generation's values will have a significant or not so significant impact on the company's values, depending on whether societal culture has shifted and whether the company is or is not actively and effectively managing its own values.

The larger a company becomes, the more problematic it is to effectively manage its culture. At stage 4, the company needs a hiring process in place to clearly identify people who fit with the company's values and it needs to be able to adapt this hiring process to changes in the larger societal norms. Without careful management, it is at this stage that newcomers typically do not share the experiences of the original founding group. The later they arrive, the less they will understand the core values and shared history of the old-timers. This divergence in perspective sets the company up for a potential "cultural civil war" simply as a by-product of its success and growth.

By the time a company reaches stage 4, it needs to develop a formal method for managing corporate culture. Corporate culture management should become an important part of the planning process, and resources should be devoted to (1) performing a cultural audit to identify potential problem areas; (2) clearly articulating the existing culture and the new culture, if different; (3) identifying gaps between the current and desired cultures; and (4) developing a plan for transforming or maintaining the corporate culture. The latter step should include a process for regularly monitoring the culture to ensure that it is promoting the organization's goals. In brief, a stage 4 company should have a formal culture management plan and planning process, one that incorporates all ten tools.

Culture Management at Stages 5 and 6

By the time a company reaches stage 5, its culture management capability should be in place. The future challenges of culture management will come from its further growth, both in size and diversification as well as from the possibility of mergers and acquisitions. As the company moves into different lines of business, it will have to adapt and then effectively communicate a new culture that is supportive of this effort. This process begins in stage 5 and is completed in stage 6. If this growth comes from startups, then the cycles of stages 1 through 4 will have to be repeated in the new ventures. If the growth comes through mergers and acquisitions, the key issue will be cultural assimilation. This is analogous to the transformation in culture that is required to support the transitions to stage 3.

Culture Management at Stage 7

The final stage of culture management involves revitalization of the enterprise. This can occur at any of the previous stages of growth. When an organization goes into decline and needs revitalization, a key reason will typically be some kind of cultural failure. The culture will have inadvertently morphed from functional to dysfunctional. We examine several examples of dysfunctional cultures in Chapter 9.

Final Comment

An important element of effectively managing corporate culture relates to how culture does change and should change over time. Although this change tends to take time (unless there is a major event such as a merger or acquisition), culture and the process of culture management need to change or adapt to meet the demands at various stages of organizational growth because of changes in organizational size. Even if culture is not being actively managed, it *will* change (mutate) because of new hires, changes in the environment, and other factors. Without active management, the culture might well change in an undesired, dysfunctional direction.

Criterion of Successful Management of Corporate Culture

How do we know that a company's culture has been successfully managed? The answer: when its culture is imprinted on the members of the organization; when it is something that they live and breathe and take for granted as a way of life. If the culture is being managed effectively, it helps create a connection between the employee and the company that is difficult to break.

The highest accolade that an employee at McDonald's can receive is to be described as having catsup in his or her veins. This expression connotes that the person is a true believer in the McDonald's culture. At IBM, the test of cultural imprinting was that if you awakened any IBMer in the middle of the night and asked, "What are our core values?" he or she would be able to recite the three core beliefs of IBM's culture without hesitation. Thus a prerequisite to a successfully managed culture is that it be imprinted on people and second-nature to them. This means it has become part of their DNA.

Conclusion

Culture management is not a six-steps-and-done process. It cannot be just an "initiative."

Although culture generally changes slowly (except when there are certain major events, such as a merger or acquisition), it requires adjusting as the organization grows in size, complexity, and geographical dispersion of people. This means that the culture management process must become a way of life in an organization.

This chapter presented the culture management process and identified ten culture management tools. The next chapters describe how companies have used these tools in identifying and managing each of the five specific dimensions of corporate culture discussed in Chapter 1.

Part II

Management of the Key Dimensions of Corporate Culture

4 Managing the Customer Orientation Dimension of Culture

This chapter deals with how companies can and should manage the customer orientation dimension of culture. We examine and analyze how certain companies have achieved success by creating and effectively managing a culture that emphasizes the importance of the customer and customer service. They are Starbucks Coffee Company, the Walt Disney Company, and Southwest Airlines.

Although we focus primarily on customer orientation, it must be noted that cultural variables are typically interrelated. For example, how customers are treated at Starbucks depends on how Starbucks treats employees. Accordingly, we use some of the same case studies in chapters dealing with other dimensions of culture.

Managing Customer Orientation at Starbucks

In our judgment, Starbucks is a consummate model of how corporate culture leads to organizational success. We begin with in-depth discussion and analysis of how the company created a culture of customer orientation and in so doing became a business icon.

In a little more than two decades, Starbucks has become a worldwide brand synonymous with lattes and cappuccino. In 2009, it had more than eighty-five hundred company-owned stores and even more licensed stores. The company has more stores in California than all of its major competitors combined. Yet Starbucks accomplished this with a commodity that has been around for quite some time.

The Secret to Starbucks' Success

How did Starbucks become what it is today: the leading brand and purveyor of specialty coffee worldwide? As described in Chapter 1, the company's success is attributable to culture and, in particular, to how it manages the customer and people (employee) orientation dimensions of culture, rather than to coffee. (We will cover the employee orientation dimension of Starbucks' culture in Chapter 5).

How Starbucks Manages the Customer Experience

This section examines how Starbucks manages the customer orientation dimension of its culture and how this contributes directly to success. To understand how Starbucks treats customers and the role of that treatment in its success, we need to examine the history and development of Starbucks as a company.

The original stores did not sell coffee drinks. They sold fresh-roasted coffee beans, imported teas, and spices. Sometimes the individual behind the counter would brew a pot and serve free samples in Dixie cups.

By the end of the 1970s, Starbucks had four retail stores, a mail-order unit, and a wholesale company. Sales were $2 million per year. Howard Schultz, who is now chairman and CEO, joined Starbucks in 1982 as director of retail operations and marketing.

The Strategic Insight: "The Third Place"

Schultz had been with Starbucks for approximately one year when he visited Milan to attend a trade show. While walking the streets of Milan back and forth from his hotel to the trade show, he had the classic flash of entrepreneurial or strategic insight that was ultimately the foundation of Starbucks' success. Specifically, he marveled at the ubiquity of the Italian coffee bars. After a few days, he began to be drawn into them because "it was so romantic."

Schultz describes his experience: "I saw the same faces and the camaraderie. The coffee bar was an extension of people's homes and was truly part of the fabric of the Italian culture. It struck me right across the head: this is something dynamic and unusual."[1]

Specifically, Schultz's key strategic insight was recognizing that the product, which is to say, the value proposition derived by the customer, was not the coffee per se. Instead, the product was the experience provided to the customer visiting Starbucks, nominally to purchase a coffee beverage but actually to go there to participate in a café milieu. This was the notion Schultz brought back to the United States and drew on to reconceptualize Starbucks and create a new business space.

The name he gave to this idea was "the third place." It referred to the physical places in people's lives. The first place was home; the second was where they worked. As envisioned by Schultz, the third place in a person's life would be the Starbucks café, where he or she could experience a sense of social interaction, while enjoying a finely brewed cup of coffee, a cappuccino, or a latte.

The Grand Experiment

The next step was putting Schultz's idea to the test. But the founders of Starbucks viewed his insight with disinterest and lack of enthusiasm. It took Schultz a year and a half to convince them to allow him to test his idea. He went back to Italy to do more research, and when he returned he was more convinced than ever that he was on to something.

In April 1984, Starbucks tested the idea by opening up a small coffee bar inside a new store. Instantly, a metamorphosis occurred. Starbucks had transformed its business from being a purveyor of whole bean coffee to something very different. The beverage was the catalyst. The atmosphere of the store changed. The customer count grew. The relationship with the customer changed. Starbucks people were able to develop closer relationships with customers because of the instant gratification and romance people received from the beverage served in this environment.

Although whole bean coffee remained the core business, Schultz changed the game at Starbucks. It was the juxtaposition of two simple elements to create a more complex, and in some ways more wonderful, thing, as the combination of hydrogen and oxygen creates water.

In spite of the experiment's success, the original owners of Starbucks balked at adapting their company to Schultz's vision: an American version of the Italian coffee bar. They did not want to change their concept of the business; they wanted to sell coffee beans, not beverages. They did not want to become a café, or a hybrid specialty retailer/café.

The Precursor of Starbucks: Il Giornale

Schultz decided to leave Starbucks to create his own company according to his vision. He called his new company Il Giornale (after the Italian daily newspaper); it was founded in 1985.

Within a year, one of the original Starbucks founders acquired another company, Peet's Coffee, located in Berkeley, California. The founder was averse to a dilution of ownership. Accordingly, Starbucks assumed debt rather than issue equity. As a result, after the acquisition the company's debt-to-equity ratio was 6:1, a very high and risky ratio.

Metamorphosis into Starbucks

In August 1987, Schultz went back to Starbucks with a buy-out offer and a vision to take the concept well beyond the boundaries of Seattle. The high debt burden on the owners of Starbucks made them receptive to Schultz's offer. Il Giornale acquired the assets of Starbucks and changed its name to "Starbucks Corporation."

Culture Management at Starbucks

From the inception of Starbucks, corporate culture was very important to Schultz. Unlike many other companies at a comparable stage of development, there was an explicit statement of Starbucks' "guiding principles," described in more detail in Chapter 3.

Starbucks' guiding (cultural) principles include dimensions relating to the treatment of customers and of people who are members of the Starbucks organization ("partners," as they are called). It also includes dimensions relating to the environment and profitability. The key dimension or principle concerning us in this chapter is the one dealing with customers: "Develop enthusiastically satisfied customers all of the time." The notion is a cornerstone of the Starbucks experience and value proposition and thereby an underlying reason for its success.

Like all companies, Starbucks has service failures as well as successes. But here is an anecdote of how Starbucks deals with customers and service failures. One of the authors was citing Starbucks in a presentation on organizational success and failure. A member of the audience said that she had a "Starbucks experience story to tell." She told of visiting a Starbucks store in North Carolina, and having been disappointed about the freshness of the coffee being served. She then said that she wrote to the corporate office in Seattle to describe her disappointment. According to her, she received a phone call as a follow-up and a letter with a coupon for a complementary beverage. She said this was a satisfactory resolution for her; but the story continued. About a year later, she received a follow-up call from Starbucks asking how her experience had been during the past year, and whether she was now a satisfied customer! This second follow-up call truly astounded her.

Training People to Develop Enthusiastically Satisfied Customers

How does Starbucks motivate its people to develop enthusiastically satisfied customers all the time? It does not do it by dropping a potion or magic pill into the coffee. It does it the old fashioned way: through training in its guiding principles, in how to treat its customers, as well as in how to treat coffee.

All café employees, or baristas, go through a training program on entry into the company. This training introduces them to the company's guiding principles as well as how to brew and serve coffee. Accordingly, it not only trains them technically but also embeds them in the social psychological aspects of the Starbucks experience that the company wants its customers to have.

This dual aspect of training (i.e., the combination of technical and cultural training) can be seen in the company's "coffee passport program," where new partners (employees) are given a 104-page booklet about coffee. The booklet includes a map of coffee-growing regions; information about the farming of coffee, roasting of coffee, and the fundamentals of coffee brewing; coffee tasting terms; and a list of Starbucks coffee types.[2] According to Joseph Michelli, author of *The Starbucks Experience*, "Partners are expected to not only use the passport as a reference, but complete verified tastings of all Starbucks core coffees twice a year."[3] They are also given one pound of Starbucks coffee each week at no cost to them in order to enhance their knowledge, understanding, and appreciation of the company's coffee.

Starbucks baristas are encouraged to become "coffee masters," a designation for partners who have achieved a defined level of coffee expertise.

Like the black belts earned by Six Sigma experts, coffee masters wear a black apron to symbolize their achievement. To receive the designation of coffee master, the baristas must complete a defined training program (usually over three months), pass a series of tests, and lead a number of coffee tastings.

Starbucks pays great attention to all aspects of the customers' store experience. This includes choice of materials in its store design and the flow of the store, as well as its ambiance. There are checklists of things that must happen at the store level, such as cleaning the counters and how long coffee can be heated to await serving before it gets disposed of.

What Starbucks Has Become

Schultz believed the kind of organization that Starbucks was and how it did business would become a source of sustainable competitive advantage. In his words, "The values of the company and the guiding principles became a unique sustainable competitive advantage."[4] In effect, Schultz understood the role of culture as a building block of organizational success, even though he did not know the concept of corporate culture per se as a management tool. Instead, it was an intuitive insight for him.

Starbucks has become the leading brand of specialty coffee. Its stores and logo are ubiquitous. By the end of 2009, Starbucks had grown to more than to $9.8 billion in net revenues. The company states that it envisions a total of about thirty thousand stores being possible. This means Starbucks has the potential to become a company with more than $30 billion in revenues.

Starbucks is an extraordinary story. It has become an iconic brand and world-class company purveying a commodity product. The secret ingredient is its culture and how it is managed.

Deconstructing Starbucks' Success

From this discussion, it should be clear that Starbucks' success is attributable not to the coffee but rather to the relationship it has created with customers. The company does not view the sale of coffee as a transaction. Instead, its "product" is the experience.

Starbucks' success is based on a number of ingredients, among them having customers view its stores as a key place in their lives (the "third place"). This does not happen by bricks and mortar alone. It happens as a result of the relationship among the brand, the physical place, and the people at Starbucks—the employees and the customers. Another ingredient to success is how its partners (employees) treat customers. Starbucks communicates its philosophy as well as technical procedures by means of the dual-purpose training program.

Managing Customer Orientation at Disney Theme Parks

The Walt Disney Company is justifiably renowned for its theme parks: Disneyland, Disney World, and similar parks on the outskirts of Paris and in Hong Kong and Tokyo.[5] Although one of the obvious strengths of Disney is its portfolio of characters, the real secret of Disney's success in its theme parks is attributable to how it treats guests.

By 2009, Disney was hosting more than 116 million visitors at its theme parks and resorts annually.[6] It derived more than $10.6 billion in revenue, from entrance fees as well as products the visitors purchased at the parks.

How Does Disney Accomplish This?

Disney Theme Parks achieves a high level of customer service with employees who are largely unskilled and who are trained by the company in its distinctive culture. Disney has developed a highly sophisticated, but elegantly simple, culture management process to help its people understand the importance of and ability to deliver exceptional service to customers.

The components of this culture management process are (1) a special language or vocabulary used at the theme parks, (2) well-defined roles and role descriptions specifying the desired behaviors, and (3) a training program with both formal and on-the-job training.

Using Words to Create a Culture

One of the tools of culture management used by Disney theme parks is a special vocabulary. Disney has created an elegantly simple way to change the mind-set of its employees. The company understands that words have two types of meaning: denotative and connotative. Denotative meaning is the technical aspect of words; for example, a frog is a small aquatic animal. Words also have connotative meaning. For a frog, the connotations might be warts, croaking, and slime. Disney uses words with the type of denotation needed to support the culture it wants to have and that it wants employees to embrace.

Disney uses its own unique and special language to communicate and reinforce a culture among employees—who, as noted in Chapter 3, are called "cast members"—of providing the highest-possible level of customer service. The company begins with the foundational notion that all employees are actually participating in a live performance. The stage for this live, gigantic performance is Disneyland or Disney World. It is a truly romantic construct.

Accordingly, when visitors come to Disneyland or Disney World for a day of entertainment, Disney wants its cast members to embrace the notion that they are all actors in a live performance. This includes not only the obvious characters such as Mickey and Minnie Mouse and Goofy but everyone interacting with the guests, including custodial people, ticket sellers, and guides on the jungle cruise. They are all cast members.

Words matter, and they help create a mind-set. There are significant differences in denotation between the concept of a customer and that of a guest. Although a customer should be treated very well, there is an even higher connotation of good treatment when it comes to guests. Similarly, there is a difference in mind-set between an employee and a cast member. The latter suggests an aura of fun and status; it is subtly higher in esteem than the construct of an employee.

Disney also uses other words to reinforce the core notion that people are participating in a live performance. It uses the terms "on stage" and "off stage" to refer to the physical aspect of the theme parks. A cast member who is in a place where there are guests is on stage and expected to behave "in character," or according to his or her defined role. "Off stage" refers to anything that is behind the scenes, such as behind closed doors or in "the under park."[7]

Using Roles and Role Descriptions to Create a Culture

Disney defines roles for each cast member. Clearly, the Disney characters have prescribed roles that come closest to traditional stage roles, but the tour guides also have prescribed roles and dialogue, with "approved variations."

Using Training to Create a Culture

Like Starbucks, Disney also uses a dual-purpose training program designed not only to communicate the technical aspects of each role but also to help people embrace the core values of the customer service oriented culture. Training begins with a course called Disney Traditions 1. The objective of this course is to help all new hires understand and embrace the special vision of founder Walt Disney: that Disney is in the business of making people happy; it is "the happiest place on earth." They learn that they are cast members. They also learn the special language and vocabulary of the Disney theme park. Once people have gone through the Traditions course experience, they are then trained in their specific roles.

Taken together, what Disney does to manage customer orientation at its theme parks is truly magical. It has created a very special program of imbuing people with values toward customers, and making their experience at a Disney theme park very special indeed.

Managing Customer Orientation at Southwest Airlines

It would be rare to read or speak about the concept of effective corporate culture without mentioning Southwest Airlines. To many company leaders, business analysts, and researchers, no company does culture better than Southwest. Experts consider the company's culture—though intangible—its most significant asset and a key contributor to growth and outstanding financial performance. In fact, Herb Kelleher, one of the company's founders, was quoted as saying: "I've always told our people that the intangibles are much more important than the tangibles. Others can always reproduce the tangibles. . . . We want people to get off the airplane with a big smile on their face, saying, 'Boy, that was an unusual experience.'"[8] In brief, what Kelleher suggests is that culture is a key source of competitive advantage and one that contributes greatly to Southwest's success.

Southwest Airlines (originally known as Air Southwest) was founded by Rollin King and Kelleher in 1967 but did not actually have its maiden flight until June 18, 1971. The idea for creating the company was to offer people a convenient means to travel between major cities in Texas—Houston, Dallas, and San Antonio—at the lowest possible price. People who would normally have driven the relatively short distances between these cities could now fly, and fly more frequently. As stated by Kelleher, the company basically created a new "market segment."[9] The company continued to grow, in terms of passengers, cities served, and revenue.

Formula for Success

As Southwest expanded, it retained its original formula with respect to routes, planes, and ways of operating: (1) using a point-to-point route system, (2) increasing the number of flights and offering these flights at fares that were dramatically lower than existing ones, (3) expanding slowly into relatively noncompetitive markets (at least initially), (4) flying only one type of aircraft, and (5) having a culture—embraced and reinforced by employees—of doing whatever it takes.

Instead of adopting the hub-and-spoke system that is the standard among major U.S. airlines, Southwest used and continues to use a point-to-point route system. With the hub-and-spoke, large numbers of passengers are fed into a major hub and then distributed to connecting flights. The problem with this system is that if a flight is delayed significantly, passengers and planes can end up stranded. In addition, late planes in one location can result in systemwide delays. With a point-to-point system, flights are typically short in duration and there are comparatively few connections at a given destination, which reduces the incidence of delays. In addition, Southwest typically has frequent departures in those cities where they do have connecting flights (Phoenix and Las Vegas, for example). The bottom line: planes in the air make money. Planes on the ground do not.

Until very recently, Southwest avoided going head-to-head with major carriers, choosing instead to serve relatively uncongested and noncompetitive airports (such as Chicago's Midway, the Los Angeles area's Burbank, and Dallas's Love Field, where the company began). This allowed Southwest, until the early 1990s, to grow its customer base without a great deal of direct competition.

Southwest has always flown only one plane, the Boeing 737. The plane is not necessarily *the* competitive advantage, although its size (accommodating between 122 and 137 passengers) seems to fit the idea of running frequent, short-haul trips. Instead, flying only 737s means the company is purchasing parts for and having mechanics and crew work on just one type of aircraft. This, along with flying into relatively uncongested airports, contributes to very short turnaround time—often less than thirty minutes. Keeping planes off the ground and in the air means happy customers (because the planes arrive and leave on time) and more revenue for the company (because that is how an airline makes money).

Each Southwest employee's job description includes something about "doing whatever it takes." This is translated into, among other things, flight attendants (and even pilots) sharing responsibility for cleaning the cabin. Having people who embrace the idea of going beyond their job to support company goals contributes to timely turnaround and satisfied customers.

Southwest's success has, over the years, attracted competitors. People Express, for example, was founded in 1980 to compete with other forms of transportation for business and leisure travelers. Like Southwest, the company offered extremely low fares. But unlike Southwest, the company did not effectively manage its growth and was bankrupt within five years. Eventually, more established carriers, such as United with its Shuttle service on the West Coast and Delta Express (and later Song) on the East Coast, lowered prices in an attempt to compete with Southwest's low cost structure. The problem was that even though these larger carriers could lower prices, they did not (and probably could not) change their corporate culture. The culture of "how we operate" was simply too ingrained. The initial forays of the majors into Southwest's market affected its profit, but doing so also affected their own. With all their existing systems and ways of doing business, the majors could not compete effectively, and most of those ventures were not profitable.

The Results

As of 2010, Southwest was flying to sixty-eight cities in thirty-five states with a fleet of 537 Boeing 737s. The company had annual revenue in excess of $10 billion and, until 2009, was consistently profitable (even when other U.S. carriers were losing money, or in some cases filing for bankruptcy). In addition, the company won many awards over the years for customer service and satisfaction and ranked in the top twenty on the *Fortune* list of most admired companies for more than a decade.

The Foundation of Southwest's Culture: "Luv" and Fun

The company was and still is based at Love Field in Dallas, and, whether a coincidence or not, "Luv" has been a very important part of the company's culture, image, and business. (In 1977, Southwest stock was listed on the New York Stock Exchange as LUV). There is a real focus on caring for employees and customers, as well as on having fun. Many articles have been written since the company's founding about the impact its unique culture has on success. (A fairly comprehensive list of these articles can be found on the Southwest website.)[10]

Evidence of Southwest's focus on culture is everywhere for an outsider to observe; it is transparent, though not replicable. Just pick up a copy of their *Spirit* magazine any month, or visit their website. Each month in *Spirit*, the CEO or president opens with a message that is typically culture-related, something about Southwest customers or people, both terms always being capitalized in every communication from any part of the company; the community; or some aspect of company performance. There is also in every issue an article profiling the "Star of the Month," a team member who has excelled. Finally, there is a profile of a customer. The company website includes a statement of the company's values (in the form of a mission) as well as a "Nuts About Southwest" blog in which employees, management, and customers can post comments, share ideas, or upload videos.

Southwest Airlines is a model of superior corporate culture management. We discuss specific aspects of the company's culture throughout this and the next four chapters.

Focus on the Customer at Southwest Airlines

There are two parts to Southwest's mission statement, one focused on customers and the other focused on people (its employees). Here is the Customer Mission Statement:

> The mission of Southwest Airlines is dedication to the highest quality of Customer Service delivered with a sense of warmth, friendliness, individual pride, and Company Spirit.[11]

In addition to the mission statement, a twenty-plus-page "Customer Service Commitment" can be found on the company's website.[12] This document presents information on airport operations, irregular operations (including what the passenger can expect if delayed), fares and ticketing, reservations, overbooking, tickets and refunds, the company's fleet, baggage, frequent flyer program, and how to contact Southwest. All of this information is presented in plain English so that it is very easy for anyone to understand. Most important, on page 1 is this statement: "We tell our Employees we are in the Customer Service business—we just happen to provide airline transportation. It is a privilege to serve your air travel needs." The message to employees and to customers: we are serious about customer service.

To show their appreciation for customers, Southwest regularly sends birthday cards to the members of its Rapid Rewards (frequent flyer) program, along with other gifts (e.g., a set of booties to wear through security after shoes are removed) and greetings (one of the authors received an "anniversary" card from the Rapid Rewards program, along with a coupon for a free drink).

Having a statement about the value placed on customers and customer service and sending little tokens of appreciation are not what's led to Southwest's success. Many companies offer statements about how important the customer is, and any company can send stuff to its customers (although in all the years that the authors have been members of all of the major carriers' frequent flyer programs, we have never received a birthday card!). What really makes the difference is how Southwest's people treat their customers. As with Starbucks, the dominant philosophy at Southwest is "Treat your employees well and they will treat their customers well." We discuss the treatment of people more in the next chapter.

If you have flown Southwest more than once you can probably recount at least one fun thing an employee did that made you feel special and appreciated. This can range from entertaining ways of completing the safety briefing to playing games with passengers who are delayed, to apologizing for flight delays (even if they are not that significant). Southwest employees are also encouraged to help solve customers' problems and are empowered with decision making authority. People "are trusted to use their different personalities to act creatively and originally to treat customers with unique flair."[13] Again, anyone who frequently flies Southwest probably also has a story about how an employee helped solve a problem.

Executives take customer complaints, and customer compliments, very seriously. Stories abound about customers writing a letter to the company and receiving a response from the president or CEO.[14] Southwest executives—including the CEO—spend hours every day reading and responding to mail (and email) from customers. Current and former executives frequently refer to what they learned about the customer experience—good and bad—in interviews, in discussion with company personnel, and on the company's "Nuts About Southwest" blog.

Ensuring that employees treat customers in a manner consistent with the company's values starts with the hiring process. As stated frequently by Southwest executives—among them Colleen Barrett, the company's former president—Southwest "hires for attitude and trains for skills. For example, with flight attendant candidates, Southwest conducts group interviews to observe how the applicants interact with other people."[15] All employees—even those who seldom interact with customers—go through customer service training, starting basically on day one of their employment. This helps ensure that each and every employee understands the value placed on the customer and on customer service.

Southwest also frequently recognizes its employees for going the extra mile in the interest of customer service. This is done through profiles in *Spirit* and through stories on the website, as well as through administration of rewards.

The result of all these efforts is that people like, and some people *love*, flying Southwest. The company has continued to grow and remains relatively stable financially, even as its competitors are declaring bankruptcy, downsizing, and reducing the quality of their service.

Conclusion

We have examined how three successful companies (Starbucks, Disney, and Southwest Airlines) manage the cultural dimension of customer orientation. Although each company is in its own business, all have achieved great success with a common core strategy: ensuring that their people embrace the importance of satisfying customers and providing a special experience. In promoting this value, these companies use one or more of the culture management tools described in Chapter 3.

Customer Orientation Culture Management Tools

What can be learned from the experiences of these companies and how they use the tools of culture management (presented in the last chapter) to successfully manage the culture dimension of customer orientation?

Have a Formal Statement of the Customer Orientation Value

Both Starbucks and Southwest have formal statements focusing on customers. The third company, Disney, focuses on ensuring a positive experience for its customers, but it does not have a formal culture statement explicitly defining its customer and customer-service value. Disney's values focus instead on the product being delivered and how it is delivered, so that, as stated on their website, the "values make our brands stand out."[16] This can have an impact on customer service and satisfaction.

Having a written statement of what the value *should* be helps everyone in the company understand what the expectations are with respect to treatment of customers. As stated previously, it is not enough to simply have a statement of the value. Instead, the value needs to be communicated and consistently managed, such that it is real for all employees. This is accomplished through use of other tools.

Use Communication, Including Language, to Reinforce the Customer Value

All three companies use special words or special methods to communicate aspects of their customer-oriented culture. Starbucks refers to its baristas. Disney has an entire language—using terms such as guests, cast members, on-stage, and off-stage—that creates a special mind-set for customer satisfaction. The language is unique to each company but fits the nature of the business it is in. At Southwest, "Customers" is always capitalized as a way of communicating their importance to the business.

Recruit and Select People Who Are Customer-Oriented

All three companies take great pains to hire service-oriented people. The hiring process at Southwest, in particular, is focused on finding people with what they call "a servant's heart," that is, people who fit with and who will embrace the company's focus on the customer. All three companies seem to adopt the belief that skills can be learned, but culture cannot.

Use Orientation and Training Processes to Help Employees Understand the Customer Orientation Value

All three companies use extensive training as a tool to help promote their customer-orientation values. This training begins on the day an individual is hired; culture is an important component of new employee orientation. Ongoing training is focused not just on the technical aspects of customer service but also on making real for all employees the value each company places on the customer and on customer service.

Reward and Recognize Those Who Represent the Customer Value

As is true at Southwest, those who go the extra mile to promote customer service and support the value placed on it by the company should be recognized for their efforts. This recognition does not have to be in the form of a financial reward. A detailed account of what an employee did that supported the customer orientation value (like that included in Southwest's *Spirit* magazine) rewards the individual in question and also helps others understand what the value looks like.

Have Leadership Practices in Place That Support the Customer Value

At Southwest, anyone and everyone—employees and customers—can communicate with even the most senior executives about customer service issues. Most important, response to the issues raised is timely. As evidenced by the story presented in this chapter, Starbucks' corporate leadership is also concerned about, and takes the time to respond to, their customers. This is not to suggest that all companies should offer customers access to senior executives. It is to suggest, however, that leaders need to find ways to show clear support for, and model behavior consistent with, the company's customer-orientation values.

Align the Structure to Support the Customer Orientation Value

All three companies, in some way, embed the customer orientation value in every individual's role description. At Disney, the role of the individual in this regard is clearly prescribed or scripted. At Southwest, the individual is empowered to execute his or her role in a way that supports the value placed on the customer. The key is to help *all* employees understand the role they play in supporting and making real the value placed on the customer.

Final Comment

The tools described here can be used in one way or another by any company. This means that achieving a culture emphasizing customer orientation is within the reach of virtually every business, if they seek to attain it.

5 Managing the People Orientation Dimension of Culture

This chapter focuses on how companies can and should manage the people orientation dimension of culture. This dimension concerns the way in which companies deal with or manage their people. It is based on explicit or implicit assumptions about how people ought to be treated as well as the role of that treatment in organizational performance. From our research and experience, we believe that if the people orientation dimension is managed effectively it can have a significant impact on both customer satisfaction and overall organizational success.

As in Chapter 4, we examine and analyze selected companies where the cultural value that they place on "treatment of people" has contributed to their success. In this chapter, we focus on Starbucks, Google, Walmart, and Southwest Airlines. We attempt to understand and deconstruct their success to gain insights that are generally applicable to other companies.

Although we concentrate primarily on people orientation, note again that cultural variables are typically interrelated. To repeat a familiar example, how customers are treated at Starbucks depends on how Starbucks treats its people.

Managing People Orientation at Starbucks

People who look for the secret to Starbucks' success in the coffee, or in the design of its stores, are looking in the wrong place. As noted in Chapter 4, the belief at Starbucks is that how the company treats its people affects how they treat the company's customers, and this creates the company's success. How does Starbucks treat its people to motivate them to treat customers well?

First, Starbucks refers to its employees (and to a great extent treats them) as partners. The word *partner* suggests something very different from *employee*. Although there is nothing wrong with being an employee, being a partner implies a different kind of relationship with the company. This can have a subtle positive impact on the mind-set of Starbucks staff, but it is insufficient unless backed up by other aspects of the way people are treated. Words and phrases without action could be empty, or even worse, lead to cynicism.

At Starbucks, the words are backed up and reinforced by company actions. In contrast to many if not most retail businesses, Starbucks gives full benefits to all employees working more than twenty hours per week. Although this increases costs, the company believes the policy helps them recruit and retain a higher caliber of people and is therefore optimal economically in the long run.

Starbucks also reinforces the partner notion through the company's innovative stock option program, called the "Bean Stock" program. All employees are eligible to own shares of the company's stock and thereby benefit from its success. The company originally developed this program prior to going public. As Howard Schultz has said, "Bean Stock means everything to Starbucks. It enables us to work as hard as we have been working."[1]

Starbucks reinforces its focus on treatment of people through one of its original Guiding Principles: "Provide a great work environment and treat each other with respect and dignity."[2] The sixth principle, added later, is also relevant to treatment of people: "Embrace diversity as an essential component in the way we do business."[3]

The net result is that Starbucks has created a culture where people feel valued. This is reflected in the company being selected as one of *Fortune's* "100 Best Companies to Work for in 2010."[4] It is also echoed in superior economic success.

Starbucks' Success in Decline

Unfortunately, nothing lasts forever. During the past few years Starbucks, like many companies, has suffered reverses. In part, this is attributable to the economic crisis that began in 2008, as well as to increasing competition from other companies such as McDonald's. However, Starbucks itself is also probably to blame. One contributing factor to its decline was its choice of a CEO to replace the retiring Orin Smith. Jim Donald, an experienced and capable executive, joined Starbucks in October 2002 as president, North America, where he managed business development and operations for all Starbucks stores in the United States and Canada; in March 2005 he was promoted to president and CEO. During his tenure, the company grew to more than fifteen thousand stores in forty-three countries. Prior to joining Starbucks, Donald served from 1996 to 2002 as chairman, president, and CEO of Pathmark Stores, an East Coast regional supermarket chain. His thirty-plus years in retailing included being handpicked by Sam Walton to help lead Walmart's development and expansion of the Wal-Mart Super Centers, where he oversaw all merchandising, distribution, store design, and real estate operations from 1991 to 1994. He also served in a variety of senior management positions with Albertson's and Safeway, where he had a reputation for improving the financial performance of stores under his supervision.

In spite of all of this background, Donald was unsuccessful at Starbucks. In 2008 Schultz reassumed the position of CEO. In discussing future CEOs at Starbucks, Schultz stated that the company would never again hire someone from the outside (that is, someone who did not understand the company's special culture) to occupy the position of CEO.[5]

Managing People Orientation at Google

Google, a publicly held corporation headquartered in Mountain View, California, developed a powerful search engine that enables it to earn revenue and profits from advertising. As of December 31, 2008, the company had 20,222 full-time employees.

The name "Google" originated from a misspelling of the word "googol," which refers to 10^{100}, the number represented by a 1 followed by one hundred zeros. Like *Xerox* and *FedEx*, *Google* has become a verb used in everyday language. It means to use the Google search engine to obtain information on the World Wide Web."[6]

Larry Page and Sergey Brin founded Google on September 4, 1998, while they were students at Stanford University. Its initial public offering, on August 24, 2004, resulted in raising $1.67 billion, implying a market value for the entire company of approximately $23 billion. Today, the company has become one of the most powerful brands in the world.

In 2001, Eric Schmidt, who was formerly CEO at Novell and chief technology officer at Sun Microsystems, joined Google as CEO. When he came in, Page and Brin assumed the titles of president-products and president-technology, respectively. Together they form what has been termed "Google's Troika."[7] The troika clearly is a classic leadership molecule (as described in Chapter 3).

The Role of Corporate Culture in Google's Success

At Google, culture has been an explicit source of competitive advantage. Early in the company's history, Brin and Page instilled a strong and distinctive set of corporate values (as we saw in Chapter 1): (1) don't be evil, (2) technology matters, and (3) we make our own rules.[8] All of these values, in one way or another, define the types of people Google wants to attract and retain. They also help define the people orientation dimension of the company's culture.

The unofficial company slogan is "Don't be evil." This slogan refers to business integrity: "We never manipulate rankings to put our (advertising or content) partners higher in our search results. No one can buy a better PageRank."[9] This mantra is used at Google operationally, day to day. Eric Schmidt, CEO of Google, cited an incident at a meeting where an engineer said of a proposal, "That would be evil." The issue concerned how advertising would be linked with search. A discussion ensued, and the conclusion was that the engineer was correct: it would be evil, and it was not adopted.[10]

The second value ("Technology matters") infuses the core strategy for Google. The company is committed to using leading-edge technology to improve search results and assist its advertisers. Google has invested heavily to continuously improve the technology that supports search results.

The third value, "We make our own rules," implies that Google goes its own way on a variety of issues. These have included Google's refusal to give financial "guidance" to Wall Street or to attempt to smooth earnings to create the appearance of steady growth. The specific practice of not giving guidance is actually "Warren Buffet's Way" and is not unique to Google.[11] However, it is relatively unconventional, with only a few companies operating in this manner. More important, it suggests a mind-set: be different!

Google has also adopted relatively unconventional approaches for creating innovation. It has encouraged engineers to spend 20 percent of their time working on projects of their own choosing. This type of practice is not unique to Google; it has been used at 3M and a number of biotech companies such as Amgen for some time. Nevertheless, it is not a common approach. In brief, Google likes to think of itself as different. To a great extent, it *is* different from most companies, but not quite as much as it would like to think. It has borrowed, or at least mimicked, cultural practices from other companies, notably Buffet's Berkshire Hathaway as well as Amgen and 3M.

The Tools of Culture Management at Google

Google is serious about its culture and about management as a source of competitive advantage. It uses a number of interesting tools to promote and reinforce the culture, including having a job titled chief culture officer, unconventional (though not totally unique) interviewing techniques, and a "Happiness Survey."

Google's Chief Culture Officer

In the summer of 2006, Google gave that title to Stacy Savides Sullivan, who was then director of human resources. Only a handful of other companies have a similar position. Sullivan's role is, in her own words, to "work with employees around the world to figure out ways to maintain and enhance and develop our culture and how to keep the core values we had in the very beginning—a flat organization, a lack of hierarchy, a collaborative environment—to keep these as we continue to grow and spread them and filtrate them into our new offices around the world."[12] She also indicated that one of her greatest challenges in a company that is experiencing hypergrowth is to hire people who possess the kind of traits that Google is looking for in a "Googley" employee.[13] According to Sullivan, this is "somebody who is fairly flexible, adaptable and not focusing on titles and hierarchy, and just gets stuff done."[14]

Unconventional Interviews

There are no standard questions to identify this type of Googley employee. However, Google might ask what seems to be an off-the-wall or way-out question in order to see how the person responds and thinks. They are not looking for a correct answer, because such questions do not really have an answer. Instead, they are trying to figure out how people think and the approach or steps they take to try to solve a problem.

A Happiness Survey

Google includes a survey of employees' happiness with the company as part of a broader annual company survey. Recognizing that human capital was the company's major driving asset to enhance its search product and create new software products, Page and Brin wanted to find out how happy people were with Google and what it was going to take to keep them working at the company.

A "Fun Fund"

As a wealthy company, Google can do some things to enhance the culture of its company that others cannot do so easily. For example, it has allocated a budget for people to "do whatever they want." They can do "some cool things," like purchase massage chairs, pinball machines, and virtually anything they want. The company is famous for its gourmet food, which is available to its employees at no cost. The company also has doctors. The rationale is that healthier people are more productive people.

Results of the Google Culture

In addition to the company's financial success, it has become an attractive place for people to work. Google has been listed several times as one of *Fortune* magazine's "100 Best Companies to Work For." This is a major source of competitive advantage for Google. Because it is a company based on creation of intellectual capital, the ability to attract and retain people is a critical factor in the company's success. Google has been successful in attracting talent even from mighty Microsoft and has hired away people at all levels of Microsoft.[15]

Managing People Orientation at Walmart

Walmart is potentially a controversial example of successful people orientation as a cultural variable because the company has had lawsuits alleging labor problems. At the same time, Walmart is a gigantic company that has been extraordinarily successful with products that are not unique. If you look closely, you will find that in spite of any imperfections this is truly a company that has experienced success, at least in part, because of the way it manages the people dimension of its culture.

Walmart recognizes the powerful role culture can play, and it believes people make the difference in its success.[16] The company has a set of principles that make up the "Walmart Way." One is: "To build a great company, you must create a culture where everyone shares the same values, purposes, and expectations of success."

The Cultural Foundation at Walmart

The cultural foundation at Walmart was created by the personal values and philosophy of its founder, Sam Walton. This is the same way culture is formed at all companies in their early stages. The culture was shaped by the day-to-day decisions and actions taken by Walton, which sent messages about his values and beliefs. Walmart's explicit or stated values include integrity, respect, teamwork, communication, excellence, accountability, and trust.[17] These values, though seemingly homespun and simple, establish a cultural context for day-to-day behavior.

Integrity means that it is wrong to lie, cheat, or steal. Respect means that all employees are to be respected regardless of race, religious belief, gender, position, or job title. Teamwork means that each person can depend on others and that no one needs to do something alone. Communication refers to dialogue in both up and down directions; it refers to listening, as well as talking. Excellence refers to continuously striving to improve. Accountability means that everyone is responsible for his or her own actions and is expected to perform at an acceptable level. Trust is the basis of all human relationships. All Walmart associates (as employees are called) are expected to act so as to engender trust among those with whom they work—including other associates, customers, suppliers, and members of the community.

Although these are the stated core values of Walmart, when we look a little deeper there appear to be three key cultural areas (derived from these values) making up the Walmart Way and contributing to the company's success: (1) a culture of respect for people, (2) concentration on customer satisfaction, and (3) a focus on continuous improvement. Our primary concern in this chapter is respect for people.

How Walmart Manages the People Orientation Dimension of Its Culture

How does Walmart operationalize or manage this aspect of its culture? It uses a variety of methods.

Respect for People

Like Disney and Starbucks, Walmart does not use the term *employees*. It refers to its people as associates. The intended connotation is that people are important and deserve respect, with the implication that *employee* is a bit demeaning. As Don Soderquist, former COO of Walmart, stated: "We work hard to provide an environment where everyone can contribute and be successful. We treat people as more than a pair of hands to do jobs: we treat them as sources of new ideas."[18]

The Saturday Meeting

One of the legendary cultural rituals at Walmart is the Saturday Meeting. This is a pure cultural process and tool. The intent of the Saturday Meeting is to give people an opportunity for involvement and communication. In the days when Sam Walton ran the meeting, he would discuss sales and then ask whether anyone had something they wanted to say. The Saturday Meeting made it possible for all associates to see the whole of the business and remind them of its fundamental purpose: to make sales. Sometimes buyers would display new items for all to see.

As the size of Walmart increased, the personal contact with Sam Walton was replaced to some extent by information technology. The sales report was distributed electronically and made available on the Friday evening before the Saturday meeting. The sales report was also displayed on a screen for all to see.

The meeting was crafted to create a sense of belonging to Walmart as a "community." It engendered a sense of competition with the rest of the world. It also reinforced people's sense of belonging to a group that was almost familylike. In a sense, it was a version of the "industrial clans" of Japanese companies.

The Walmart Cheer

Another tool to reinforce the sense of a business clan is the Walmart Cheer. It is possibly the most well-known symbol of the Walmart culture. It sounds very much like a sellout crowd heard at a football game or pep rally:[19]

> Give me a W!
> Give me an A! . . .
> What's that spell?
> (Answer:) Walmart!
> Whose Walmart is it?
> (Answer:) It's my Walmart!

Results of Effective Culture Management at Walmart

Walmart has grown to be the largest corporation in the world. In 2008, it had more than $379 billion in sales revenue. For the ten-year period from 1999 to 2008, the company consistently achieved more than 20 percent return on equity.

During 2008, Walmart was one of the relatively few companies that continued to be profitable in spite of the economic crisis. It was one of a handful of companies whose stock price actually increased in value for the year, while the average stock lost approximately 45 percent of its value!

Walmart has received its share of criticism, and even lawsuits from employees. It has imperfections and makes mistakes. Nevertheless, the company remains committed to cultural principles, and as its success demonstrates, those principles are working quite well.

Managing People Orientation at Southwest Airlines

The first part of Southwest's mission (presented and described in Chapter 4) focuses on customers; the second focuses on people.

> We are committed to provide our Employees a stable work environment with equal opportunity for learning and personal growth. Creativity and innovation

are encouraged for improving the effectiveness of Southwest Airlines. Above all, Employees will be provided the same concern, respect, and caring attitude within the organization that they are expected to share externally with every Southwest Customer.[20]

This statement, according to the popular press, reflects the values of the founders. According to founder and former CEO Herb Kelleher, "It began by us thinking about what is the right thing to do in a business context. We said we want to really take care of these people, we want to honor them and we love them as individuals. Now that induces the kind of reciprocal trust and diligent effort that made us successful."[21] As illustrated by Kelleher's statement, at Southwest employees do indeed "come first."

Making It Real

As was the case with the customer mission presented in Chapter 4, it is one thing to say "We value our employees and want to treat them well." It is quite another thing to actually do it. But Southwest does, and they do it well.

A quick visit to the company's blog[22] shows how much the employees value their relationship with Southwest and how much Southwest values them. There are numerous entries about employees who have gone above and beyond the call of duty, employees expressing their appreciation for something the company has done (as an example, a company event), and stories about expected and unexpected rewards and recognition. An April 2009 blog entry, which featured a nine-minute video, celebrated the twenty-one winners of the "Operation Kick Tail" incentive contest. Employees were given the opportunity to submit "Kick Tail-a-Grams," commendations recognizing their fellow employees for "positively outrageous customer service" and "living the Southwest Way." More than 180,000 entries were received, from which the twenty-one winners were randomly selected. Each winner received $10,000. The awards were made at company meetings, as well as by surprise visits to the field that reflected the Southwest culture of fun. A baggage handler was given a small briefcase and told to open it, revealing the sum written in bold on the inside. A gate agent was given a fictitious boarding pass, with his own name, the destination "To the Moon," and the amount written on it. The winners' names appeared at the end of the video. All of this was done with a sense of humor—a key value of the company—but at the same time it conveyed an important message: we (not just management, but all employees) value people and the contributions they make to our success.

At Southwest, the Human Resources Department is called the "People Department" because employees are viewed as more than resources. As suggested by the Employee Mission Statement presented earlier, employees are treated as people and in a real sense viewed as internal customers who have needs that the company works hard to satisfy.

Two Keys to Successful Management of the People Value: Hiring and Training

As was true of the customer value, management of the people value begins with the hiring process. A visit to the Southwest Airlines careers website would tell any prospective employee—even someone who knew nothing about the company—a great deal about what is expected. The first statement is from CEO Gary Kelly: "Our People are our single greatest strength and our most enduring long-term competitive advantage." This is followed by pictures of their employees in action, even a flight crew all dressed like Elvis. There is also a tab on this website called culture, which offers a definition and presents "Live the Southwest Way," shown in Exhibit 5.1.

The message is clear: Southwest is looking for candidates who want to have fun, but who also have a "warrior spirit" and a "servant's heart"—an interesting combination of qualities. The company wants people who will do whatever it takes and go the extra mile to do whatever is needed. The fact

Live the Southwest Way		
Warrior Spirit	**Servant's Heart**	**Fun-LUVing Attitude**
• Work hard	• Follow the Golden Rule	• Have FUN
• Desire to be the best	• Adhere to basic principles	• Don't take yourself too seriously
• Be courageous	• Treat others with respect	
• Display a sense of urgency	• Put others first	• Maintain perspective (balance)
• Persevere	• Be egalitarian	• Celebrate successes
• Innovate	• Demonstrate proactive customer service	• Enjoy your work
	• Embrace SWA family	• Be a passionate team player

Exhibit 5.1. The Southwest Way.
Data derived from numerous sources, including the Southwest website (http://www.southwest.com/careers/culture.html).

that Southwest typically receives nearly a hundred thousand applications in some years for only two to three thousand positions suggests that working in this culture is attractive to prospective employees. Again, it isn't what is written that's important; it's what the company actually does.

The culture of the company, with respect to both people and customers, is clearly reflected in the interview process. Candidates are typically asked to describe how they effectively used humor in a work situation (because having a sense of humor and using it is valued at Southwest). The company frequently interviews people in groups to see how they interact with others, because they want people who value teamwork. Interviewing teams sometimes ask candidates to prepare a five-minute presentation on themselves for an audience. The presenter is not as important as the reaction. The interviewing team watches the audience to see who is cheering on the presenter and who is using their time to polish their own presentation. The "unselfish" candidates—those who are focused on others—are the people Southwest wants.[23] The focus on fun and not taking oneself too seriously is illustrated in a well-told story about a group of eight prospective pilots. These candidates were kidded about their dress (all were in dark suits with black shoes and black socks). They were then encouraged to loosen up and change into Southwest's Bermuda shorts. Six of the eight applicants accepted the offer and interviewed for the rest of the day in shirts, ties, and Bermuda shorts. All six were hired.[24]

Once hired, new employees are introduced to the company's culture and history and given initial job-specific training. This typically involves one to two weeks in the classroom, followed by two to three weeks on the job. Each new employee is assigned a "training coordinator" whose role is to help guide the on-the-job training process. Throughout the initial training, the company is careful to observe whether the individual is a good fit with respect to embracing and living the Southwest values. According to Kelleher, people either like it or they don't:

> It normally would take about six months after which some would say: "I'm liberated. This is what I always wanted. I can actually say what I think." Others would say: "I have to get out of here. I need the security and comfort of a highly structured organization." The first set of people would stay and be happy, becoming much more productive than they had ever been because now they

could stop worrying about process and start focusing more on substance. The second group would leave because they simply weren't compatible.[25]

In fact, the word *compatibility* and the concept are part of the Southwest language. There is nothing wrong with the company or the rejected employee; they just aren't compatible.

Financial Rewards Aren't Everything

Although Southwest pays the highest wages in the industry and has a profit-sharing plan that makes all employees owners (a first in the airline industry), according to Kelleher money does not represent the biggest reward for employees: "Compensation doesn't cause people to give that last 10 percent that is often crucial. . . . So honoring them, respecting them, and keeping in touch with them about everything that is going on in their lives, their illnesses, anniversaries, birthdays, and promotions"[26] turns out to have value far beyond salary remuneration. For example, Colleen Barrett, president emeritus of Southwest, began the practice of sending a birthday card to every employee—something that the company continues doing today. Southwest also has a strong focus on promoting from within—an important ingredient to maintaining and nurturing its culture.

The company holds many events at which specific employees are recognized for their contribution. Another role these events play is to show *all* employees how much the company appreciates their efforts, and to promote the notion of having fun. These events include:

- The annual Chili Cook-Off (in April).
- The Halloween Party, at which everyone (including the executives) dresses up. (CEO Kelly has appeared as Dorothy from *The Wizard of Oz.*)
- "Message to the Field" Meetings, which are held at several locations around the country. Employees devote time to designing T-shirts and preparing for various contests that occur during the meetings. These events also typically include tailgate parties.
- The Company's Anniversary Meeting (in June), where employees are recognized for their years of service, as well as their dedication to customer service and the examples they set with respect to the Southwest Way.

- A number of nonscheduled events that help show employees that the company cares. One is Hokey Day, when members of the company's Culture Committee go to one of the "stations" (airport locations). They greet an incoming flight, give the crew snacks, and clean the plane for them. These events are typically a total surprise for the crew.

Constant Communication

As is true of the focus Southwest places on staying in touch with customers, the company is also in constant contact with employees via the intranet, weekly telephone messages from the CEO for all employees, monthly articles in *Spirit* magazine, and the quarterly "Knowing the Score" message that presents information about the company's financial performance (important to employees because they all own part of the business). In addition, employees have access to anyone and everyone in the company they need to help solve problems and address issues. Executives' doors are open. The goal is to keep everyone connected.

Results of Southwest's Management of People Orientation

Industry analysts and Southwest executives seem to agree that the focus on people (which, like customers, is always capitalized in any of the company's communications to illustrate how important it is) has been a significant ingredient in the company's success. Southwest experiences low turnover; as of 2010 there were seventeen original employees still working for the company. The high level of customer satisfaction the company receives supports the notion of treating employees well so they will in turn treat customers well. In addition, the bottom line is that Southwest has experienced the best record of profitability among U.S. airlines.

Conclusion

We have examined how four successful companies manage the cultural dimension of people orientation. Each is in its own business but has achieved great success with a core strategy common to them all: they make their people feel valued.

People Orientation Culture Management Tools

All four companies share the core value of treating people well, though each expresses it in its own way. Further, there are some differences with respect to the type and use of culture management tools.

Have a Formal Statement of the Treatment of People Value

All four companies have formal culture statements related to people. Starbucks' statement is a sentence and Southwest's is a paragraph, but in both the message is clear: people are important. In fact, at Southwest there are only two parts to the mission (values) statement, one focused on customers and the other focused on their people (employees). All four companies have found ways to help make their people orientation value real for all employees by using other culture management tools.

Use Communication—Both Language and Methods— to Reinforce the Value Placed on People

All four use special words to communicate the people aspect of their culture. Starbucks refers to baristas, Google refers to Googley employees, Walmart to associates, Southwest to people.

At Walmart and Southwest, there are specific communication mechanisms in place to promote and support the people value. These communication mechanisms, in both cases, are multidirectional, not one-way. Important information is shared with employees about what is occurring within the company, but more importantly employees are encouraged and given specific opportunities to share their ideas about what can be done to improve and enhance their experience. The message is "We value your input!" Input is also valued at Google, where employees have an opportunity to share their perspectives on the company's Happiness Survey.

Recruit and Select People Who Fit

Google and Southwest use creative methods to select people who will be effective members of the team. At Google, this means selecting for flexibility, adaptability, and the ability to get things done. At Southwest, it is selecting people with a sense of humor who can work as a member of a team, and have a servant's heart. The lesson from these companies is that embedding culture as a key variable in the hiring process can greatly contribute not only to successful management of the culture but also to positive company performance.

Use Training to Promote the Focus on People

Starbucks (as described in Chapter 4) and Southwest both conduct technical training and also training in the company's values for all employees, beginning with their first day on the job. The training helps employees understand the company's people orientation value. In addition, the act of conducting ongoing training for employees helps reinforce the concept that people are one of the company's most important assets.

Retain People Who Fit

At Southwest, the training coordinator assigned to each new employee is charged with assessing the extent to which the individual fits with the company's culture. Those people who are incompatible (as the company terms it) leave of their own volition or are asked to leave. The goal is to protect and preserve the company's culture by ensuring that those selected for employment do indeed fit.

Use Rewards and Recognition to Help Promote the People Value

All four companies profiled in this chapter have a variety of rewards, financial and nonfinancial, that recognize employees for their contributions and show they are appreciated. Starbucks and Southwest have employee stock ownership programs, which help employees feel connected to the company and think like owners—because they are. At Google, there is the Fun Fund, which employees can draw on to do things that interest them. Finally, each company has specific events that are intended to recognize the value of employees to that company.

Have "Leadership Practices" in Place That Support the People Value

At Starbucks and Southwest, senior leadership is involved in ensuring the people orientation dimension of culture is "real" for employees. At Starbucks, Schultz reentered the company as a way of helping to revitalize not only the culture but the company as a whole.

At Walmart and Southwest, there are specific events at which leadership has the opportunity to share information and interact with employees. Their message: We care what you think!

Embed the People Value into the Company's Structure

At Google and Southwest, there are distinct functions tasked with helping leadership communicate, manage, and reinforce the company's culture. At Google, there is a chief culture officer. Southwest has a Culture Committee (discussed in detail in Chapter 10).

The human resource function in all of these companies plays a key role in supporting the people orientation dimension through design and implementation of the hiring, new employee orientation, and training processes. In companies that manage their culture effectively (as is the case in the companies examined in this chapter), the human resource function is a true partner to leadership in this process.

Final Comment

Although there are similarities, each company has particular methods of managing its culture, some of which can potentially be used by other companies. These methods include the Happiness Survey and the Fun Fund used at Google; use of corporate role models and constant communication with employees at Southwest; and certain rituals such as the Walmart Cheer.

Regardless of their differences, all of these companies are excellent sources of ideas for managing the key cultural dimension of people orientation.

6 Managing the Performance Standards and Accountability Dimension of Culture

Performance standards and accountability is one of the most crucial but relatively neglected (and to some extent mismanaged) aspects of organizational culture. If a company does not clearly define and have effective ways for managing its culture with respect to standards of performance and accountability (quality, customer service, achievement of goals, etc.), employees can come to view anything as good or effective performance. If standards and accountability are not emphasized in the culture, one can hardly expect them to be a focus of actual behavior.[1] This chapter addresses how companies can and ought to manage the performance standards and accountability dimension of culture.

Managing the performance standards and accountability dimension has an impact on all other culture dimensions because it identifies company standards of performance with respect to such elements as quality and service; what and how much employees are held accountable for; and who is rewarded for what. Our research on corporate culture shows that the performance standards and accountability dimension is an independent statistical factor, distinct from all other factors.[2] This research further supports the idea that the dimension is an explicit part of a company's culture.

As in Chapters 4 and 5, we again examine and analyze selected companies that have actually achieved success by effectively managing the performance standards and accountability dimension of culture to gain insights into how they did it. Hewlett-Packard, Smartmatic, and Infogix are all technology companies but are distinct from one another in various significant ways. The most important difference is in their approaches to performance standards, performance management, and accountability in their cultures. Polar opposites from Infogix in their approach, Hewlett-Packard and Smartmatic are classic examples of the prevailing paradigm of performance management culture, while Infogix represents a potentially new paradigm for performance management culture (based on the principles of the Deming philosophy combined with certain aspects of the traditional paradigm).[3]

Managing Performance and Accountability at Hewlett-Packard

Hewlett-Packard (HP) is legendary for its culture. Headquartered in Palo Alto, California, HP is a technology company operating in 170 countries around the world.

In 1939, Bill Hewlett and Dave Packard started the business as a two-man firm in a one-car garage in Palo Alto. Their first product was an electronic instrument used to test audio sound equipment. By 1979, the company had increased in size to fifty-two thousand employees with annual revenues of more than $2.4 billion. In fiscal year 2009, the company achieved revenues totaling $114.6 billion. As in virtually all entrepreneurial companies, the values of the founders are the basis of the company's culture. They are expressed in "the HP Way," the company's philosophy of management.

The HP Way

The HP Way consists of a set of shared values and corporate objectives.[4]

Core Values

The corporate values listed here are a key component of the HP Way:

- *Passion for customers.* We put our customers first in everything we do.
- *Trust and respect for individuals.* We work together to create a culture of inclusion built on trust, respect, and dignity for all.
- *Achievement and contribution.* We strive for excellence in all we do; each person's contribution is critical to our success.
- *Results through teamwork.* We effectively collaborate, always looking for more efficient ways to serve our customers.

- *Speed and agility.* We are resourceful and adaptable, and we achieve results faster than our competitors.

- *Meaningful innovation.* We are the technology company that invents the useful and the significant.

- *Uncompromising integrity.* We are open, honest, and direct in our dealings.[5]

These values are a set of guiding principles for how people in the company should deal with each other and with customers, as well as certain standards for operating the business. In fact, all are stated in terms of standards of performance and what people are being held accountable for (an example: "We put our customers first"). Two of the corporate values—achievement and contribution, and speed and agility—directly relate to performance standards and accountability. In addition, the HP value of uncompromising integrity can be thought of as a standard of performance and possibly a form of accountability.

Corporate Objectives

The phrase *corporate objectives* at Hewlett-Packard is not the classic use of this term. As stated on the company's website, "HP's corporate objectives have guided the company in the conduct of its business since 1957, when first written by co-founders Bill Hewlett and Dave Packard."[6]

- *Customer loyalty.* We earn customer respect and loyalty by consistently providing the highest quality and value.

- *Profit.* We achieve sufficient profit to finance growth, create value for our shareholders, and achieve our corporate objectives.

- *Growth.* We recognize and seize opportunities for growth that builds upon our strengths and competencies.

- *Market leadership.* We lead in the marketplace by developing and delivering useful and innovative products, services, and solutions.

- *Commitment to employees.* We demonstrate our commitment to employees by promoting and rewarding based on performance and by creating a work environment that reflects our values.

- *Leadership capability.* We develop leaders at all levels who achieve business results, exemplify our values, and lead us to grow and win.

- *Global citizenship.* We fulfill our responsibility to society by being an economic, intellectual, and social asset to each country and community where we do business.

The core overarching belief underlying the HP Way, as expressed by Packard, is that "it is necessary that people work together in unison toward common objectives and avoid working at cross purposes at all levels if the ultimate in efficiency and achievement is to be obtained."[7] He was actually referring to an enduring set of corporate objectives, rather than a set of annual objectives.

Management of Corporate Values at Hewlett-Packard

How does Hewlett-Packard actually manage corporate values in general, and standards of performance and accountability in particular? The company uses a variety of related tools.

Definition of the HP Way

A primary tool for managing the performance standards and accountability dimension at HP is its statement of the HP Way, including its sets of objectives and values. As previously noted, these are stated on the company's website and serve as constant reminders of the way HP works.

Employee Selection

Another tool that Hewlett-Packard uses to manage this dimension of culture is its selection methods and process. The company strives to select people who will fit the culture and devotes a great deal of effort to selection of employees. The process is reminiscent of selection (screening) for membership in a fraternity or sorority. An interview team facilitates selecting employees who fit with the company's culture and values. This team spends at least an entire day with the job candidate. As an HP manager put it: "It starts with the hiring decision. Everybody we hire, we hire forever. At least that's the premise. We are not hiring for a program or for specific short-term skills."[8]

Management by Objectives

HP uses a classic MBO (management by objectives) process as the major mechanism through which the company can influence standards of performance and hold people accountable. This begins with a planning process generating key result areas (key areas of focus), objectives, and goals. Performance against goals is measured and leads to both evaluative as well as corrective feedback. The evaluative measurements are used as an input into the performance evaluations and reward process.

Long- and short-range objectives are established for the company and group and then cascaded down to specific operating units. Objectives are outcomes to be achieved, not tasks. As described by Gregory Rogers in a 1995 Harvard Business School case about Hewlett-Packard: "The entire MBO process was part of annual tactical and strategic planning that defined a job's objective and its major responsibilities and performance measures."[9]

The Hewlett-Packard MBO system is the key mechanism through which the company can influence standards of performance and hold people accountable. This enables HP to motivate people to embrace the values of achievement and contribution and of speed and agility, as well as to translate them into real day-to-day behavior on the part of employees. The Hewlett-Packard MBO process is closely linked to and supported by its performance evaluation and reward system.

Performance Evaluation and Reward Systems

At many companies, the process of performance evaluation is considered a nuisance, an administrative task of relatively minor importance that takes time away from getting the job done. At Hewlett-Packard, the process of performance management and evaluation is taken very seriously. Managers are expected to invest a great deal of time and energy to ensure that an individual's pay level within the salary range is a reasonable reflection of his or her performance compared to other people in similar positions. The immediate supervisor is the first to evaluate an individual's performance. Then, for the outliers (both high- and low-performers), it is adjusted on the basis of a ranking process, conducted by managers, which compares employees in different departments.[10]

The Model as a Whole

The Hewlett-Packard system of managing standards of performance and accountability is important not just as a practical example but also as a classic example of the MBO system for motivating adherence to these corporate values. This is as good as it gets.

Although Hewlett-Packard has done an exceptional job of making this system work for them over a long period of time, many other companies have been less successful with this approach. As described later in this chapter, there are a variety of problems or difficulties in making the approach work. These difficulties have led to experiments with other types of nontraditional (non-MBO systems) for performance management. One of the most interesting and significant of these experiments is being conducted by another technology company (Infogix), as described later in this chapter.

Managing Performance Standards at Smartmatic

Smartmatic is a privately owned, multinational company that designs and deploys end-to-end, custom technology solutions to enable government agencies and large enterprises to fulfill their mission with the utmost efficiency. Founded around a core team of elite engineers guided by the principle of continuous improvement in process, performance, and results, Smartmatic delivers leading-edge technology to clients in four key business divisions: (1) electronic voting systems, (2) intelligent and integrated security systems, (3) identity registration and authentication of large population groups, and (4) technology research and development and consulting. Currently headquartered in London, the company was founded in Caracas, Venezuela. In 2010, revenues were about US$200 million, and the company employed about 250 people. Smartmatic views itself as a "Silicon Valley type" of company that happens to have sprung out of Venezuela.

Smartmatic has developed a statement of eight core values (one of which deals explicitly with performance) and related behaviors:

Integrity
- Commits to honesty and truth in every facet of behavior
- Establishes mutual respect and trust when dealing with others
- Demonstrates legal conduct and work as an example to others
- Acts and behaves in accordance with own words

Candor
- Is able to act forthrightly in all communications
- Speaks own mind and makes others understand his or her objectives

- Is able to change and adopt new behaviors as a result of learning and feedback
- Creates an environment where others can learn from their own mistakes
- Gives and solicits informal feedback and coaching at all levels to perform better

Commitment

- Fully supports and implements decisions
- Is totally committed to the achievement of company goals (strives to achieve what is "almost impossible")
- Pursues targets with the determination to achieve them; does not give up, especially in the face of adversity
- Pursues continuous improvement and development, professionally and personally
- Overcomes barriers in order to achieve results

Innovation

- Why are things the way they are?
- What can be done?
- It is an attitude; how can it be done?
- Challenges the status quo and pushes for continuous improvement
- Comes up with a lot of new and unique ideas
- Champions new initiatives within the scope of own job
- Encourages others to be creative and innovative
- Adopts a flexible approach to difficult situations, leading to effective and creative solutions

Excellence

- Delivers in accordance to commitments
- Executes assigned tasks with diligence and quality
- Simplifies systems and processes to eliminate unnecessary work
- Consistently delivers with high standards of excellence with no mistakes

Vision

- We want to do and want to become something that nobody else wants to do or wants to become; we visualize a world others don't, and that makes us special
- Understands organization's business objectives and translates them into specific principles
- Balances day-to-day activities with a focus on the long-term
- Aligns goals, objectives, and resources with business needs across functions
- Anticipates and removes potential roadblocks, and develops contingency measures when needed
- Understands priorities and workloads of colleagues
- Monitors progress and adapts plans according to circumstances

Teamwork

- Shares information openly
- We all win together and we all fail together
- Anticipates and facilitates resolution of conflicts
- Listens attentively and invites responses
- Genuinely cares for people and demonstrates empathy
- Encourages people to work as a team
- Promotes a sense of belonging to the organization

Managing people (if applicable)

- Effectively delegates important tasks and encourages risk taking
- Understands diversity in the way of thinking of his or her team members, fostering agreement
- Successfully follows up all details pertaining to the work he or she is responsible for
- Is able to make sound decisions under conditions of uncertainty or complexity
- Takes timely actions to address performance issues
- Keeps people well informed about the business plans of the organization
- Encourages others to speak their minds[11]

A great strength of this approach to managing culture is the definition of the overall cultural values in terms of specific related behaviors that demonstrate the value. For example, someone exemplifying the teamwork value shares information openly, listens attentively, deals with conflict effectively, and encourages people to work as a team.

The Smartmatic value of excellence is the company's value that deals with performance standards and accountability. As defined at Smartmatic, excellence in performance is demonstrated in terms of specific related behaviors, as when a person:

- Delivers in accordance to commitments
- Executes assigned tasks with diligence and quality
- Simplifies systems and processes to eliminate unnecessary work
- Consistently delivers with high standards of excellence with no mistakes

In brief, the behaviors that demonstrate the value in action are identified in these four bullets. Most culture statements of values refer to general concepts of integrity, innovation, and so on without giving sufficient specificity to translate the value into actual day-to-day behavior. As stated by Victor Ramirez, Smartmatic's SVP of human resources, "We added behaviors to the values statements to convert the values into reality."[12]

The Smartmatic Performance Management Process

Shortly after joining Smartmatic in 2006, Ramirez designed a system for performance management that is another significant aspect of how Smartmatic manages excellence in performance (as well as its other values). The Smartmatic performance management system is impressive because it is a true system in the technical sense of the word.[13] As the company states in a document that describes this system, "Managing performance enables Smartmatic to focus on clear goals, set direction and priorities, and establish mutual expectations between the organization and the employee. Furthermore, it drives a culture of continuous improvement, supports individuals to meet their development aspirations and strengthens our company capability."[14]

The system has four key parts: (1) the performance management cycle, (2) the definition of responsibilities of the manager and the associate whose performance is being managed, (3) the set of Smartmatic values and related behavior, and (4) the two-dimensional Performance Evaluation Template.

The Performance Management Cycle

Managing performance at Smartmatic is not an annual process consisting of just filling out a form. Instead, it is an ongoing business cycle of helping people identify their accountability, deliverables expected, behaviors they should demonstrate, measures of individual performance and needs for future development, connection to the business strategy, and what they will be rewarded for.[15] The performance cycle is a relatively typical MBO-type process and consists of (1) performance planning and objective setting (every January), (2) midyear review, and (3) year-end review.

The performance-planning and objective-setting step begins with the company defining its objectives. Next, divisions and departments establish their own objectives to support those of the company as a whole. Finally, individual objectives are developed to support the divisional and departmental objectives and thereby company objectives. This is a straightforward, solid example of a classic MBO process. A key to making this work is collaborative discussion between manager and associate to identify SMART goals, which are defined as *s*pecific, *m*easurable, *a*mbitious, *r*elevant, and *t*ime-bound."[16]

Steps 2 and 3 of the cycle consist of reviewing actual progress against goals. The first review occurs at midyear and is an opportunity for manager and associate to recognize success, identify any problems or potential problems in achieving goals, and develop action plans for addressing problems. During the year-end review, the manager reviews the associate's self-evaluation as well as other key associates' inputs. So far, this is all classic MBO stuff, solid but unspectacular. Examining it closely, though, reveals a magical or "secret sauce" element.

The subtlest and most important aspect of this process involves the *content* of the review. Instead of being merely a performance review, it is actually a "performance-culture" review. Specifically, the manager and the associate discuss and evaluate the performance achieved against objectives *as well as demonstrated values and related behaviors.* At some companies, performance is the only thing that matters, but at Smartmatic what matters is the combination of performance with demonstrated behavior that adheres to cultural values.[17] Ramirez says, "If you do what we want you to do and also do it *the way we want you to do it*, you will be a role model."[18]

Definition of Responsibilities

Another component of the Smartmatic performance management process is definition of responsibilities for the manager and the associate being evaluated. Having this information in written form helps ensure that all employees—managers and their direct reports—understand the important role each person plays in ensuring the success of the process. In addition, this information helps all parties understand what they can expect from one another. Manager and associate responsibilities are summarized here, along with elaboration of the SMART goals introduced just above:

Responsibilities of the manager

Holding primary accountability for performance and development of their direct reports

Ensuring individual goals and objectives are aligned to business goals

Setting SMART objectives with clear measures and agreeing on mutual performance expectations with the associate

Conducting regular two-way performance reviews with the associate, giving feedback on strengths and identifying areas for development

Supporting the associate on appropriate development plans to strengthen performance in the role

Planning and conducting thorough, quality year-end performance reviews and evaluations that include obtaining feedback from others in the organization on the associate's performance

Demonstrating fairness and consistency in performance evaluation and compensation management

Encouraging and supporting stretch performance at all times and engaging the commitment of all associates

Responsibilities of the associate

Providing input and agreeing on annual objectives

Continuously reviewing individual performance against goals

Demonstrating values and behaviors in delivering performance results

Preparing for performance review

Demonstrating willingness to undertake demanding goals and remain flexible in a constantly changing environment

Renegotiating agreed deliverables on the basis of changing circumstances, including change in priorities

SMART objectives:

Specific: clearly stated

Measurable: measurable outputs defined according to criteria (quantity, quality, time, and so on)

Ambitious: achievable with stretch but still realistic

Relevant: relevant to the business needs and goals of the department or organization

Time-bound: within a clear timeframe

Set of Smartmatic Values and Related Behavior

As shown earlier, one of the subtle gems of the Smartmatic performance management system is including behaviors that reflect the value statements. This element makes the system real for people and enables the company to operationalize values such as integrity, innovation, and excellence. "Behaviorally anchoring" the values—that is, defining what effective performance looks like with respect to each value—makes it easier for managers and associates to evaluate performance with respect to the value.

Two-Dimensional Performance Evaluation Template

The final feature of the Smartmatic performance management system is a template for performance evaluation that combines the two dimensions of performance and related cultural behaviors desired by the company. This two-dimensional template is shown in Exhibit 6.1. The overall evaluation combines the dimensions of (1) achievement of objectives (*what*) and (2) related values and behaviors required to deliver the results (*how*), using the agreed rating labels and descriptors.

This is an essential tool in helping all employees understand that at Smartmatic it isn't just about the performance achieved but also the extent

Superior Results, Unsatisfactory Behavior 3.1	Superior Results 3.2	Exceptional Performer 3.3
Consistently contributes at a superior level of performance on all job objectives; however, performance falls below expectations on Smartmatic values/behaviors.	Consistently contributes at a superior level of performance on all job objectives and also demonstrates Smartmatic values/behaviors.	Consistently contributes at an exceptional level of performance on all job objectives and Smartmatic values/behaviors. Recognized as a role model both within the group and in a wider population. Few people achieve this level of performance.

Good Results Unsatisfactory Behavior 2.1	Strong Performer 2.2	Superior Behavior 2.3
Fully meets expectations on all job objectives; however, performance falls below expectations on Smartmatic values/behaviors.	Fully meets expectations on all job objectives and Smartmatic values/behaviors. This is a positive and fully acceptable level of performance.	Consistently demonstrates superior behavior and fully meets expectations on all job objectives.

Unsatisfactory Performer 1.1	Good Behavior, Unsatisfactory Results 1.2	Superior Behavior, Unsatisfactory Results 1.3
Performance falls considerably short in relation to job objectives and Smartmatic values/behaviors, despite repeated explanations and coaching.	Fully meets expectations on Smartmatic values/behaviors; however, performance on job objectives falls below expectations.	Consistently demonstrates superior behavior; however. performance on job objectives falls below expectations.

Partially Met Expectations	Fully Met Expectations	Exceeded Expectations

Exhibit 6.1. Smartmatic values/behavior, rating labels, and descriptions.
Data from Smartmatic internal document.

to which everyone is behaving consistently with and in support of the company's values.

Compensation and Rewards

Although not explicitly part of the performance management system per se, Smartmatic has a comprehensive compensation and reward system that is closely tied to it. This system includes a mix of base salary, short-term variable compensation for performance, and long-term variable compensation for performance. As a result, it establishes incentives and reinforces performance, both technical and in terms of behavior consistent with company values.

Managing Performance Standards and Accountability at Infogix

Difficulties with the traditional paradigm of performance management and accountability have led to some experiments with other types of nontraditional (non-MBO) systems for performance management. Infogix is conducting one of the most interesting and significant of these experiments.[19] The company uses a somewhat unorthodox approach to performance management[20]; in fact, the approach is so radically different that it required a new name or construct to describe it: "performance optimization."

Company Description

Infogix is a software company that supplies information integrity software solutions to help major corporations ensure accuracy, consistency, and reliability of their operational, financial, and management information. It is a pioneer in the information integrity space. To understand how Infogix manages the cultural dimension of performance standards and accountability, it is important to put this in the context of its business philosophy. Accordingly, we first briefly review the company's history and then examine how it manages this culture dimension through the performance management process.

Company Origins

Madhavan Nayar started Infogix in 1982 as a one-man consulting firm. Nayar, who holds degrees from universities in India and the Illinois Institute of Technology, pioneered the concept of information integrity software solutions at a time when few had realized the need for specifically designed systems that helped customer organizations ensure the validity and accuracy of information. Today, Infogix is a world leader in its industry, with nearly two hundred team members as well as offices in major cities across North America and Europe.

Adoption of the Deming Philosophy

During 1993, the senior leaders at Infogix learned about the management philosophy of W. Edwards Deming. On April 1, 1994, after several months of study and deliberation, they adopted the Deming philosophy and created the foundation of Infogix's culture with respect to performance standards and accountability.

There are many facets to the Deming philosophy of management, but here we describe only those most relevant to the purpose of this chapter.[21] Deming advocated a set of key ideas that constitute the foundation of his philosophy:

- *Appreciation of a system*: understanding the overall processes involving suppliers, producers, and customers (or recipients) of goods and services
- *Knowledge of variation*: the range and causes of variation in quality, and use of statistical sampling in measurement
- *Theory of knowledge*: the concepts explaining knowledge and the limits of what can be known
- *Knowledge of psychology*: concepts of human nature[22]

These notions, and in particular appreciation of the system and knowledge of (statistical) variation, are critical to understanding the Infogix approach to management of the culture dimension of performance standards and accountability. As Deming explained, *appreciation of a system* involves understanding how interactions (i.e., feedback) between the elements of a system can result in internal restrictions that force the system to behave as a single organism automatically seeking a "steady state" or equilibrium. This steady state determines the output of the system, rather than the individual elements doing so. As a result, the structure of the organization, not the employees alone, holds the key to improving the quality of output.[23]

Knowledge of variation involves understanding that everything measured consists of both "normal" variation that is due to the flexibility of the system and "special causes" that create defects. Quality involves recognizing the difference in order to eliminate special causes, while controlling normal variation. Deming taught that making changes in response to normal variation would only make the system perform worse. Understanding variation includes the mathematical certainty that variation will normally occur within six "standard deviations" (a classical statistical measure of variation) from the mean (or statistical average).[24]

On the basis of these four key notions, he then developed a set of what are termed "Deming's fourteen points"[25]:

1. Create constancy of purpose toward improvement of product and service, with the aim to become competitive and stay in business, and to provide jobs.

2. Adopt the new philosophy. We are in a new economic age. Western management must awaken to the challenge, must learn their responsibilities, and take on leadership for change.

3. Cease dependence on inspection to achieve quality. Eliminate the need for inspection on a mass basis by building quality into the product in the first place.

4. End the practice of awarding business on the basis of price tag. Instead, minimize total cost. Move toward a single supplier for any one item, on a long-term relationship of loyalty and trust.

5. Improve constantly and forever the system of production and service, to improve quality and productivity, and thus constantly decrease costs.

6. Institute training on the job.

7. Institute leadership. The aim of supervision should be to help people and machines and gadgets to do a better job. Supervision of management is in need of overhaul, as well as supervision of production workers.

8. Drive out fear, so that everyone may work effectively for the company.

9. Break down barriers between departments. People in research, design, sales, and production must work as a team, to foresee problems of production and in use that may be encountered with the product or service.

10. Eliminate slogans, exhortations, and targets for the work force asking for zero defects and new levels of productivity. Such exhortations only create adversarial relationships, as the bulk of the causes of low quality and low productivity belong to the system and thus lie beyond the power of the work force.

11a.   Eliminate work standards (quotas) on the factory floor. Substitute leadership. 11b. Eliminate management by objective. Eliminate management by numbers, numerical goals. Substitute leadership.

12a.   Remove barriers that rob the hourly worker of his right to pride of workmanship. The responsibility of supervisors must be changed from sheer numbers to quality. 12b. Remove barriers that rob people in management and in engineering of their right to pride of workmanship. This means abolishment of the annual or merit rating and of management by objective.

13.   Institute a vigorous program of education and self-improvement.

14.   Put everybody in the company to work to accomplish the transformation. The transformation is everybody's job.[26]

The fourteen points can be viewed as a set of values and practices making up the Deming philosophy or cultural foundation of a "Deming company."

Point 11 (both parts) of this philosophy directly challenges the classic paradigm of management as represented by Hewlett-Packard. The most fundamental challenge to the classic paradigm is elimination of the management-by-objectives approach.

Impact of Implementing Deming at Infogix

The process of implementing the Deming philosophy at Infogix had a profound and extensive impact on the organization. It affected the company's culture, the performance management process, the company structure, and the nature of people who stayed or left the company. We focus here on only the performance management aspects of the implementation.[27]

In sharp contrast to traditional performance management practice, use of quotas and other numerical objectives linked to incentives and compensation was discontinued at Infogix. Similarly, formal performance evaluations and salary adjustments tied to performance evaluation were also eliminated.

The reaction of most of the company's team members was skeptical, and some were quite negative. As a result, many of the star salespeople left the company. During the eighteen months after adoption of the Deming approach, almost 95 percent of the sales force departed and was replaced. During 1994, companywide employee turnover exceeded 50 percent. An employee survey revealed that employee morale was far below the industry average.

Over the next several years, additional issues or problems surfaced in applying the Deming philosophy and approach at Infogix. Despite these challenges, the approach was institutionalized and became the core of the Infogix culture.

Creating a System for Performance Optimization at Infogix

Performance optimization is a term coined at Infogix to refer to an innovative variation on the conventional notion of performance management.[28] The Infogix performance management system comprises some of the same components as a traditional performance management system, with the exception of two key features: (1) it does not measure individual performance as such, and (2) it does *not* link performance directly to rewards. This is consistent with the Deming philosophy and the beliefs of company leader Nayar, who believes strongly that rewards ought to be based on *company*, rather than individual, performance. This means that the performance of individuals is not measured, as it would be under the traditional approach. This in turn has an impact on the company's culture as it relates to performance standards and accountability.

Although the performance optimization system does not include rewards for individual performance for the reasons outlined here, Infogix does grant rewards for individuals. The individual reward strategy is to provide "base" competitive pay and "compensate" (give variable compensation to) leadership group members according to company performance.

Problems Implementing the Infogix
Performance Optimization System

The planning process was the first component of the performance optimization process to be introduced at Infogix. The system used the concepts of key result areas, objectives, and goals as the focus of planning at the corporate and unit levels. These elements of the plan are the basis for performance standards and accountability.

Although it was relatively easy to introduce the planning model to the core team, several related issues required resolution for the model to really work effectively. There were elements of Infogix's special culture that made it difficult to integrate the model into the organization on a day-to-day basis. For example, discussions at planning meetings revealed that the Deming philosophy was, in fact, often misinterpreted to mean that organizational members didn't need to worry about their jobs because they would be there for them whether or not they performed. The lack of a formal culture statement defining the desired organizational culture as it related to performance standards further exacerbated the problem. There were similar difficulties in people not understanding the accountabilities and responsibilities within self-managed work teams. Several situations arose where team members could take advantage of the Infogix system to suit their needs. This had negative implications for overall company performance and competitive position within the industry.

A key adjustment to the system ultimately contributing to the effectiveness of Infogix's performance optimization system was development of detailed measurements for objectives and goals. As a CPA once told us, "What gets measured gets counted!" This means that the things that are measured are the most important factors in influencing people's behavior in an organization.

At Infogix, a great deal of time and care was put into developing measurements of goals. In part, this is because Infogix is a highly intellectual organization filled with many well-educated and highly technical people. In addition, this is the orientation of the company leader, who is precise about terminology and the need for operational definitions. The net result was a detailed set of measurements for every objective and goal. These measurements are critical to making the plan operational and specific, as well as to setting explicit performance standards that serve as a basis for accountability.

Results and Benefits of the System at Infogix

The performance optimization system at Infogix remains a work in progress. One major benefit of the performance optimization system is greater focus on priority objectives. In the Infogix plan, these are the most important areas of focus for the coming one to three years. Identifying these priorities helps people understand what is most important and where the emphasis must be for the company to achieve its long-range vision.

A related benefit of implementing the performance optimization process is that there has been a cultural change at Infogix: Planning and performance review is now a way of life and is part of the "Infogix Way."

A third benefit concerns the productivity and accountability of people. The specificity of the measurements has increased the extent to which people are accountable for specific results rather than just vague responsibilities. In addition, the plan has become a tool for systematically monitoring overall performance of the company as well as specific business units.

Financial performance is one of the ultimate tests of a company's success. As with other information technology companies, Infogix had to deal with the collapse of information technology investment since the boom that led up to Y2K. In addition, Infogix faced the Great Recession commencing in 2008. As a privately held company, Infogix's financial information is proprietary. Nevertheless, we can say that the company is strong financially and has gotten stronger over the past five years, in contrast to some of the larger companies in this space such as Compaq (which was acquired by Hewlett Packard) and Sun Microsystems. The ultimate criterion for any company is this: Are we stronger at the end of a time period than at the beginning? The answer for Infogix is definitely yes.

Comparison of the Classic Approach and Infogix

Hewlett-Packard and Smartmatic take what can be characterized as a classic approach to performance management and accountability, while Infogix takes an unconventional experimental approach. What are the similarities and differences? What are the problems of each approach? What can be learned from the two different approaches?

The Classic Approach

The classic approach is represented by Hewlett-Packard, a successful world-class company, and Smartmatic, a rapidly growing entrepreneurial technology company. HP uses a variety of long-established tools for culture management, among them employee selection, socialization, training, and an MBO-type performance management process to help achieve high standards of performance and accountability. Although the process emphasizes teamwork, it focuses on individual performance and evaluates (and rewards) individuals for their contributions.

Similarly, Smartmatic uses a well-designed integrated performance management system to manage the performance and accountability of people. This system involves establishing SMART goals, providing ongoing feedback on performance against these goals, evaluating individual performance, and recognizing performance through explicit rewards.

The Infogix Approach

With respect to performance management and accountability, the Infogix approach uses a combination of planning and measurement to focus behavior on performance standards as individuals work in teams. Consistent with the Deming philosophy, there are no direct rewards for individual contributions.

Evaluating the Two Approaches

The approach used by Hewlett-Packard and Smartmatic is tried and true. The great strength is that it works reasonably well and is familiar to many companies and many people. By contrast, the MBO approach also has well-known and well-documented limitations that can lead to various kinds of dysfunctional behavior. Specifically, a poorly designed performance management system can lead to "goal displacement" or "measurementship."[29]

Goal displacement is inadequate congruence of goals, created by the motivation to achieve some goals sought by the organization at the expense of other intended goals. Goal displacement may be caused by several things, notably suboptimization, selective attention to goals, and inversion of means and ends.

Suboptimization occurs when the performance of an organizational subunit is optimized at the expense of the organization as a whole. It is caused by factoring overall organizational goals into subgoals and holding individuals and units responsible for them. It is a common problem and difficult to avoid in large, complex organizations such as Hewlett-Packard.

Selective attention to organizational goals is closely related to suboptimization. It occurs when certain goals of the organization are pursued selectively, while other goals receive less attention or are ignored. In this case, a rule or guideline that is part of the control system is followed absolutely, even if it contradicts or prevents achievement of the goal. The original goal is replaced by the goal of following the rules.

A third type of goal displacement is caused by inversion of means and ends. This occurs when a performance management system tries to motivate attention to certain instrumental goals, which become ends in themselves because of rewards and thereby prevent achievement of other goals.

Measurementship involves lack of goal congruence created by motivation to look good in terms of the measures used in performance management systems, even though no real benefit is produced for the organization. It involves manipulating the measures used by a system, also known as playing the numbers game. There are two primary types of measurementship: "smoothing" and falsification.

Smoothing is an attempt to time activities in a way that produces the appearance of similar measures in different time periods. For example, a manager may wish to smooth calculated net income in two adjacent periods. If profit is expected to be unusually high during the first period, this figure can be smoothed by incurring expenditures in the first period that would otherwise have been made in the second period. Falsification is reporting of invalid data about what is occurring in an organization in order to make a person or activity look good in the management system.[30]

Another type of problem with traditional approaches to performance management and accountability is "decline of reward impact." Just as food stuffs are perishable, the impact of rewards is as well. Over time, rewards seem to lose their effectiveness. For example, if a person receives $10,000 in one year as a bonus and then receives the same $10,000 in the following year, there is an observable tendency for the same level of reward to have less impact in the second and subsequent years. As Nayar of Infogix points out, the reward has an effect similar to that of an addictive drug or medication, with greater and greater quantities needed over time to achieve the same effect or impact.[31]

All of these things are true limitations of the classic MBO approach, but it still appears to be the best approach presently available to facilitate implementation of the cultural dimension of performance standards and accountability.

The performance optimization approach based on the Deming philosophy combined with certain aspects of the traditional approach used at Infogix is promising, but it remains a work in progress. Since it is less developed than the traditional approach, implementation requires a great deal of effort and cost. The experiment at Infogix has gone on for more than a decade. In addition, because most people in the workforce are familiar and comfortable with the traditional approach, great pains need to be taken to recruit, select, and retain people who will embrace the Deming approach, where there are no direct rewards for performance. Also, because the Infogix approach has not been in existence as long as the traditional approach, it is not easily packageable and must be custom-designed. This suggests it is probably more suited to smaller companies like Infogix with a few hundred employees than to larger companies like Hewlett-Packard with many thousands of employees.

Conclusion

This chapter has described how three companies in the technology space manage the performance standards and accountability dimension of culture. They all use some of the same tools in managing this dimension, but there are some differences, based in part on how the dimension is defined.

Performance Standards and Accountability Culture Management Tools

As can be clearly seen throughout the chapter, two of the most important tools for managing the performance standards and accountability dimension of culture are (1) developing and using a reward system to recognize behavior consistent with the values, and (2) embedding values in performance standards. These and the other tools used by the companies examined in this chapter are described below.

Formal Statement of the Performance Standards and Accountability Value

Hewlett-Packard and Smartmatic use formal statements of their unique culture as a way of helping employees understand what is expected of them. The written values statements at these two companies are literally everywhere. Infogix adopted Deming's fourteen points as the basis for its performance standards and accountability value. In all three cases, then, there was some type of formal statement of this value.

Use Communication (Language and Methods) to Support the Value

Infogix uses the term performance optimization to signal a difference in approach with respect to how the performance standards and accountability value is defined at the company. Hewlett-Packard and Smartmatic also have specific terms used in the context of their MBO-type programs that help reinforce the performance standards and accountability dimension of their cultures.

All three companies have clearly focused a great deal of attention on communicating to all employees what the expectations of performance are and how they will be managed. In addition, all three companies use performance review and evaluation meetings to identify, discuss, and help team members understand the progress being made against goals at the company, team, and (in the case of HP and Smartmatic) individual levels.

Recruit and Select People Who "Fit" with How the Value Is Defined

At Hewlett-Packard, all values are embedded in the company's recruiting and selection process. A great deal of effort is invested in ensuring that those who join the company will fit. At Infogix, the unique aspects of the company's culture and approach to performance management are shared during the recruiting process so that prospective employees can decide if this approach will work for them.

Reward and Recognize Behavior Consistent with the Value

All three companies reward employees on the basis of performance against culture standards. At Hewlett-Packard and Smartmatic, these rewards are individual, reflecting these two companies' more traditional approach to performance management. At Infogix, the rewards are team-based and reflect the Deming approach.

Embed the Value in Performance Standards

Even though all three companies link the performance evaluation process to their culture, Smartmatic is the most direct. At Smartmatic, employees are evaluated against technical as well as cultural performance standards. Implementing a system of this kind requires time (and patience), but the return on investment can be great. In brief, everyone in the company will understand and strive to behave consistently with the company's desired culture.

Final Comment

As these cases demonstrate, performance management and accountability is not just a simple matter of techniques and tools; it is rooted in a cultural philosophy of how people ought to be managed or led and what the fabric of a culture ought to be.

7 Managing the Innovation and Change Dimension of Culture

The notion that companies can somehow be "built to last" is a pleasant fiction.[1] Nothing lasts forever, not redwood trees, not empires, and certainly not companies. At times there are periods of stability for companies and nations that give the illusion of permanence; but it is a mirage.

This has been shown with powerful force by the "Great Recession" of 2008–09. The financial tsunami crushed many companies that had distinguished histories and long periods of survival. Lehman Brothers, Bear Stearns, Merrill Lynch, and Countrywide Financial disappeared as independent entities. AIG, Citigroup, and General Motors (once the mightiest of them all) were humbled and brought close to bankruptcy—saved only by massive federal government bailouts. All were once undisputed leaders and best-in-class companies. Today, they are object lessons in management failure.

Could effective management of their corporate culture have made a difference in their fall from grace? We believe that the answer is clearly yes.[2] Specifically, all of these companies failed, to some extent, to effectively manage change and innovation.

This chapter deals with how companies can and should manage the innovation and change dimension of culture to help ensure that they remain healthy, both financially and in terms of organizational effectiveness.[3] As we explain in the first sections, change and innovation are not synonyms and should be treated as two separate but related dimensions of culture that need to be managed. We address managing change as a separate aspect of culture (as well as managing innovation) in this book because our research identified it as a causal factor in successful organizational and financial performance.

As in previous chapters, we examine and evaluate selected companies that have achieved and sustained success by emphasizing a culture of change and innovation. In this chapter, however, we begin by describing and defining change and innovation, the difference between these two concepts, and how they are related.

The Concepts of Change and Innovation

As discussed in the first chapter, humans and chimpanzees have about 99 percent of their DNA in common. Even so, there are distinct differences between the two. The same applies to change and innovation.

The Nature of Change

There are many definitions of change, but all connote making something different in some particular way. The difference can be small (incremental change) or radical (transformational). It can involve shifting from one (or the current, equilibrium) state or phase to another, which in turn results in a transformation or transition. Although change can result in transformation, transformation is different from change. Change involves anything different from the norm, while transformation involves a metamorphosis from one state to another. As a caterpillar grows, it changes. A metamorphosis or transformation occurs when it becomes a butterfly.

Change can be planned or unplanned and done systematically or ad hoc and piecemeal. Change can be categorized as incremental, major, or transformational. Incremental change is barely noticeable and is not material or significant. An incremental change occurs when a new piece of equipment or a new software application is introduced. A major change occurs when there is a switch in software to an enterprise-type system, or when a new manufacturing plant comes online. Transformational change occurs when a company switches from a direct-selling model to use of distributors, or from distributors to an online sales model (like Dell Computers).

How do companies manage change? Some build the concept of virtually perpetual change into their culture. Others tend to resist all change, at any cost, even facing potential destruction of the company through atrophy.

The Nature of Innovation

Innovation is a special type of change. As used here, *innovation* is the process of designing changes in an organization or component of economic activity (such as a product or service) in order to create competitive advantage. By definition, innovation involves planned changes; but it can also result by accident. Accidental innovation occurs when something is "discovered" that was unplanned or unexpected. For example, the drug called Viagra was originally investigated by Pfizer for its properties as a blood pressure control medication. Its use to overcome erectile dysfunction was an accidental (but propitious) discovery.

Importance of Cultural Dimensions of Change and Innovation

Managing change and managing innovation are critical aspects of long-term sustainability and success. For example, rapidly growing organizations embracing change as a "way of life" tend to experience less difficulty in making the required transitions at different stages of growth.[4] Those viewing change as threatening tend to experience significant problems. In one $100 million organization, the owner/entrepreneur nominally supported the changes needed to take his company into the future. Yet he resisted when confronted with the need to change his company's planning process, product line, structure (including delegating more decision making responsibility to members of his management team), and corporate culture. Instead of changing, he held on to the old ways of doing things, until his firm began to lose market share. Once this happened, he blamed his senior management team and replaced them—for the second time in as many years.

Where innovation is a way of life, companies tend to sustain their position as market leaders. 3M is a classic case of a company that embeds innovation in its culture. It stimulates innovation with a strategy and practice of permitting product R&D people to bootleg (divert) time for a pet project. This form of "lawlessness" is not only tolerated but encouraged as a key aspect of the 3M culture. Such a practice would be anathema in many companies. (As we shall discuss later, this cultural practice resulted in development of the now ubiquitous and highly profitable product called "Post-it.") We noted in Chapter 5 that Google follows a practice similar to 3M's by encouraging software engineers to spend 20 percent of their time working on projects of their own choice.

In some cases, the innovation aspect of culture is carried to an extreme, resulting in a dysfunctional culture, or what might be called the "not invented here syndrome." In these companies employees believe they, the products they offer, the way they do business, their systems, and other factors are so unique that there is nothing to be learned from others. As a result, an excess of resources (time and dollars) is invested in reinventing the wheel. This leads to performance problems and can result in an overall decline in the company's financial results.

Innovation and Change in Corporate Culture

Innovation as a cultural dimension is often included in corporate value statements, and attempts are made to manage it explicitly. This is not typically true of the broader notion of change. Formal corporate culture statements rarely include a value related to change per se. Companies tend to react to change rather than proactively manage it. For example, the Johnson & Johnson Credo—J&J's statement of core values—includes mention of the importance of managing innovation, but not change. This is not an isolated example. The Smartmatic values statement (shown in Chapter 6) also includes a value for innovation, but not for change.

This distinction is important because unless something is the subject of specific focus, it tends to be managed ineffectively or not at all. There are, however, examples of companies that manage change well even if the word does not appear in the formal statement of values. In this chapter, we present case studies of how companies successfully created cultures that emphasize change or innovation, and subsequently achieved overall success[5]: Johnson & Johnson, 3M, Southwest, Toyota, and GE. We also revisit Smartmatic, discussed in the previous chapter in the context of performance management. J&J, 3M, and Smartmatic illustrate management of innovation, while Southwest, Toyota, and GE demonstrate management of both innovation and change. We attempt to clarify and deconstruct their success to gain insights generally applicable to other companies.

Managing the Innovation Cultural Dimension at Smartmatic[6]

Smartmatic has created a mind-set among its people that inevitably leads to every member of the company embracing innovation as a cornerstone of culture and operations. How was Smartmatic able to make this happen? It used a variety of methods to instill innovation as a core value, beginning with the story of the company's birth. Just as the story or myth of the birth of Rome (by legend, Rome was founded by two wolves) has a profound impact on people's mind-set, Smartmatic's story has a considerable influence on employees.

"Innovation Is in Our DNA"

According to the company's CEO, Antonio Mugica, "We were born as an innovative company, and innovation is in our DNA."[7] Articulating and repeating this theme is an effective method of cultural management because it establishes the identity of Smartmatic as an innovative company.

We noted in Chapter 3 that a sign or marker of a successfully managed culture is that the culture is second nature to people. It becomes part of their fabric of being; the way they see and do things. This has been accomplished at Smartmatic. Employees see themselves as innovative and view it as part of their heritage, and their DNA.

Formal Statement of Innovation as a Cultural Value

In addition to the story of the founding, Smartmatic uses its formal statement of values and related behaviors (described in Chapter 6) to convey a culture of innovation. One of the company's eight core values ("Encourages others to be creative and innovative") deals explicitly with innovation; it is an effective reminder of what is important at Smartmatic.

The Smartmatic Identity and Core Strategy

Smartmatic not only has a history of being an innovative company; it has also created a rationale for the critical role of innovation as central to survival. As Mugica says, "We see ourselves as a tiny company competing with giants. We see ourselves as an underdog. This means that the only way for us to win is to be different in everything we do."[8] As a result, differentiation in everything Smartmatic does is embraced as a core strategy, which leads directly to the value of innovation.

The scope or focus of innovation at Smartmatic is significantly broader than it is at most companies. Although most view the domain of innovation as product development or manufacturing, Smartmatic broadens the concept to include every activity. Mugica cites GE as an example of how innovation in financing can be critical to an organization's success. As is well known, GE Credit Corporation was established as a vehicle to assist present and potential customers in purchasing its products. As a result, this financial unit of GE became essential to the company's performance, contributing as much as 40 percent of overall profits.

This perspective leads people at Smartmatic to question everything: How can we be creative in manufacturing? How can we be creative in finance? How can we be creative in other ways to give us a competitive advantage? Mugica skillfully uses the position of underdog as a spur to this mind-set. The premise is that Smartmatic must be more creative and innovative than the larger competition if it is to survive and prosper. Innovation must infuse everything they do, from new product development to ideas for changing the firm's financial model for customers.

"A 'Can Do' Attitude; and an Anti 'Can't Do' Attitude!"

An implicit value set supporting innovation at Smartmatic relates to having a "can do attitude" and dismissing the "can't do attitude." As Mugica puts it, "My approach is: Don't tell me it cannot be done. Tell me what you need, to get it done!" This perspective leads people to think creatively about how to complete tasks, achieve goals, and the like—which frequently leads to innovative ways of doing things. Mugica cites an example: in the fall of 2008, the company undertook a project with the government of Bolivia to register five million voters in just seventy-five days! Other companies decided this was impossible or too difficult and passed on the project, but Smartmatic embraced the challenge. In October 2009 they successfully completed the project. The assignment was valuable to Smartmatic not only as a source of revenue but as another example of how the company can do whatever it sets out to do; and as we know, success leads to more success, while failure leads to more failure.

Willingness to Take Risks

The willingness to take calculated risks, a core value of Smartmatic not found in the formal values statement, infuses everything the company does. It also supports innovation. People willing to take risks are also ready to try different approaches and implement new ideas. The voter registration project was a highly significant risk for Smartmatic.

Candor and Self-Criticism

The candor and self-criticism value explicitly included in Smartmatic's values statement also supports the focus on innovation. According to Mugica: "We need to be candid to ourselves. Are we really significantly better than our competitors? If we believe we are, and we are not, we are in trouble."[9] The willingness to critically examine decisions and actions supports innovation; the very act of asking questions about the effectiveness of a process, system, or other function can lead to ideas for improvement.

The Role of Company Vision in Culture Management

Another factor contributing to innovation being embraced at Smartmatic is that the company's vision supports the culture, and vice versa. "Culture and vision are mutually reinforcing," says Mugica. The company's vision is, "We imagine technology with profound social impact raising civilization. We are focused on getting there."

The Role of Stock Ownership in Culture Management

Smartmatic uses stock ownership to reinforce culture in general and the core value of innovation in particular. When asked who has stock ownership at Smartmatic, Mugica replies: "Everyone. The cleaning lady has shares." This is based on the belief that ownership changes how people think about their jobs.

Thinking Differently

Overall, the key to Smartmatic's management of innovation is that the company thinks differently than other companies do, and this in turn encourages its people (and creates an expectation) to think differently. This is by design and is part of Smartmatic's core strategy. If there is any similarity between Smartmatic and other companies, it is to businesses in Silicon Valley. Hewlett-Packard, Apple, and Google are all role models for Smartmatic.

Lessons from Smartmatic's Management of Innovation

Smartmatic uses a number of methods to manage its culture, but the most important is "cultural osmosis." As noted previously, founders of a company imprint their values upon the company through what they say and do. What people see on a day-to-day basis as decisions are made and actions are taken affects their thinking and actions. Accordingly, the values and viewpoints of the founder or founding group become the initial values of the enterprise. At Smartmatic innovation has become a core part of everyone's mind-set, through a form of cultural osmosis (described in Chapter 3), in which innovation is a by-product of everything done by people.

Managing Innovation at J&J

Johnson & Johnson is a leading world-class company with more than $63 billion in revenues and operations around the world. J&J consists of many subcompanies, including some entities such as Neutrogena, Centecor, and LifeScan that were acquired. Innovation is a core value in the J&J Credo. The Credo states that "research must be carried on, innovative programs developed. . . ." J&J is often cited as one of the most admired of all companies, and innovation has historically been a driver of its success.

How does J&J manage innovation? The company has a sophisticated but simple method of influencing the behavior of its component companies to motivate them toward innovation, while leaving them sufficient autonomy to be self-managed to a considerable extent. Specifically, J&J asks individual subsidiaries such as Neutrogena to report on whether sales include revenues from introducing various types or levels of innovative products over the preceding three to five years.

The categories used by J&J in asking for subsidiary reports on innovation are incremental, major, and transformational innovations. Incremental innovation refers to anything that involves less than 5–10 percent of the product; major innovations involve more than 10 percent but less than 100 percent of the product; and transformational innovation refers to change in more than 100 percent of the product. Using this method, J&J was able to motivate Neutrogena to do a transformational innovation. Specifically, the company launched a cosmetics line, resulting in more than doubled revenues and quadrupled profits.

Managing Innovation at 3M

Like J&J, 3M is also a world-class company famous for innovation, which has long been part of its core competitive strategy.[10] A classic example of innovation is Post-it Notes, which probably inhabit every office in the world.

Motivation of Innovation at 3M

For decades, 3M has motivated innovation by following an idiosyncratic set of practices. As we noted in Chapter 3, R&D people are encouraged to bootleg 15 percent of their time and budget to work on projects of great personal and professional interest. The underlying concept is that if people believe in a potential product and are willing to gamble on its development, the company will eventually benefit. This enables people to circumvent the traditional 3M bureaucracy for approving product development projects.

This process was responsible for development of the Post-it Note. The entire history of 3M involves developing products with a high degree of adhesion or tackiness (Magic Tape, packing tape, and so on). However, one material being tested for such purposes failed all the traditional 3M criteria for products because it had a low degree of adhesion; it was unique in a negative way. Despite this, the 3M culture permitted scientists to investigate the properties of this "low-quality" low-adhesion material. This quality led to developing Post-It Notes, a product with just enough adhesiveness to be "temporarily permanent" as a vehicle for posting notes on books, letters, or other objects.

In effect, 3M manages the culture of innovation by permitting people to pursue projects of their own choosing. They then use successful projects as a role model to stimulate other innovations.

Managing Innovation and Change at Southwest Airlines

Innovation is an essential part of Southwest's culture. In fact, the word is included in the company's employee" mission: "Creativity and innovation are encouraged for improving the effectiveness of Southwest Airlines."[11]

There is also a section on the Southwest careers website called "The Freedom to Create and Innovate."[12] Listed in this section are "some of the history-making ideas that came straight from our creative and innovative Leaders and Employees" such as the Ten-Minute Turnaround and Ticketless Travel. The company does not explicitly include the value of change in the formal statement of is culture (that is, in its mission statement), but Southwest also embraces the need for change, in the context of its values.

The Innovation Cultural Dimension at Southwest

From the beginning of the company, Southwest has been about innovation. The founders, in effect, created an entirely new market by making air travelers out of those who would normally have taken a bus or car and by increasing the frequency of air travel on the part of those who, in the past, couldn't afford to travel very often by plane. The company had the first profit-sharing plan within the airline industry, launched in 1973. This was also innovative, and at the same time it supported the company's culture, which focuses on customer service and having employees think like owners.

Southwest promotes innovation through the company's open-door policy. Employees are encouraged to ask questions, share ideas, and make suggestions. They have direct access to anyone in the company—even the CEO. When a question is asked or idea is submitted, the sender can expect to hear back from the recipient within a week. According to former CEO Herb Kelleher, "if it looks like a good idea we'll want to test it, so we send it to marketing or wherever it may fit and ask them to experiment with it in the field for a month or so and see what happens."[13] If, on the other hand, the decision is made to not pursue the idea, the sender will receive a response that includes a full explanation for not pursuing it. The sender can then resubmit the idea, if he or she feels that something was missed or not considered.

Employees are encouraged to challenge ideas and take risks in the service of improving company effectiveness and supporting the company's values. There is also tolerance for mistakes and the view that much can be learned from them. Consequently, fear of failure is low at Southwest. There are many stories of executives who implemented new ideas that turned out to be "mistakes," with some costing the company a great deal of money.

Although the mistake makers expected to be terminated, they were not. Instead, their experiences became stories that others could learn from— stories that supported the focus on innovation.

Innovation and thinking outside the box seem to be ongoing processes at Southwest, with the constant focus on identifying ways to improve the company's effectiveness. The following story is an illustration. For a time, other airlines included Southwest on their computerized reservation systems. When these other airlines launched their own low-cost carriers (such as the United Shuttle on the West Coast), they eliminated Southwest from their systems (on January 31, 1995). This led to travel agents having to hand-write Southwest tickets—a tremendous inconvenience. A group representing the American Society of Travel Agents had a meeting with Kelleher to discuss the problem. Kelleher described what happened next: "I told them we'd solve that by going ticketless. After they had left my office I called our People to find out how we could do this and discovered that five or six of them had been working on going ticketless for almost a year. They had done this on their own initiative."[14]

The Change Cultural Dimension at Southwest

Change is also a part of the Southwest culture that is sometimes described as the company's desire to remain "adaptable." Kelleher describes it this way: "When you're in a business where the capital assets travel 500 miles per hour, you have to be quick and responsive."[15] Even though change is an important aspect of Southwest's culture, the changes that are adopted and pursued all need to fit with the company's values and its strategy. According to Kelleher, "If someone proposes a service that doesn't fit our values, we would say no, we don't do that."[16]

Southwest's culture of making changes only within company values continues to be a key component of its current success. When other airlines began charging passengers a fee for each checked bag, Southwest retained its Bags Fly Free program. Doing otherwise would have "gone against the essence of Southwest," and CEO Gary Kelly did not want to "'nickel and dime' customers."[17] The result: Southwest reported $11 million in earnings for the first quarter of 2010, one year after losing $91 million![18]

Employee and Company Recognition of Innovation and Change

Those who are innovative and embrace change are recognized by Southwest through employee awards. The Founder's Award salutes those "who go above and beyond the call of duty on a consistent basis—in community service, outstanding job performance, implementation of creative solutions to complex problems, and bringing innovative ideas and programs to the company."[19]

As a company, Southwest has been recognized for its focus on innovation. In 2009, Kelleher received the Steve Fossett Innovation Award from the U.S. Travel Association. This award recognizes a "world-wide, travel-industry leader who has broken new ground, pushed boundaries, and revolutionized the industry, leaving a legacy of long-lasting change."[20] Southwest also received the 2010 American Advertising Federation's Innovation and Leadership Award for "uniquely inventive advertising programs."[21]

It is clear that Southwest's focus on innovation and change is very much a reality within the company and contributes to the company's success. In addition, those outside recognize how innovative the company has been and continues to be.

Managing Change and Innovation at Toyota

As stated previously, the basic problem with managing change as an ongoing aspect of culture is that, unlike innovation, it does not tend to be explicitly stated as part of the culture of many companies. For example, none of the culture statements cited previously (Starbucks, Google, Ritz-Carlton, Walmart, IBM, 3M, Johnson & Johnson) include a statement about change. Nevertheless, change is an important aspect of a company's culture, whether it is explicit or not; this is why we are addressing it here.

Toyota, a quintessentially Japanese firm, treats change as an explicit part of the core culture. It explicitly embraces the notion of change as a core cultural attribute.

Prologue

It must be noted at the outset that Toyota offers us an opportunity to see both the benefits of a culture that embraces change as well as the dysfunctional aspects of culture when a core cultural value is violated. Our rationale for its inclusion is simple: for more than fifty years, Toyota strived to build a world-class reputation for product quality, and it succeeded admirably. It did this based on a culture of innovation and change.

In 2009 the company surpassed General Motors and became the largest producer of automobiles in the world. This achievement was fleeting, though, because of the "sudden acceleration problem" encountered by several of Toyota's brands and models in 2008–2010. Toyota has been severely criticized for attempting to cover up this problem. Although we are aware of the troubles Toyota has experienced, here we first deal with the culture of innovation and change at the company, as it has purportedly existed for about fifty years. We view this as the cultural equilibrium state of Toyota. The problems surrounding the sudden acceleration phenomenon are, from our point of view, a "cultural aberration" that is relatively short-term in duration, not a permanent departure from the company's long-held strategy and beliefs. Although there are important lessons to be learned from Toyota's fall from grace, there are also important lessons to be learned from Toyota at its best. Both notions are discussed here.

The Concept of *Kaizen* and Kaizen at Toyota

During the 1980s, with the economic rise of Japan, we learned about the Japanese concept of *Kaizen*. This concept embodies the notion of "continuous improvement in all aspects of a business."

The value of Kaizen is one of the core values of Toyota and seminal to "the Toyota Way." Specifically, the notion of Kaizen at Toyota is that "we are relentless in our pursuit of improvement, never easily satisfied, constantly making improvement efforts and steadily encouraging innovation (the Toyota Way)."[22]

Throughout its history, the leaders of Toyota embraced the value of Kaizen. There are many examples, as cited by Liker and Hoseus:

- "We are working on making better products by making improvements every day." (Kiichiro Toyoda)
- "Don't think mechanically. Even a dry towel can produce water when ideas are conceived." (Eiji Toyoda)
- "Kaizen activities are the incubator of innovation. This is because Kaizen activities create the atmosphere of change." (Akira Takahashi)

- "Be ahead of the times through endless creativity, inquisitiveness, and the pursuit of improvement." (Toyota Precepts)[23]

Putting These Values into Action at Toyota

How does Toyota put these values into action? "Quality circles," one of the key tools Toyota uses, have been adopted throughout the world. The quality circle process is based on having work teams select a problem they want to work on and then using a structured process of analysis and problem solving to deal with it.

Quality circles became a fad in the United States during the 1980s, but disappointment with their results led to a gradual dénouement of the concept. This suggests that either something in the Japanese culture made the practice work there or its application was flawed in the United States. Possibly both were true.

There is nothing magical about using quality circles to implement the concept of Kaizen. They are a tool shown to work in certain situations, but to fail to meet expectations in others. Perhaps the secret of why quality circles continue to work at Toyota is that their use has become a way of life—an integral part of the Toyota Way—and not merely a managerial flavor of the month.

Results

In 2009, Toyota Motor Corporation became the number one automobile manufacturer in the world. For sixty-eight years, General Motors had been the leading producer, even though the company has long been criticized for its stodgy culture and tendency to resist change. One is compelled to ask whether the fundamental differences in culture between Toyota and GM had any role in this reversal of fortune.

Epilogue: A Moment of Crisis for Toyota and the Toyota Way

Unfortunately, even a carefully constructed culture does not last forever. If it is not nurtured, it can become tenuous. In spite of carefully constructing a reputation for quality products, Toyota began to experience serious problems with its automobiles during 2008–09. Sudden acceleration occurred in some of Toyota's vehicles and was blamed for causing several fatal accidents. Initially, Toyota attributed the problem to a floor mat jammed against the accelerator pedal. The problems began to spread and criticism of the company began to mount, with some customers shunning Toyota vehicles and purchasing other brands.

On February 5, 2010, the company's president, Akio Toyoda, grandson of the company's founder, issued an unprecedented public apology. Toyoda said he was "deeply sorry about the inconvenience and concern caused to our customers and others" and said that the company had reached "a moment of crisis." [24] The company recalled more than nine million vehicles worldwide in an effort to fix the problem.

What caused this problem at Toyota? According to Satoshi Hino, author of a book on the company's culture, in the fourteen years in which corporate operations were not headed by Toyoda family members, Toyota's core values "came under strain" as managers extended the company's image and products.[25] He said that the managers were distracted from adhering to the Toyota Way—the values and principles instilled by the founders—with the drive to become the biggest automaker in the world, a push to increase manufacturing in North America, and the company's debut in Formula One racing.[26]

In late February 2010, a contrite Toyoda told members of the U.S. Congress that his company's rapid growth had "confused" the priority it places on safety.[27] This is a classic culture value conflict, suggesting that somehow Toyota's system of culture management failed to keep up with growth. In brief, there was a conflict between (1) Toyota's desire for growth and the goal to become the largest automobile manufacturer in the world and (2) the value of customer orientation. Alerting customers to the potential product hazard would have hurt the company's chances of overtaking GM as the largest auto manufacturer in the world. In addition, company documents indicated that Toyota's focus was to minimize recall costs.[28] As one released document reveals, Toyota management took credit for saving the company hundreds of millions of dollars by persuading U.S. regulators to limit or avoid safety recalls.[29]

Another aspect of culture and how the company operated, related to decision making, might also have contributed to Toyota's problems. This is a large-scale business with global operations in manufacturing, distribution, and product design. Even so, the practice was to have all significant decisions made at the highest levels—in Japan.[30] In an organization of this size, a command-and-control model of management is intractable and simply will not work effectively.

This incident cost Toyota in terms of both credibility and market position. As Rebecca Lindland, an auto industry analyst at IHS Global Insight, wrote, "Toyota has long been seen as a company that puts customers before profits, and unfortunately this document [the released document referenced above] indicates otherwise. This is almost a worst-case scenario."[31]

The Economic Costs of Cultural Failure

The failure of Toyota to behave consistently with its reputation for quality and focus on the customer has already resulted in serious economic costs. It has also hurt loyalty to the Toyota brand. With customer perceptions of product quality shaken, other brands have begun to boost their market share. Toyota owners are reported to be migrating to Ford, Honda, Hyundai, and Nissan.[32] In addition, the company is exposed to class action lawsuits that will continue for many years, possibly resulting in punitive damages.

Clearly, this is a dramatic example of the value of a strong functional culture as an economic asset and the economic cost or liability of a dysfunctional culture to the bottom line. It also shows the fragility and potentially perishable nature of corporate culture when it is not continuously managed well.

Can Toyota recover? Undoubtedly yes. It will require a significant change effort, however, not only in innovation per se but in other aspects of the Toyota culture. In this regard, the Toyota core value of openness to change will be tested.

Managing Change and Innovation at GE

General Electric is another company that embraces change and innovation as part of its culture. According to the company's website, "GE is imagination at work. From jet engines to power generation, financial services to water processing, and medical imaging to media content, GE people worldwide are dedicated to turning imaginative ideas into leading products and services that help solve some of the world's toughest problems."[33] This is part of what has been dubbed "the GE Way."[34]

The GE Way defines the company culture and includes core values related to change and innovation. According to Robert Slater, "Leaders who adhere to GE values are expected to create a clear, simple, reality-based, customer-focused vision; they are supposed to have a passion for excellence; *to stimulate and relish change.*"[35]

The company's culture is captured in the "GE Values Guide."[36] One of the core values is to "see change as opportunity . . . not threat."

GE thinks of culture as being *among* its innovations. According to the company's website, "At GE, we consider our culture to be one of our innovations. Over decades our leaders have built GE's culture into what it is today—a place for creating and bringing big ideas to life. Today, that culture is the unifying force for our many business units around the world." Innovation is so much a part of GE that there is a tab on the home page of their website labeled Innovation.

As discussed in Chapter 3, GE wants to retain people who fit or embrace its culture—including the company's focus on innovation and change—and enable those who do not to leave the company.

What is the bottom line? GE is one of only a few companies to have continued to be successful for a very long period (more than a hundred years). We believe its focus on innovation and change is a fundamental reason for this success.

Conclusion

Of all the cultural dimensions, the constructs of innovation and change are possibly the most ethereal and elusive. They are abstract notions but real elements, and some companies have done a very good job of capturing them in their culture.

This chapter examined companies that manage innovation and change well. There are many more examples of companies managing innovation as an explicit dimension of culture, and fewer that explicitly manage change as a core dimension of culture. Toyota and GE are examples of the latter.

Innovation and Change Culture Management Tools

The companies described in this chapter use many of the same tools in managing the innovation and change dimension of their culture.

Have a Formal Statement of the Innovation and Change Value

All six companies include in their values statements something about innovation, change, or both. At Smartmatic, innovation is highlighted as a specific value. In some of the other companies, the focus on innovation appears as a statement (within the Credo at J&J, as part of Southwest's Mission, and so on). At Toyota and GE, the formal statement of values also includes the word *change.* Including statements about innovation and change help employees understand that these concepts are important to the company's success.

Use Communication to Reinforce the Innovation and Change Value

All six companies have many stories about individuals, teams, or the company as a whole benefiting from innovation or change. At Southwest, there are also stories about unsuccessful change efforts serving to reinforce the idea that it is OK to make mistakes. Stories help employees understand the importance of the value; they also help define what the value is and what it looks like in practice.

At Southwest, there is a commitment to giving feedback on ideas within a specific period of time, whether the idea is accepted or not. Open lines of communication help foster both innovation and learning.

Finally, some of these companies—notably Southwest and GE—make a practice of formally recording innovations. At Southwest, the list of employee-generated innovations appears on the website. This practice helps reinforce the idea that innovations are valued and helps promote the innovation value.

Reward and Recognize Those Who Represent the Innovation and Change Value

All of the companies profiled offer incentives for innovation. At 3M, a major incentive is that those individuals whose ideas create and launch successful new products can sometimes become the head of a division offering that product. At Southwest, there are a variety of employee awards for innovative ideas. As was true of the other values, this recognition does not need to come in the form of financial rewards or promotions. Sometimes, the very telling of a story about something innovative that an individual or team did that benefited the company can be a reward in and of itself.

Embed the Innovation and Change Value in Company Processes

All of the companies profiled here have specific processes that promote innovation, creativity, and change. At these companies, looking for ways to improve performance, effectiveness, and ways of doing things is constant. At the same time, however, it is also true that these companies recognize that change needs to be made in the context of other company values.

A Final Comment

Perhaps the greatest lesson we can learn from these examples is that for these abstract constructs to have real impact they must become part of the way of life in an organization. They must become part of the "Smartmatic Way," "the Johnson & Johnson Way," "the 3M Way," "the Southwest Mission," "the Toyota Way," or "the GE Way." If this happens, then they are converted from ethereal notions and have real tangible impact. Otherwise, they are just words—words that sound impressive but have no real organizational impact.

8 Managing the Company Process Orientation Dimension of Culture

The final dimension of culture is that of *company process orientation,* the view people hold about specific aspects of how the company operates. The ability to effectively implement *all* systems and processes that exist within a company can be positively or negatively affected by the real culture, but this chapter focuses on four of what we consider to be the most important aspects: planning, decision making, communication,[1] and the processes and systems a company uses to promote social responsibility, or what some label being a "good corporate citizen." Within every company, there are values, beliefs, and norms that define behavior as consistent or inconsistent with effective implementation of these systems; this behavior has a direct impact on how the system actually functions.

In each section of this chapter, we begin by defining each of the four systems using a continuum. In the case of planning and decision making, this continuum reflects how these systems should evolve as a company grows in size, whereas in the case of communication and social responsibility the continuum is not based on size per se. After discussing each continuum, we discuss the impact that the real culture can have on system implementation. Throughout, we present examples of companies that have effectively aligned their organizational culture with effective system execution. This chapter is structured somewhat differently from those covering the other dimensions; it is organized by the four systems, as opposed to a specific company.

Managing the Planning Value

On one end of the planning system continuum is what might be called the "What am I going to do after lunch?" approach. The company's management is basically reacting or responding to external or internal threats and opportunities. No true planning is taking place. At the other end of the continuum is a system that produces a written document—a strategic plan—detailing where the company is (external and internal opportunities and threats), where the company wants to be or what it wants to achieve over the long run (typically three to five years out), and how the company will move from where it is to where it wants to be. The plan is used as a guide to help all employees understand where the company is going and what they need to do to support achievement of its long-term goals, with management regularly monitoring performance against the plan. In between these two extremes of reacting versus very formal planning are many variations with respect to how companies plan.

The effectiveness of whatever planning process a company nominally adopts (which means, what it declares it is using) will be affected by its culture. For example, a company might be using a highly structured approach to planning that produces a written playbook for where it is going and how it wants to get there. It might even be making a substantial investment (of finances and time) in this process. If, however, the company's culture does not include valuing planning as opposed to firefighting or crisis management, the planning process will break down and not function effectively. Taken to an extreme, team members will spend most of their time looking for fires to fight (or sometimes lighting fires to fight) because this is what is rewarded and recognized. They will ignore the plan. This in turn can result in a company underperforming or missing significant opportunities. The bottom line: the planning value of a company must support effective implementation of whatever planning process or system is adopted. How this value should be defined depends on the company's size, structure, and other company values. In brief, it needs to fit with everything else.

The Planning Value at Southwest Airlines

Southwest Airlines prides itself on being, according to cofounder Herb Kelleher, "quick and nimble."[2] As discussed previously, there is a strong focus on employees and customers. Both of these values or ways of operating are reflected in how the company does planning. Although the company has a clearly defined purpose and a strategy for achieving it, it does not have what might be thought of as a traditional strategic plan. Instead, the company uses what Kelleher describes as "scenario planning."[3] Basically, the company's executive planning committee meets periodically to develop future scenarios and ask, "If this happened, what would we do?"[4] The result of these discussions is a collection of plans that Southwest can implement, if and when a specific event occurs. An example of this planning process in action is described in the book *Nuts.*[5] The Southwest planning team anticipated that United Airlines would counter their efforts to enter the California and West Coast market and so developed a plan to address this. As United was preparing to launch its now-defunct United Shuttle service, Southwest was purchasing Utah-based Morris Air. This purchase gave the company more 737 planes and also allowed it to establish itself in the Pacific Northwest, thus creating even more competition for the fledgling Shuttle.

Southwest's culture supports and is supported by this approach to planning at levels below that of the executive team. Employees throughout the company are empowered to take action whenever they feel it is in the company's interest. But they are also well aware at all times of what the company's purpose, strategy, and financial performance are. Because they are all stock owners, they understand that every decision must be made in the context of the overall strategy and in the best interest of company performance. What this means at Southwest, however, is that things can and should *change*. But when they do, employees know that management has a plan for ensuring that this change is made in the most effective manner possible.

Managing the Planning Value at Infogix[6]

In Chapter 6, we examined the performance optimization system developed at Infogix. The system includes a well-designed planning component, which is supported by the company's culture. Planning has always been a part of Infogix's culture; the company has a well-established strategic planning function and the leaders of the operating groups pride themselves on their strategic capabilities. The planning process (developed by the authors and used at Infogix), shown in Exhibit 8.1, is quite formal and systematic.

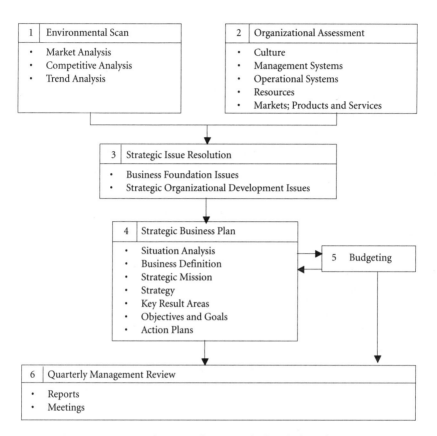

Exhibit 8.1. Management Systems' strategic planning method, applied at Infogix.

The process begins with collection and analysis of information about the environment in which the company operates and its internal capabilities. Assessment of internal capabilities uses a specific framework, called the Pyramid of Organizational Development, which will be described in more detail in Chapter 10.[7] This framework helps take the SWOT (strengths, weaknesses, opportunities, and threats) analysis that is a part of most planning processes to the next level of sophistication. Instead of just identifying internal strengths and weaknesses, the pyramid framework focuses a company on identifying strengths and opportunities to improve with respect to six dimensions or building blocks of organizational success: markets, products and services, resources, operational systems, management systems, and organizational culture. Research has shown that these six dimensions have a significant impact on long-term organizational success.[8] Hence it is important for companies to understand where they are and what they can do to improve with respect to each dimension.

Infogix has a data-driven culture. This helps support effective implementation of this sophisticated approach to external and internal assessments. Team members are willing to invest the time needed to collect the information on which the company's plan will be based.

Analysis of external and internal assessment data results in identifying specific issues to be resolved. Resolution of these issues is the basis for the company's strategic plan. The foundation of the strategic plan, using the approach presented in Exhibit 8.1, is (1) the business definition (or concept), (2) the strategic mission, and (3) the core strategy. The business definition (or concept) defines the business that the company is in. The strategic mission identifies what the company wants to become. The core strategy specifies, in a big-picture manner, how the company will compete. To effectively create and define these dimensions requires that the culture of the company support thinking strategically. This is the case at Infogix. As described in Chapter 6, Infogix created a "new" market and is focused on helping to shape it. This is reflected in these elements of the company's plan.

The next levels of the plan are key result areas, objectives, and goals. Key result areas identify the critical success factors on which a company should focus to promote long-term success. In the approach to planning presented in Exhibit 8.1, key result areas are the dimensions of organizational success included in the pyramid framework (markets, products and services, resources, operational systems, management systems, and corporate culture) plus financial results. In brief, the plan is organized using these dimensions. Objectives—broad statements that define the company's strategy—are then established for each key result area. Finally, goals—specific, measurable, time-dated results to be achieved in the coming year—are established for each objective. For a company to maximize its effectiveness in completing these steps, there must be a focus on results as opposed to activities. As described in Chapter 6, the Infogix culture supports this, with respect to performance standards and accountability. Hence the company's plan is very much based on results to be achieved rather than actions to be taken.

Step 5 involves creating a financial plan to support the nonfinancial strategic plan. This is accomplished at Infogix through a process of identifying the resources required to achieve each goal. The company's culture emphasizes effective use of resources and hence is supportive of this process.

The final step in the planning process, and one that makes it a true process, is quarterly management review. As described in Chapter 6, the Infogix culture stresses the importance of measurement and using measurements as input to regular, systematic assessments of performance. In some companies, effective planning suffers because it is "the thing we do after we do everything else." In these companies, review meetings can end up postponed because there are more pressing matters. At Infogix, quarterly review meetings are viewed as very important and are cancelled or rescheduled only if there is a real emergency. In brief, the culture supports the idea that planning should be a way of life.

Managing the Decision Making Value

From a systems perspective, decision making in a company involves identifying who has the *authority* to make which decisions and the *process* that is used to make decisions. From a cultural perspective, decision making authority is frequently translated into the extent to which managers and employees feel empowered. Within companies, the decision making authority continuum ranges from all decisions needing to be made by management (and sometimes only senior management) to providing all employees with the authority to make decisions within their areas of responsibility. The decision making process continuum ranges from making decisions based only on gut feel and instinct (a shoot-from-the hip approach) to decisions made using information and analytical techniques to identify, evaluate, and choose among alternative courses of action to achieve a goal.

Small entrepreneurial companies tend to operate with a more directive ("telling") style of decision making because the owner is in constant contact with all employees and it is, after all, his or her business. Within these companies, the decision making process tends to be more informal, more based on gut feel. As companies grow and new levels of management are created, management theory and practice suggests that decision making should be delegated to the lowest possible level of the company. The owner/entrepreneur or senior management can no longer make *all* decisions, and the organization's culture should support this reality. However, if the way in which senior management operates is to override decisions made at lower management levels, if lower levels of management are punished for making mistakes, or if those who are responsible for implementing decisions are not involved in making them, then the real culture will not support delegation of decision making authority and responsibility, and all decisions will continue being pushed up to senior management.

As companies grow and develop, the decision making process needs to become more formal, systematic, and defined. Having a well-defined and effective decision making process in place actually helps promote delegation of decision making authority. However, if the real culture promotes continuing to make decisions based on opinion or gut feel, the formal process will be underused or ignored completely, and as a result the quality of the decisions that are made will suffer. One additional note: there are some companies in which a culture that values systematic decision making can be carried to an extreme. In these cases, the company may suffer from "analysis paralysis": timely decision making is lacking because decision makers are investing too much time collecting and analyzing information. In brief, they are overkilling the decision making process.

The Decision Making Value at Southwest Airlines

Not surprisingly, Southwest Airlines "empowers its managers and front-line staff—those who deal directly with the customers—to act as 'problem solvers,' often making decisions on the spot that can save the relationship with the customer."[9] The formal decision making process is based on the premise that if all employees understand the company's purpose and mission (values), then decisions will be made in the best interest of the customer and the company's employees. In addition, the fact that all employees hold shares in the company helps promote the idea that in making decisions employees should think like owners—because they actually are.

The culture of the company very much supports empowering employees. People are not punished for making a "bad" decision or for making one that may not be consistent with company rules. In fact, the company shares stories of employees who have made decisions of this type, as a way of helping everyone understand and embrace the value placed on empowerment.

For example, a captain made the decision—against company rules—to return to the gate with a passenger who had boarded the wrong plane. Instead of being criticized, he was congratulated.[10]

One of the authors experienced this ability to make decisions in action at the Oakland airport a few years ago.

> While trying to leave on an earlier flight out of Oakland, I was told that my reservation had been inadvertently cancelled. Basically, I now had no seat reserved on any flight, and it was Friday afternoon. I had obtained the boarding pass for the original flight the day before (before the reservation was cancelled) and had already gone through security. I fully anticipated having to go back down to ticketing and wait in several lines—ticketing, security, etc. Instead, within minutes, the customer service agent had printed a boarding pass for an earlier flight, one that left within ten minutes of the time he began to solve my problem.

This is not an isolated event. Simply visit the company's website or read any of the published information from customers about how Southwest's people have effectively solved problems in real time. The bottom line: empowerment is very much a real part of the Southwest culture.

There is another aspect to the Southwest culture that relates to the decision making process: a bias for action. This doesn't mean that decisions are made in the absence of information. Instead, information is presented and discussed, and a decision is made as quickly as possible. With respect to major, strategic decisions, this ability to take quick action is in part supported by the process the company uses to plan: continually identifying, analyzing, and developing plans to address future scenarios. At a more operational level, it is supported by the company's culture, which promotes the idea of "trying things" as long as they fit within the company's values. There are countless stories of quick decision making, including Kelleher "approving" a decision to completely reorganize the company's maintenance department after reviewing a three-page memo from the chief operations officer and then having a four-minute conversation.[11]

The formal decision making style and process used at Southwest supports its ability to achieve goals and is consistent with other aspects of how it operates, and with its culture—that is, having a solid focus on customers and employees, keeping things simple, and being quick to act.

The Decision Making Value at Google

At Google, there is a strong focus on "consensus" and data-driven decisions. These values are reflected in what Google calls its "10 Golden Rules."[12] Among them are these three:

- Hire by committee. Virtually every person who interviews at Google talks to at least half-a-dozen interviewers. . . . Everyone's opinion counts. . . . Yes, it takes longer, but we think it's worth it.

- Strive to reach consensus. Modern corporate mythology has the unique decision maker as the hero. We adhere to the view that "many are smarter than a few" and solicit a broad base of views before reaching any decision. At Google, the role of the manager is that of an aggregator of viewpoints, not the dictator of decisions. Building consensus sometimes takes longer but always produces a more committed team and better decisions.

- Data-driven decisions. At Google, almost every decision is based on quantitative analysis. We've built systems to manage information, not only on the Internet at large but also internally. We have dozens of analysts who plow through the data, analyze performance metrics, and plot trends to keep us as up to date as possible.

As described in earlier chapters, the hiring process a company uses is one tool or mechanism for managing corporate culture. At Google, the team decision making approach in hiring helps increase the probability that those who are hired will fit with the company's culture, and it also communicates to a prospective employee how important team decision making is.

Consensus or team decision making fosters "synergism," whereby the decision made by the group is typically more effective than one made by a single individual. In a true consensus approach, all opinions receive equal weight; there is no ultimate decision maker. Thus the message is that "all opinions are valued and valuable." This seems to fit with other aspects of the Google culture. The consensus approach to decision making also helps promote a sense of team—something that is important within the overall Google culture.

Being data-driven promotes effective decision making by helping to focus decision makers more on facts than on opinions. Given the nature of the employees that Google needs and that it attracts, being data-driven makes sense. Also, it fits with and supports the nature of Google's business; the company is, after all, in the business of providing information to Internet users.

Google's approach to decision making and the culture that supports it certainly have a number of positives. However, there are also some potential drawbacks to this approach that must be managed. First, team hiring and team decision making can take a great deal of time, particularly if these processes are not managed effectively. In brief, opportunities can be missed. Second, being too data-driven can lead to analysis paralysis. Some web postings by former employees suggest that both of these problems are starting to surface at Google. Those ex-employees describe the hiring process as "drawn out" and "inefficient," sometimes taking as long as nine months.[13] Some question whether this investment of time is worth it, but others recognize that it is a mechanism to preserve the company's culture. With respect to decision making, some suggest that there are times when trying to be data-driven and reach consensus leads to exceedingly slow decision making. One former employee described the frustration of "debating miniscule design decisions"—such as the exact shade of blue to be used and the size of a border—as contributing to that person's decision to leave the company.[14] At the same time, this person went on to thank the company and to say that he or she would miss the "incredibly smart and talented people" who work there.

Although Google's decision making approach and decision making culture have clearly contributed to its success, the comments from ex-employees suggest that there may be some opportunities to more effectively manage this aspect of culture as the company looks to the future.

Managing the Communication Value

The role of communication in corporate culture is complex and interesting because it has a dual aspect: communication is simultaneously a value (or component of) and a process for managing a company's culture. In this chapter, we are referring to communication as a component of culture, rather than as a tool for (or process to facilitate) culture management.[15]

Communication, in this context, is defined as "what information is shared, who it is shared with, how it is shared, and when it is shared" *inside* a company. At one extreme of this continuum are companies in which the communication system is very informal and ill-defined (sometimes result-ing in people not receiving the information they need when they need it, or receiving inaccurate information). At the other extreme are companies that have formal systems of communication that are designed to provide everyone in the company with the information they need, in an effective format, and in a timely manner. Regardless of where the company is on this continuum, the real culture can positively or negatively affect how the system actually works. For example, a culture that supports continuous and open sharing of information can make up for the lack of a formal commu-nication system. All employees will work together to ensure that everyone has the information needed to perform their role effectively and support the company's success. Alternatively, if the culture of a company promotes the notion that information is power, then even the most formal communica-tion system won't work because people will avoid sharing information.

The Communication Value at Southwest Airlines

A quick visit to Southwest Airlines' website suggests that the company has a highly formal and well-developed system of communication, focused on sharing with employees everything they need to and want to know. There is a constant stream of information flowing throughout the company, daily, weekly, and monthly. Some of the methods used by Southwest are listed in "The Freedom to Stay Connected" in the careers section of the company's site.[16] In reviewing this list, it is interesting to note that all of these commu-nication methods and tools focus, directly or indirectly, on reinforcing the company's culture. Southwest recognizes that every communication repre-sents an opportunity to help nurture one of the company's most important assets: culture.

In addition to the mechanisms listed on the company's website, there is an open-door policy that operates throughout the company. Employees are encouraged to make suggestions, provide feedback, and ask questions of anyone within the company. As described in Chapter 7, they can expect that any message they send will be responded to by someone within a few days. The message is, "Not only will we share with you what we know, but we want to know what you know, as well." There is a fairly constant stream of ques-tions and issues being shared and discussed on the company's blog in which

Gary Kelly, the company's CEO, and other members of senior leadership frequently make posts (and this is just the part of the website that is public).

Southwest's communication system supports and is supported by the company's culture. In addition, how employees and leaders use the system reflects the company's culture and helps reinforce some of the other important values that contribute to Southwest's success.

The Communication Value at Walmart

Under the culture section of the Walmart website, in a section titled "Learn About Our Culture," are several items that relate to how the company manages the value attached to communication. They are referred to here as "rules" or "customs" that support the company's three Basic Beliefs and Values (discussed previously in chapter 5). Specifically, the website identifies:

- Open Door. The door is always open. At Walmart, our management believes open communication is critical to understanding and meeting our associates' and our customers' needs. Through our "open door" policy, associates are free to share suggestions, ideas, and voice concerns. . . . Associates can trust and rely on the open door. This means that managers will treat all discussion fairly, with an open mind, and without bias. . . . They'll work with you to mutually resolve any issues or problems you may have.

- Sundown Rule. It's really a twist on "why put off until tomorrow what you can do today?" Observing the Sundown Rule is very simple. Whether it's a request from a store across the country or a call from an associate down the hall, we do our very best to give our customers, and each other, same-day service.

- Grass Roots Process. "Listen to your associates. They're the best idea generators." Sam Walton said that, and he believed it. . . . We're still listening. The sheer size of our company limits how many stores executives can physically visit each year. But Sam's philosophy lives today in our Grass Roots Process. A key part of that process is the associate opinion survey—it gives every single associate a way to voice their ideas, suggestions, and concerns. . . . Using the survey, we continually find ways to improve our customer service and how to better serve our associates.[17]

The open-door policy at Walmart operates a little differently than it does at Southwest Airlines. At Walmart, every employee ultimately has access to whatever level is needed to secure resolution to a problem. However, he or she needs to go through the chain of command—beginning with the immediate supervisor. This practice goes back to Sam Walton, and according to Don Soderquist, the company's former vice chairman and COO, it contributes to helping identify and resolve problems that might go unresolved, if this policy were not in place.[18] This is an example of a communication process that, in a sense, is driven by the company's culture.

The grassroots process gives all employees a mechanism to provide input to the company on what can be done to improve performance. The opinion survey results are broken down by operating unit and shared with all employees. According to Soderquist, the intent of this effort is "to communicate to our associates that we would do our best to take better care of them if they would do their best to communicate with management."[19]

The values related to communication—reflected in Walmart's customs and rules—are reinforced through the company's meeting structure, which was described in Chapter 5. Friday morning meetings of officers and division heads, Saturday morning meetings for management personnel, and weekly or even daily meetings in stores and warehouses are mechanisms through which the culture can be shared, discussed, and reinforced. In addition, these meetings serve as a formal mechanism to collect and disseminate information.

The Communication Value at the Ritz-Carlton Hotel Company

Ritz-Carlton has a specific communication process or mechanism in place for disseminating information, collecting it, and reinforcing the culture. This is called "the line-up." The concept, according to President Simon F. Cooper, "comes from the early restaurants of France, where the chef got his whole team and all the waiters and waitresses and the maitre d' together at 5:30 in the evening. It's a sort of roundtable."[20] The line-up happens at every Ritz-Carlton Hotel, everywhere in the world, at the beginning of the shift. According to Cooper, the process takes about fifteen minutes, and part of the agenda is the sharing of a "wow story." Part of the Ritz-Carlton language, this describes something an employee has done that exemplifies the value the company places on customer service—in brief, something that led to a customer saying "Wow." Line-up meeting time is also used to share announcements, acknowledge staff contributions, and discuss or reinforce specific aspects of the Ritz-Carlton Credo. The meeting is thus both a way of reinforcing the company's culture and an important communication mechanism.

All employees—or the company's ladies and gentleman, as they are called—are asked to offer input to the company's annual SWOT (strengths, weaknesses, opportunities, and threats) analysis. They are also asked for input to what has been described as a "river of quantitative and qualitative data points"[21] in a variety of areas. This information helps the Ritz-Carlton executive team understand where the company is and how it is performing against what they refer to as "key success factors." In addition, collecting this input from employees helps communicate that their opinions are needed and valued.

Managing the Social Responsibility and Corporate Citizenship Value

Social responsibility and corporate citizenship is defined as "the principle that companies should contribute to the welfare of society and not be solely devoted to maximizing profits."[22] The contribution can be financial, physical (e.g., development of new recreational facilities), educational, human (providing paid time for employees to engage in community improvement activities), or environmental (such as focusing on being green).

The factors that are the basis of the continuum for this company system or process are "what we do, why we do it, and when we do it." On one end of the continuum are companies where there is an informal process for making decisions about the contributions to be made and how they will be made. At this end of the continuum, a company responds to requests for contributions case by case because there is no strategy to guide these decisions; the company tends to make changes in operation that are socially responsible only as they become aware of them or as they are required (as by law) to make them. At the other end of the continuum are companies with a well-defined and purpose-driven social responsibility process. They are proactive in identifying and implementing initiatives that will benefit the communities in which they operate. Implementation of these initiatives is just part of the way they do business.

The Social Responsibility and Corporate Citizenship Value at Southwest

Southwest Airlines' website has a significant amount of information about its social responsibility system or process. The basics are outlined in a twenty-one-page document titled "Southwest Cares: Doing the Right Thing (2008)."[23] It is organized into four sections: Our Planet, Our Communities, Our Employees, and Our Suppliers. The first two sections describe Southwest's social responsibility and corporate citizenship processes.

The planet section of this document focuses on what the company is doing to improve and protect the environment. In this section, there is a detailed description of the steps the company is taking to:

- Reduce greenhouse gas emissions by retrofitting its fleet and by using efficient flight paths
- Reduce waste and increase recycling efforts throughout the company (including on aircraft)
- Increase fuel efficiency
- Make the transition from fossil-fuel-burning to electric ground equipment
- Reduce water use
- Conserve energy
- Minimize noise impact within the communities the company serves

The planet section also presents information on the "Green Team." This is a group of employee volunteers who focus on "identifying environmentally responsible efforts already in place, searching for areas of improvement, making recommendations for environmentally responsible business practices, and putting a 'green' filter on future business decisions."[24] Finally, the section includes "third party verification" of the information by Burns & McDonnell, an engineering and consulting firm.

The communities section spotlights the programs and processes Southwest uses to give back to and support the communities in which it operates. This part of the company's social responsibility system has three levels: individual employees who "provide help where it is needed"; Southwest's Charitable Giving and Community Relations Teams, which make corporate donations and work to maximize volunteerism; and the Corporate Community Affairs Team, which works to develop relationships that can "positively impact the communities we serve."[25] Each level supports the company's Share the Spirit program (a formal activity since 2006), which is all about giving back to the company's "hometowns" (cities that the airline serves). In fact, Southwest makes a practice of getting to know any new hometown and what's important to it before they officially begin flying there.[26]

In addition to the "Doing the Right Thing" document, the Southwest Cares section of the company's website has fairly detailed descriptions of the company's recent community involvement activities—that is, how the social responsibility system is currently being operationalized. The list includes such activities as Graffiti Wipe Out in Dallas, Habitat for Humanity in New Orleans, Operation Phone Home, Thanksgiving SHARE Basket, and Walking on Sunshine.

The culture of the company supports and is supported by the social responsibility process being used. The Southwest Cares document, in fact, begins with presentation of the company's values (customers and employees, discussed earlier in this book, as well as the values related to the planet and to Southwest's communities). Here is how they are presented:

> To Our Communities: Our goal is to be the hometown airline of every community we serve, and because those communities sustain and nurture us with their support and loyalty, it is vital that we, as individuals and in groups, embrace each community with the SOUTHWEST SPIRIT of involvement, service, and caring to make those communities better places to live.

> To Our Planet: We strive to be a good Environmental Steward across our system in all of our hometowns, and one component of our stewardship is efficiency, which by its very nature translates to eliminating waste and conserving resources. Using cost-effective and environmentally beneficial operating procedures (including facilities and equipment) allows us to reduce the amount of materials we use and, when combined with our ability to reuse and recycle material, preserves these environmental resources.[27]

It is, of course, one thing to state values like these, and quite another to ensure that this culture is reflected in how employees actually behave. The question of whether the system and culture work effectively is addressed, in part, by the data presented in the Southwest Cares document. It contains statistics on metric tons of recycled solid waste, fuel efficiency improvements year by year, and the impact of other energy-saving and waste-reduction programs. It also presents the number of volunteer hours per year contributed by employees; the amount and number of charitable donations made; specifics on certain ongoing programs such as "Adopt-a-Pilot," in which pilots spend time in fifth grade classrooms mentoring students; and the company's continuing support of the Ronald McDonald House charity (begun in 1983). The message being sent is not only that the social responsibility process is working but that measurement of progress in this area is very important to the company's success.

The Corporate Social Responsibility Value at Starbucks

Like Southwest, Starbucks has a sophisticated structure and process for managing social responsibility. In fact, Starbucks' focus on and process for social responsibility is trademarked. On the website, this is presented as "Starbucks(tm) Shared Planet(tm) is our commitment to doing business in ways that are good for people and the planet."[28]

The company produces an annual "social responsibility" (now a "global responsibility") report, which details what the company is working to achieve and progress it is making with respect to desired results in this area.[29] The 2008 report can be customized to the user's needs, so that only the information wanted or needed is presented. This in itself would seem to convey that Starbucks is interested in conserving resources!

The company has an environmental mission statement on its website as well:

> Starbucks is committed to a role of environmental leadership in all facets of our business.
>
> We fulfill this mission by a commitment to:
>
>> Understanding of environmental issues and sharing of information with our partners (i.e., employees)
>>
>> Developing innovative and flexible solutions to bring about change

Striving to buy, sell, and use environmentally friendly products

Recognizing that fiscal responsibility is essential to our environmental future

Instilling environmental responsibility as a corporate value

Measuring and monitoring our progress for each project

Encouraging all partners to share in our mission[30]

The statement reflects the processes Starbucks uses in supporting social responsibility and the culture that it wants to promote as well.

With respect to social responsibility, Starbucks had three areas of focus in 2009: ethical sourcing, environmental stewardship, and community investment.[31] Within each area, the company identified specific goals it wanted to achieve. Every year, Starbucks presents a scoreboard on the progress made in achieving its goals. A 2009 goal related to environmental stewardship was to "have 50% of the energy used in our company-owned stores come from renewable sources by 2010." (In a late 2009 report, the estimate was that 20 percent of energy was coming from renewable sources.[32]) In addition to these scorecards, the "Starbucks Shared Planet" website offers information on the progress the company is making with respect to conserving energy, reducing greenhouse emissions, increasing recycling, and curtailing water usage.

Starbucks also emphasizes community involvement. As stated on the company's website, "Our company mission to inspire the human spirit goes far outside the walls of our Starbucks stores. It means encouraging and supporting partners' [employees] and customers' involvement in their communities."[33] Starbucks has set a goal that the company's employees will contribute more than one million hours of community service per year by 2015. In 2008, 246,000 hours were contributed.

Starbucks, like Southwest, helps make the value the company places on social responsibility real by tracking performance against specific areas of concern and making this information public. Starbucks, however, takes this one step further by setting specific goals or targets with respect to what the company wants to achieve in the area of social responsibility.

Managing the Social Responsibility Value at Interactive Holdings

Managing social responsibility is not just something that large or giant companies do; there are smaller ones that embrace this value as well. One of them is Interactive Holdings, a rapidly growing end-to-end communication solutions company offering communication strategy, production, and delivery services primarily to large international pharmaceutical, biotech, and medical device companies. In this company, employees are committed to a concept called "More Than Business." This term is used frequently in conversation, and there are specific goals in the company's strategic plan that reflect what it wants to achieve in this area.

More Than Business (MTB) represents a cultural imperative for Interactive Holdings to "make a positive difference in the world as we go about our day-to-day business,"[34] as CEO Bob Befus puts it. Every year, Interactive Holdings allocates 1 percent of gross revenues to a number of initiatives the company and its employees believe will improve people's lives throughout the world. According to Befus, "Interactive Holdings and its staff members, many of whom are employee owners, are committed to setting aside funds out of gross revenues instead of profits because attempting to make a difference in the world is a very high priority."[35]

MTB funds are not all spent as cash contributions. Most are donated to nonprofit organizations as services.

A volunteer MTB Committee serves the organization by bringing focus and structure to the MTB activities. Funds are allocated to projects in three areas: multiplication, support of staff member initiatives, and specific areas of need or concern. Multiplication involves "helping other companies catch the vision for allocating 1% of gross revenues to make a positive difference in the world."[36] Staff member support matches staff member gifts or volunteer hours with funds. Some staff members have used these funds for trips to help build homes in New Orleans or to help in orphanages in Africa. Others have used them to support causes such as food drives or multiple sclerosis. The third allocation of funds permits Interactive Holdings to select a need and attempt to raise the level of support for several years in a row because the company recognizes that often the most effective efforts are those where relationships with organizations and groups are fostered and developed for a number of years. A need area could be orphans in a certain part of the world or a specific homeless problem area in the United States or abroad. Every year for three to five years, approximately a third of the company's MTB budget is allocated to the current focus area.

In 2009, on revenue of $12 million, Interactive Holdings spent $132,000 in services and cash for MTB initiatives. Services are donated at cost; retail value was in excess of $200,000. Not only does the company donate these funds but the Interactive Holdings' staff also make contributions of their time. All of those who do this value the time they spend, wherever they spend it, and come away enriched by the experience. At Interactive Holdings, the value of giving something back is very much embraced by employees. They do not view it as a burden or something detracting from their jobs or the financial rewards they receive (because most are employee-owners). The value of social responsibility is a part of their work life and very much a part of the company's culture.

Conclusion

This chapter has focused on how several companies manage the company process orientation cultural dimension. Specifically, we examined how companies manage the values that support effective planning, decision making, communication, and social responsibility and corporate citizenship systems.

Company Process Orientation Culture Management Tools

This is an interesting dimension of culture because in some cases the tools for managing these values are the processes themselves. For example, there is a communication system, and there are associated values attached to how this system should operate. At the same time, effective use of communication is a culture management tool. The tools for managing the company process orientation dimension of culture are described below.

Use Communication to Reinforce Process Orientation Values

The culture of communication in a company affects how the communication system actually works. This then has an impact on all other company systems. For example, if the value is that information is power, important information needed to make decisions or develop plans is not likely to be shared. Hence the effectiveness of the decisions or plans that are made will suffer.

In all of the companies examined in this chapter, communication processes are two-way; management provides a great deal of information to employees to help them understand the company and to effectively perform their jobs, *and* management asks for input. In addition, most of these companies have mechanisms in place to ensure that employees' concerns are heard and responded to. At Southwest, this means having a total open-door policy; at Walmart, this means having a modified open-door policy. Open and free-flowing communications helps companies quickly identify and resolve systems and culture problems.

Recruit and Select People Who Will Support Process Orientation Values

Google and Southwest (as described in previous chapters) take great care to select people who will embrace how they operate. At Google, this means choosing people who are comfortable making decisions in teams and who are data-driven. At Southwest, it means recruiting people who understand the company's values and will make decisions within these values.

Embed the Process Orientation Values in Well-Defined Systems

This is perhaps the most important tool for managing this cultural dimension. Even though Southwest and Infogix differ dramatically in their approach to planning, each company has a well-defined planning process that everyone understands and that the culture supports.

The dominant style of decision making at a company needs to be supported by an effective process, as well as the company's culture. The consensus decision making style at Google is well understood and, in a sense, "documented" in the form of some of the ten golden rules. This process appears to fit with the company's culture, but it does not seem to be working as effectively as it could be. This may be due to lack of an effective decision-making process, as opposed to being a problem with the culture per se.

A company can declare that it is socially responsible or a good corporate citizen, but living this value involves developing and effectively implementing a social responsibility performance management system. In brief, the company needs to set specific goals with respect to what it wants to achieve in this area and track progress against these goals. All three companies profiled in this chapter have systems that allow them to do so. Southwest and Starbucks have much more sophisticated systems, compared to that of Interactive Holdings. However, they all answer the basic question, "How is our company doing with respect to 'giving back' to our communities and with respect to helping to improve our environment?"

A Final Comment

It is interesting to note that of the five culture dimensions, this is the one most typically *not* defined in the context of a culture or values statement. Instead, those companies that effectively manage this dimension do so by actually implementing the systems that the values support. In brief, the system and the culture need to fit together and support one another.

9 The Dark Side of Corporate Culture

Throughout this book, we have discussed and examined how corporate culture can be an intangible asset, a source of strategic and competitive advantage, and a driver of superior financial performance. However, corporate culture also has a dark side: if managed incorrectly or left unmanaged, it can lose its positive aspects and become dysfunctional or toxic. This chapter deals with situations in which culture becomes a liability, not an asset.

We begin by revisiting the concept of dysfunctional culture, which was introduced in Chapter 1. We then identify dysfunctional cultural syndromes that companies can suffer from that in turn create problems with respect to the functionality of one or more of the five key dimensions of culture we described in Chapters 4 to 8: customer orientation, people orientation, performance standards and accountability, innovation and change, and company process orientation. Next, as in prior chapters, we examine and analyze selected companies with dysfunctional cultures to gain insight into how this unfortunate condition occurs and its consequences. We have selected some very important case examples of how companies (at various stages of their history) mismanaged their culture. Specifically, we discuss AIG, the once-great and powerful company that is the poster child for the financial collapse experienced in 2008–09. We explain how IBM, generally regarded as a company with an outstanding positive culture, mismanaged customer orientation in the 1980s and fell from grace. We discuss how American Express created a highly dysfunctional environment through low productivity and an excess of politically oriented behavior. We also cite other examples of companies with dysfunctional cultures at various stages of their history. First, however, we discuss the nature of a dysfunctional culture.

The Nature of a Dysfunctional Culture and Dysfunctional Culture Syndromes

Just as a strong positive culture is an asset but does not appear on the balance sheet, a powerful negative culture is a liability that can cause a company to underperform and even fail.[1] This section examines the nature and causes of dysfunctional corporate cultures. It also demonstrates the consequences of these types of cultures, citing actual examples.

As the term is used here, a *dysfunctional culture* is one that leads a company to suboptimal performance both in day-to-day operations and in terms of bottom-line results. A dysfunctional culture is the opposite of a functional culture. The latter is a positive constructive force, leading companies toward success. The former leads companies toward failure. Company cultures can be dysfunctional with respect to how any or all of the five cultural dimensions (treatment of customers, treatment of people, standards of performance or accountability, innovation and change, and company process orientation) are defined. Sometimes a culture is so extremely dysfunctional that it becomes toxic and causes the company to fail; other times it merely leads to relative stagnation and underperformance.

Dysfunctional Cultural Syndromes

In our experience, we have identified several types of dysfunctional cultural syndromes:

The Arrogant Company

The Gambler

Politics R Us Corp.

Hamlet Corp.

The Debating Society

The Emperor Rules

The Paranoid Corporation

These are various cultural types, each characterized by an overriding cultural flaw that can have an impact on any or all of the five cultural dimensions described in the previous chapters. Most of these syndromes are fairly self-explanatory, but they are briefly described here. We also describe the impact each syndrome can have on how one or more of the five cultural dimensions are defined within a company where a syndrome is present.

The Arrogant Company

As the label implies, this is an organization in which the culture is built around the notion that the company is demonstrably the best of breed. Typically, this type of company has been successful for a reasonably long period, and its success is institutionalized as a notion of superiority. Xerox, GM, Caterpillar, Microsoft, and AIG have all been so successful and dominant that they took on what is characterized by outsiders as a culture of arrogance. It must be noted that these companies do achieve their superiority by real excellence in one or more facets of their business management. Unfortunately, development of certain dysfunctional attitudes can sometimes accompany this excellence.

In the Arrogant Culture, there is a belief (explicit or implicit) in the continuing excellence and superiority of the company. Success is seen almost as an inevitability, and from that comes a sense of the company's invincibility. In effect, companies suffering from this syndrome take the notion that "We are number one" to an extreme form of what might be termed "corporate narcissism." This is what led many Wall Street financial firms to assume a "masters of the universe" mentality that became a principal cause of the failure of many of those same firms.

In a company that suffers from the Arrogant Culture syndrome, customers may be taken for granted ("We can do whatever we want because we are the best and customers will continue to buy from us"). Obviously, if customers have an alternative, they will slowly (or not so slowly) abandon this company, which is what happened to U.S. automobile makers in the 1970s. Employees may come to believe that anything they do is, by definition, excellent (note that this is a view of employees and a performance standard) because they work for such an excellent company. This may or may not be the case and can eventually lead to overall decline in performance.

There may be reluctance to critically examine and change company processes, practices, or systems because "they helped us become the excellent company that we are today, so why change?" There may also be a more global reluctance to change that affects a company's ability to adapt to changes in its markets or develop new products and services to better meet customer needs. In brief, this syndrome can have a significant impact on how the innovation and change cultural dimension is defined. Later in this chapter, we will see how arrogance can lead to organizational decline in the case of American Express under Jim Robinson, who was then CEO.

The Gambler

In this type of culture, the ability to manage risk has been carried to the extreme of becoming a necessity. There is almost a compulsion to take risk. As we shall see in the case of AIG, the entire business was built around the notion of managing risk, and historically the company had a core competency in doing that. This same core competency, reinforced by a long history of success, led to excessive risk and was characterized as a form of gambling by some within the firm, as well as by outsiders who have attempted to deconstruct what caused its virtual downfall.[2]

The Gambler Syndrome has its most direct impact on the innovation and change cultural dimension. In companies that suffer from this syndrome, risk taking is the norm and is rewarded (that is, it might be an explicit or implicit standard of performance). Carried to an extreme, this can result in a "bet the company" mentality. The syndrome can also affect the planning and decision making dimensions. In companies that suffer from the Gambler Syndrome, being reactive tends to be rewarded more than planning. Decision making is based more on opinion than fact and might be characterized as "shooting from the hip." Further, in companies that suffer from this syndrome, people are willing to take great risks in developing plans and making decisions.

The Hamlet Corp.

In contrast to the Gambler organization, the Hamlet Corp. is an organization unable to make timely decisions. There may be analysis paralysis, where teams feel that "we never have enough information." Decision making may be avoided completely, or individuals may try to pass the buck to others as a way of avoiding having to take responsibility for the decisions made. Companies that suffer from this syndrome also tend to be excessively risk-averse.

It is obvious that the Hamlet Corp. Syndrome has its most direct impact on the culture of decision making within an organization. In brief, the culture promotes the idea that it is best to avoid making any decision. This can also affect the innovation and change dimension. In companies that suffer from this syndrome, people are risk-averse and afraid of making mistakes. There may also be a blaming aspect to the culture. Hence people, teams, and the company as a whole have a tendency to avoid rather than embrace change. The performance standards and accountability cultural dimension may also be affected by this syndrome. People may come to believe that good performance means avoiding making mistakes. In turn, this means avoiding making decisions.

The Debating Society

This is a company typically made up of very intelligent individuals who are skilled debaters. They enjoy the process of debate as a form of "entertainment," or a process of Darwinian evolution. In this culture, scoring points in the debate is more important than achieving results, and as with the Hamlet Corp. decisions tend not to be made.

The Debating Society syndrome has its most direct impact on the culture dimension of performance standards and accountability. People in these companies may come to believe that performance is based on the number of points one scores in the debate. This can lead to excessive competition between people and functions, which can affect the communication aspect of the company culture. The culture may come to support withholding information from others because it is the mechanism through which points can be scored. The Debating Society Syndrome can also have an impact on the people orientation dimension; one's team will become one's debating partners or those that one represents. In other words, there will be a silo, not a team, mentality.

An example of a Debating Society culture and its ultimate dysfunctional consequences is Reuters, which was once the leading and dominant company in the financial information business. Reuters was founded in Great Britain. The name was once an icon in the world of newspapers, captured in the familiar phrase "Source: Reuters." As a successful company, Reuters was able to attract the best and the brightest to be employees. It recruited many people from the prestigious British universities of Oxford and Cambridge, which led to a belief in the company's intellectual capabilities. Self-confidence at Reuters bordered on arrogance.

During the early 2000s, Reuters was declining financially and suffering competition from upstarts such as Bloomberg, which was founded by a brash New Yorker who lacked a degree from Oxford or Cambridge. Bloomberg was easy to underestimate, yet Reuters seemed unable to react or change how it was doing things.

The dirty little secret at Reuters, according to insiders who were there at the time, was the company's inability to make decisions. It was described by its own people as the "Ox-Bridge Debating Society." This derisively implied that Reuters was ruled by graduates of the two elite British universities who were skilled debaters but unable to agree on the course of action that would save the company from a looming disaster. Ultimately, Reuters was sold to the Canadian information company Thomson, and is now known as Thomson Reuters.

We will see another example of the dysfunctional effects of a debating culture in the case of American Express, later in this chapter.

The Emperor Rules

This is a cultural syndrome that results from having an extremely strong and powerful CEO who tends to dominate all the decisions and all the people in the company. This person often has a mercurial personality and verbally bashes subordinates to cow them into submission. This verbal abuse is typically accompanied by terminations, so employees are intimidated and on edge. They are fearful of being castigated verbally or losing their job. The net result is a culture in which there is only one real decision maker and leader: the Emperor (or Empress) himself (or herself)!

In this type of company, the CEO is a business icon or "rock star." The company *is* its leader, who rules with imperial authority. An example of this type of company is Apple, which has been built around its CEO, Steve Jobs.[3] In fact, Jobs is so important to the company that when he announced he was taking a medical leave in 2009, it had an almost immediate and significant impact on Apple's stock price.

The Emperor Rules Syndrome can have an impact on several cultural dimensions. The people orientation dimension may promote the notion that employees at all levels need to be loyal subjects of the emperor. Loyalty, in fact, may be what is rewarded, as opposed to performance (an aspect of the performance standards and accountability cultural dimension). People may not feel empowered to make decisions; instead, they wait to be told what to do by the emperor (the decision making aspect of culture). Finally, the innovation and change cultural dimension tends to be defined by the emperor; he or she determines how open the company is to change and makes the decisions about what changes (if any) are to be made.

The Paranoid Corporation

In these companies, there is great distrust of everyone, even their own employees. People who work in these companies are always on edge and worried about competition, the economy, changing customer tastes—virtually everything that can happen that could adversely affect performance. There are functional and dysfunctional aspects to this trait. The functional aspect is that the company is vigilant about tracking and usually responding to threats. The dysfunctional aspect is that if this is carried to an extreme, it will infuse or color everything that is done.

The Paranoid Corporation Syndrome affects the people orientation dimension most directly. There can be insufficient trust among employees, which leads to lack of teamwork. Information sharing may be limited because of this lack of trust, or individuals may not trust the information they do receive from others (the communication aspect of the culture). The customer orientation dimension is also affected by this syndrome, because the culture supports the notion that customers are prone to taking advantage of the company.

Dysfunctional Cultures in Action

In the cases to follow of dysfunctional cultures in action, we will not see examples of all of these syndromes. However, we will see how several of them led to problems in some well-known and once highly regarded companies.

Mismanaging Performance Standards and Accountability at AIG

During 2008, American International Group (AIG) was at the center of the financial crisis that affected not only the United States but essentially the entire international financial system. AIG was so enmeshed in the global financial system that it was deemed "too big to fail."[4] Just a few years previously, AIG was one of the bluest of blue chip companies, with an AAA (triple A) credit rating and a legendary CEO (Maurice "Hank" Greenberg) who was highly respected. It was the leading U.S.-based insurance organization and among the largest underwriters of commercial and industrial insurance in the world. Today, AIG is the poster child for what went wrong in the financial crisis of 2008–09. How did this once-great company fall from grace so quickly?

Origins of AIG

AIG traces its beginnings to 1919, when Cornelius Vander Starr formed a fire and marine casualty insurance agency in Shanghai called American Asiatic underwriters. From this beginning, Starr expanded throughout China and Asia by creating a number of agencies writing both property and life insurance.[5] Later, the company grew through acquisitions, and in 1969 it went public. In 2008, it was listed on the NYSE and was one of the most highly successful and respected companies in the world.

Financial Innovation

The rapid decline of AIG was attributable to an esoteric financial product, the "credit default swap." In this complex financial transaction, debt is layered into bondlike securities and sold in pieces or layers. Investors in the top layer are the first to get their money back and so have less risk. Investors at the bottom layer are the last to get their investment back in the case of default, so they earn a higher rate of interest for taking increased risk. In brief, for a fee AIG would insure a company's debt in case of default.

A Statistical Mirage

Using econometric models based on years of historical data about the ups and downs of corporate debt, AIG ran computer simulations of the effects of these transactions. As AIG's top executives and the president of the financial products group understood the model's projections, the U.S. economy would have to undergo a complete economic depression for the company to have to face defaults.[6] The models showed that these swaps could be a money maker for AIG, with a 99.85 percent chance of never having to pay out any insurance. On paper, it seemed that AIG would earn millions in fees for taking on infinitesimal risk. It was a classic economic free lunch, which of course is not supposed to exist in the real world. As stated by the former president of the Financial Products Division, Tom Savage, "The models suggested that the risk was so remote that the fees were almost free money."[7]

The basic problem was that the model was based on a subtle assumption that proved to be spurious, and it produced a "statistical mirage." Specifically, the model assumed that the parent company, AIG, would always have a triple A credit rating. It also assumed that total economic collapse was statistically improbable, a classic "black swan event."[8] Nevertheless, it was not just a failure of statistics but also a failure to adhere to the core culture at AIG that ultimately led the company down the road to this disaster.

Violating a Core Cultural Norm at AIG

One key aspect of the culture at AIG that characterized the company from its beginnings was that "just about anyone could question a trade."[9] However, this cornerstone of the AIG culture changed over time under the leadership of Frank Cassano, formerly the firm's chief operating officer and the man who assumed leadership of AIG's financial products group in the fall of 2001.

Cassano, a Brooklyn College graduate, excelled in accounting and credit (the back office) but had no expertise in the art of hedging. He was regarded as "smart and aggressive, sometimes too aggressive." He was also described as "very, very good; but he was arrogant."[10] Although known for back-office expertise, Cassano was ambitious and wanted to be a player at the center of the action at AIG. He made this known to his bosses, and in 1994 he got a chance to show what he could do.

In 1998, Cassano played a key role in the company's internal credit default swap debate.[11] Almost from the beginning, he was a big supporter of the product. He (as well as others) failed to understand the risks involved and, it seems, did not grasp that he was betting the company.

Under his leadership, the Financial Products Division took on more risk. Management became more top-down, and the critical, long-held cultural norm characteristic of AIG was abandoned: "The culture that had characterized the firm from the outset—one in which just about anyone could question a trade—would change, according to people who worked at the firm."[12]

The company suffered from a certain amount of arrogance and was a victim of the Emperor Syndrome under Cassano's leadership. The combination of his ambition, arrogance, lack of skill in hedging, and alleged abrogation of the cultural norm of questioning transactions simply proved to be a toxic brew for AIG.

Deconstructing the AIG Failure

The failure of AIG can, to a great extent, be attributed to the failure of its culture. In addition, not adhering to the norm or behavioral practice of questioning transactions is a subtle thing. This type of norm can be changed or subverted by leadership, even after persisting for decades. However, there were culture management tools that could have been used at AIG to reinforce this norm and help prevent its subversion by a different leader.

The cultural norm of challenging all transactions could have been elevated to an explicit core value related to performance standards; it could have been included in a formal statement of cultural values. It could also have been part of performance evaluations, including 360 degree feedback on leadership effectiveness. This might have been done as a formal feedback mechanism using confidential surveys administered by independent third parties such as external consultants, to ensure that a leader such as Cassano was adhering to long-established cultural practices.

Could the failure of AIG have been prevented? It is impossible to know for certain. One thing is clear: there *are* culture management tools available to help mitigate the perversion in culture that happened at AIG. Throughout this book, in the context of discussing how companies effectively manage their cultures, we have identified some of these tools.

Mismanaging the Customer Dimension of Culture at IBM

IBM is one of the truly great companies in the world and has been that way for many decades. One of its key assets is its culture (previously described), which has many positive attributes. However, even mighty IBM is not immune from slipping and allowing its culture to transition from positive to dysfunctional. This happened at IBM during the early and mid-1980s, and it produced a period of great turmoil in the company. The root cause of this problem was a culture of arrogance that led IBM to stray from its historical culture, which was focused on customer orientation and satisfaction.

In 1981, IBM introduced its first PC and it was an immediate success. The PC was so successful that within a year and a half of its release, IBM had taken a very significant market share away from Apple Computer, and the company's software was becoming the standard for the industry. Customer demand was so high, in fact, that IBM was unable to meet it.

During the early 1980s, IBM was in a very strong economic and competitive position. In 1984, annual revenues were in the range of $40 billion and annual profits were approximately 10 percent of sales or about $4.0 billion. In 1986, revenues were $63 billion, with $6.3 billion in profit. IBM's profits were larger than many companies' annual sales! The company had 425,000 employees worldwide, with 225,000 in the United States. In addition, there were internal projections at IBM that forecast revenues of $190 billion by 1990 and $200 billion by the year 2000. Inside the company, one of the versions of the PC was known as "popcorn"; people joked that IBM was going to manufacture PC's like popcorn. All of this, plus the company's historical strength in mainframe computers, made the future look very bright for IBM.

The Dark Side of the IBM Culture

Unfortunately, there was one little problem with this rosy scenario about IBM's future: "the mainframe guys" (that is, the people who controlled the mainframe business at IBM) saw the PC as a threat rather than an opportunity.[13] They correctly perceived that it would evolve into a shift of power from a mainframe-based paradigm of computing to a network scenario, which would ultimately undermine IBM's hefty gross margins and thus their organizational power. The potential long-term threat was real, and there were even some early disturbing signs in the midsized computer market. For example, in 1984 IBM was manufacturing a midsized workstation computer that sold for as much as $25,000 per unit. At that time, an IBM PC was selling for about $5,000, though it did not come with a letter-quality printer. IBM did not want to produce that type of printer for the PC because the company correctly understood that this action would cannibalize the midsized computer business. This was strange, countercultural behavior from a company that had long prided itself on "producing the computer that people want at the price they are willing to pay." It was definitely not customer-oriented behavior.

The mainframe business told its customers: "You don't need these PCs. You can do everything you need with our mainframes and 'dumb' terminals." That was the truth, but not the whole truth and nothing but the truth! It was true that customers could do the same things with the mainframes and terminals, but what was not stated was that the cost would be significantly greater than with PCs. Initially, this ploy worked because IBM had credibility, but as the PC began to evolve and Sun Microsystems and others developed viable midsized computers at lower price points, both the economics and the credibility of IBM were tarnished. In addition, inside IBM there was an invisible (to outsiders) battle going on between the mainframe guys, who were still quite powerful because of the profitability they dropped to the bottom line, and the upstarts who had developed the PC business. The upstarts lost and were squashed.

Results of IBM's Cultural War

In effect, the mainframe guys won the battle and lost the strategic war. Although they defeated the PC division, this invisible cultural battle within IBM left its core mainframe business vulnerable to external competitors. It also left the company without a credible competitive weapon (its own PC) to combat the invaders from Silicon Valley.

By failing to embrace the inevitable change, IBM allowed companies such as Intel, Microsoft, Compaq, Sun, and others to become giants. By playing a prevent-defense strategy, and by abandoning its long-held cultural customer orientation value, IBM lost the game, and then went through a decade of turmoil before reinventing itself.

IBM's CEO was terminated and replaced by an outsider, Louis Gerstner, from RJR Nabisco. Gerstner was brought in to change the culture at IBM. Since he had no ties to anyone there, he had the freedom to make whatever changes were required to help the business survive, including changes in personnel and culture.[14] The company, which had never had a layoff in its history, downsized from 425,000 people to 165,000 people—losing more than 60 percent of its workforce. The power of the mainframe division would never be the same. They had won the battle but lost the war.

Dysfunctional Performance Standards at American Express

Another sad example of a dysfunctional culture was American Express under the leadership of CEO Jim Robinson during the period from 1977 to 1990. AMEX was founded in 1850 as an "express" company guaranteeing safe and rapid delivery of packages in New York State. In 1890, it created "travelers cheques" and assumed liability on any losses due to theft or fraud. In 1958, the company entered the "charge card" business, which had been pioneered by Diners Club nine years before.

Culture Under Robinson's Leadership

James Robinson III became CEO in 1977. Over the next six years, he pursued a strategy to make AMEX into a "financial supermarket." He approved several acquisitions, including Shearson Loeb Rhoads (a brokerage house), E. F. Hutton (a brokerage house), Lehman Brothers Kuhn Loeb (an investment banking firm), the Boston Company (an institutional asset manager), and First Data Resources (a merchant processor), as well as a few banks.

Under Robinson's leadership, the company was organized into separate and relatively autonomous businesses; the corporate parent became a holding company. Each division had its own management structure and considerable autonomy from the others.

Culture and Management Style

The culture at American Express suffered from a variety of dysfunctional attributes. A Harvard Business School case study noted that "both insiders and outsiders described the culture of the time as arrogant and complacent."[15] AMEX managers tended to view the competition with distain, deriding bank cards as "local shopping cards," rather than serious competition.[16]

The company's arrogance was believed to have led to a missed opportunity to partner with American Airlines on one of the first affinity marketing programs. Again according to the Harvard Business School case study, "When American Airlines approached the company in 1984 about the possibility of collaborating on American AAdvantage, a co-branded card that would credit passengers with frequent flyer miles for every dollar they charged, [AMEX] managers spurned the offer."[17]

Another dysfunctional aspect of the AMEX culture was that it was highly political and debate-oriented, not based on actual performance. This grew out of Robinson's leadership style, which, as we saw with Reuters, involved a preference for debate. As one senior executive stated: "You weren't really sure where things would go; debate and contention were the dominant mode of activity—'Let's see where the chips fly.' Jim looked at all the scenarios, letting people argue their positions and develop them all in detail. This Darwinian exercise was a killer to staff and very frustrating."[18]

As a result, the company became very political. Certain things could not be said in meetings; it became a norm that "you could not challenge up."[19]

One executive who was there at the time confided that the culture was a "triumph of form over substance. People were rewarded for thoughts and suggestions, not results. It was about how many options you could propose; there was no follow-up on what you actually completed. There was no accountability, and lots of fiefdoms. We didn't work across the organization."[20]

The Results of the Dysfunctional Culture at AMEX

By the late 1980s, the company was facing many problems and its very survival was in question. The core strategy of becoming a financial supermarket was not working. Although an attractive concept, it was not going well because the company lacked clear direction and was highly political. People were busy with their own divisional problems and retreated into a bunker mentality with organizational silos.

There was a serious threat of erosion in what had been the core business and cash cow for funding the acquisitions: the charge card business. The company was facing serious competition from other charge cards. The market had become value-oriented, and the strategy of a prestige card was not working as well as it previously had. Customers were abandoning the AMEX card and acquiring lower-cost cards.

As a consequence of his leadership failures and the dysfunctional culture he had created, Robinson was replaced by one of his lieutenants, Harvey Golub. One of the key things Golub did was change the culture that had existed under Robinson. He refocused the performance evaluation culture and process on performance metrics instead of scoring points in debate. Demonstrating a profound understanding of the role of measurement as a tool of culture management, he declared, "If you get the metrics right, you'll get the behavior."[21]

Golub also began the process of creating what he called a "principles-driven business." Managers were given guiding (operating) principles, which were effectively a set of cultural values:

1. We must provide a superior value proposition to all of our customer groups;

2. We must achieve best-in-class economics; and

3. Everything we do must enhance and support the brand.[22]

The first principle relates to treatment of customers and is a performance standard as well. The second is clearly a performance standard. The third is a performance standard that relates to a broader core strategy and strategic goal articulated by Golub: that American Express must become the "world's most respected service brand."[23] As one executive reported, "Both Harvey and Ken [Chennault, Golub's successor and the current CEO of AMEX] are driven by principles and values."[24]

By the time Golub retired, American Express had transformed its culture and operations and was once again one of the premier financial service companies in the world.

Conclusion

This chapter has examined how culture—which can be a key strategic asset and source of competitive advantage—can also become dysfunctional, toxic, and a liability.

We have identified several dysfunctional syndromes of corporate culture and described the impact these syndromes can have on specific dimensions of a company's culture. We also examined and analyzed selected companies with dysfunctional cultures to gain insight into how this unfortunate condition occurred and its consequences. We have seen how Reuters became an impotent debating society and ultimately was sold to another company. We have seen how AIG, which once had a core competency of managing risk and a culture in which almost anyone could question a trade, took on more and more risk, while the culture morphed into one in which transactions could not be criticized. We have seen how once-mighty IBM allowed its culture to become politicized, lost its orientation to customers, and became resistant to change. Finally, we have seen how American Express became arrogant and underestimated the competition, while also developing a culture that focused more on form over substance and rewarded people for ideas and not results.

We have previously cited a number of culture management practices and tools that might have made a difference in these situations and prevented some of the damage. Among these practices and tools are formal statements of culture values, consistently monitoring the company culture, recruiting and training people to socialize them in the culture, and performance management systems that promote and reward desired behavior. Unfortunately, none of these tools and practices is a perfect solution. As one example, IBM had a culture statement that focused on customers, but it was ignored or misinterpreted by the mainframe guys. Although these practices and tools can help prevent a functional culture from transforming into a dysfunctional culture, they are not a panacea.

Part III

Leading Culture Management and Transformations

10 Leading Culture Management and Culture Transformations

By now, one thing should be clear: in the best and most successful companies—like those profiled in Chapters 4 to 8—culture infuses and influences everything, and it is constantly nurtured and reinforced. In these companies, there is a formal statement of company values, and when asked, employees can identify them (in some cases, as with Ritz-Carlton, employees can recite the values verbatim). In these best-of-breed companies, not only can employees recite the values but they actually live them, and as a result customers can see them. Values are not just words on paper. Every process in the company—communication, decision making, planning, training, performance management, and so forth—reflects and supports the values. There is constant and fairly open communication throughout the company—up, down, and across—and the content of at least some of this communication is directly about the company's values. In these companies, there is also ongoing emphasis on the extent to which the culture is being lived by all employees. As a result, culture, even though intangible, has become a true strategic asset for these companies.

How does this happen? The answer is that those companies that are highly effective and successful, those recognizing that culture is a very important asset, have leaders who understand and are committed to managing this asset. In this chapter, we focus on leadership of the culture management process. We also examine specific cultural transformations that leaders may face and need to manage. As will be discussed in this chapter, the need for these transformations occurs as a result of changes in company size (growth-related changes), vision, or strategy; or as a result of business combinations (mergers and acquisitions). We conclude this chapter with identification and description of culture management best practices and a strategic lens for cultural transformation.

Leading cultural change and transformation should not be confused with the cultural dimension of innovation and change, which was the subject of Chapter 7. Innovation and change is a specific dimension of a company's culture that needs to be defined and managed. In this chapter, we are dealing with the overall process of managing, and perhaps transforming, *all five* core cultural dimensions (customer orientation, people orientation, performance standards and accountability, company process orientation, and the dimension of innovation and change).

Culture Leadership: Roles and Responsibilities

One of the primary issues every organization faces with respect to culture and management of it is identifying who is responsible—that is, who is or should be the leader of this process. As described earlier, the original culture of a company is an outgrowth or reflection of the founder's (or founding members') personality. He, she, or they are the culture leaders, and the culture tends to reflect the values that are important to that person or those people. The culture is transmitted and managed through personal interaction with the founder or founders.

As a company grows, this original culture—created or seeded by founder DNA—can be transformed through the entrance of new people with new ideas. Even if the founder or founders are still present, it will be extremely difficult for them to have daily interactions with all employees. New ways of transmitting and reinforcing the culture need to be implemented, as discussed throughout this book. In addition, new culture leaders must emerge to support or replace the founder.

Who should ultimately be responsible for culture management is not really a question of delegation of responsibility to a specific organizational role. In actuality, it is really a question of who has the core competency as well as the authority to serve as the leader of the culture management and change process. In many cases, this leadership role is shared (as described here).

The CEO's Role

When the CEO is also the founder, this person will, de facto, define key aspects of the company's culture simply because of his or her status and power. The CEO or founder is the eight-hundred-pound gorilla in the company. His or her attitudes and values will inevitably influence the attitudes and values of others whom the CEO employs.

Although the founder or CEO is most often the person responsible for defining the culture, he or she might or might not have the responsibility and the capabilities for effective culture management and change. Certain corporate leaders have a natural aptitude for culture management; others do not. This suggests that it may be better to have someone other than the CEO be responsible for culture management. Even if the CEO is not the ultimate leader of the culture management effort, he or she needs to support it.

Senior Leadership's Role

The primary, but not exclusive, role of senior leadership is to bless and support (through words and actions) the culture management and, if appropriate, change processes. If there are disagreements among strong leaders in the company, this will cause confusion and possible conflict. In extreme cases, the entire organization might become embroiled in an internal battle as bitter as a civil war.

In companies with strong, functional cultures, all the members of senior management serve in one way or another as leaders in the culture management process. Indeed, every manager must serve as a role model for behavior that is consistent with and that supports the company's desired culture; each must be, in a sense, a "cultural ambassador." In addition, there should be one or more people on the company's *senior management team* who ultimately own the culture management process. This leader or leaders will tend to be supported directly by the company's human resource function, as described in the next section.

In certain cases, management of corporate culture is a shared function. This is consistent with the concept of a leadership molecule, which we discussed in Chapter 3. For example, at Starbucks, this function was not explicitly given to a specific person. It was, instead, shared by Howard Schultz, the CEO, and Howard Behar, the SVP for retail stores. This was because of their personal orientations and their formal organizational roles. Both Behar and Schultz were passionate about the importance of culture, and both held the same sensibilities about the treatment of people and customers, as well as a strong sense of social responsibility or community orientation. When Starbucks was still a relatively small company and not yet a household name and world-class brand, one of the authors spotted a Starbucks cup on a street in Los Angeles and realized that the company must have opened its first store in LA. When the author mentioned this to Behar during a break at a strategic planning meeting in Seattle a few weeks later, Behar's response, with a furrowed brow, was, "I hope you picked it up and threw it in the trash." It was evident that he was more concerned with this than with the recognition that Starbucks was now ensconced in Los Angeles.

Role of the Human Resources (HR) Function

The HR department or unit (if the company is large enough to have a unit dedicated to this function) plays a significant role in managing corporate culture and, if needed, supporting cultural transformations. However, in companies with an effectively managed culture, this is not done in isolation. Instead, HR works as a partner with leadership to ensure that the HR systems reflect and reinforce the company's values. Some of the specific culture management tools that HR oversees are described in this chapter. Note that if the company is not large enough to have a formal HR function, or if this function is designed to be administrative in nature (that is, the focus is strictly on payroll, administration of benefits, and the like), then the responsibilities discussed here will have to be performed by another unit or a specific individual.

Developing a Formal Statement of Cultural Values

The HR function typically engages regularly with employees at every level of the company. Therefore, this unit tends to understand how employees talk and what is meaningful to them from a global or companywide perspective. Human resources can thus be a strong partner in helping leadership develop or refine (in the context of a culture change process) the company's formal culture or values statement. At the same time, it should be noted that development of these statements is a complex technical exercise, requiring specific expertise and experience. As a result, it might be

necessary for HR to engage an experienced external consultant to serve as
a facilitator and partner in developing these values or culture statements.

Recruitment and Selection Processes

As described throughout this book, recruitment and selection is an important culture management tool. Human resources can assist leadership in
using this tool effectively in a variety of ways. First, HR can develop "profiles" of the types of people the company wants to join the organization. At
times, this is an extensive process. We have worked with a leading consumer
products company to identify the profile of people who were successful in
that company and, using this information, to develop unobtrusive interview questions to determine their cultural fit with the organization. It took
more than nine months to complete the process.

Second, HR can partner with the management of specific functions or
areas of the company in developing interview questions and techniques to
identify candidates who will be a good fit with the company culture. Examples of how companies use interview questions are presented throughout
this book.

Third, HR can work with company and functional management in designing the recruiting and selection process so that it helps promote selection of people who will fit with the company's culture. This includes
everything from the application process to the process used to review applications, to who is involved in the interview process, to criteria used in
making the final hiring decision.

New Employee Orientation and Training Programs

New employee orientation programs are very important, not just from the
standpoint of helping people understand the company's culture but also for
employee retention: "Studies have shown that failure to properly introduce
and assimilate newly hired employees into the new culture is one of the key
reasons 55% of them don't make the grade or voluntarily leave within the
first two years."[1] The human resources function plays a significant role in
designing and implementing this process, and in the best companies it is
actually the driver of this process.

In addition to describing what the company does, its history, current
strategy, and so on, the most effective new employee orientation programs

also include a heavy dose of company culture. Culture can be woven into this process in a variety of ways. Amgen used a video of Kevin Sharer, now CEO and then COO, to welcome people to the company. In one of these introductory videos he said, "Welcome to Amgen. By now you have learned that culture is important at Amgen and that we have a strong set of values. If you embrace those values, you are likely to be successful at Amgen. If not, you are likely to experience some bumps in the road."[2]

The HR function also plays a significant role in ensuring that ongoing technical training includes and reflects the company's culture. HR may not be involved in developing or delivering all of this training, but members of the HR team can act as consultants to those who are responsible. In this role, HR professionals can look for opportunities to include the company's values in the training that is being delivered.

Performance Management Systems and Rewards

The HR function can make an important contribution to culture management through its role in designing the performance management system and related reward and recognition practices. Human Resources can work with leadership in designing performance appraisal processes that focus not just on performance against goals but also on the extent to which employees are living the company's values. This was illustrated in the example of Smartmatic's performance management system, discussed in Chapter 6, which was designed by the company's SVP of human resources, Victor Ramirez.

In addition, HR can serve as a partner to leadership in designing employee reward and recognition programs (including compensation) that recognize those who best represent the company's values. In Chapters 4 through 8, we presented several examples of companies that have successfully designed and are using reward programs to reinforce their values.

Leadership Development Program

Another culture management tool that HR plays a significant role in managing is leadership development. The HR function can assist leadership in identifying developmental needs of managers at all levels; identifying or designing programs to meet these needs; and, most important, ensuring that design and delivery of these programs effectively supports the company's culture. In addition, HR can work with leadership to develop specific programs that focus on enhancing the culture management skills of managers throughout the company. Sophisticated companies such as GE, IBM, Disney, Starbucks, and Southwest Airlines all use training and development programs not only to develop competencies but also to transmit culture.

Corporate Events

Every event held at a company is an opportunity to communicate and reinforce the culture. At a minimum, any event can communicate the value the company places on its employees—that is, how much they are appreciated. Events can also be used to recognize individuals for their role in managing the company's culture or their effectiveness in serving as representatives of the culture. The HR function, in partnership with leadership, can work to ensure that every event fits with and supports or reinforces the company's culture.

Culture Communication

As the case studies throughout this book show, constant communication with employees—up, down, and across—is a very important culture management tool. The HR function can serve as a partner to leadership in developing and disseminating culture-related messages, through employee newsletters, email, and other forms of communication. Human resources can also serve as a mechanism through which employees can provide feedback to the company on culture-related issues.

We have also observed HR groups offering input on "scripts" for the CEO and other senior leaders to use in highlighting the culture as part of the annual meeting. Some HR groups use interview formats to talk with the CEO about the culture in a question-and-answer session, in a live or taped video broadcast.

Annual Monitoring of the Culture

The human resources function in a company is, in a sense, the keeper of the cultural flame. Even though HR does not ultimately own culture and culture management—the ultimate owner is senior leadership—its people are a valuable resource in ensuring that culture receives continuous focus and management. In this regard, HR is typically responsible for the annual or biannual monitoring of the culture, as well as for interpretation of the data. This can include surveying employees about the extent to which the culture is real or in other ways assessing the effectiveness of culture management efforts.

Cultural Transformations That Leaders May Face

In addition to ongoing management of culture, leaders also have to be aware of and able to manage cultural transformations. Some are inevitable, brought about simply because the company has grown in size. Others come about by design or are the by-product of an event such as an acquisition. It should also be noted that if a company (such as Southwest Airlines) understands the importance of culture as an intangible asset and has focused on it from the very beginning of the business (which is rare), the transformations described here, when encountered, will tend to be nothing more than business as usual.

There are four primary types of cultural transformation that an organization might experience: (1) from early-stage entrepreneurship to a professionally managed firm, (2) revitalization (turnaround), (3) business vision (strategy) transformation, and (4) business combination (merger, acquisition). In addition to these four primary types, organizations sometimes engage in compound transformations, consisting of more than one type simultaneously. This in effect constitutes a fifth type of cultural transformation. We describe all five types of cultural transformation next.

Professional Management Cultural Transformations

The need for this first type of transformation typically begins at about $10 million in annual revenue, with about a hundred employees, although it may occur when an organization reaches a much larger size. During this transformation, leadership needs to help all employees—whether they have been with the company for a number of years or joined more recently—understand and embrace a culture consistent with having more formal systems and processes in place to effectively manage the operations of a large company. At the same time, leadership needs to ensure that the positive aspects of the entrepreneurial culture are retained.

This transformation typically involves developing or refining, communicating, and reinforcing a culture that supports, among other things:

- All employees, regardless of tenure or department, feeling they are part of one team (or part of the company family) and they are valued (people orientation)

- Continued focus on the customer and customer service (customer orientation)
- Holding all employees accountable for performance against goals and for supporting the new systems and processes that are being put in place (performance standards and accountability)
- A focus on embracing, not resisting, change (innovation and change)
- Planning as opposed to firefighting, systematic decision making and empowerment, an effective communication process, and a focus on social responsibility (company process orientation)

During this transformation, there may be a cultural clash—a crisis—in which there is a battle or invisible war between the professionals (in marketing, production, finance, and so on) who were recruited as the company grew and the early-stage recruits. The battle is often expressed in terms of who is valued; but in effect it is really a larger battle over the soul or sensibility of the company. The underlying cultural issue is whether the company will remain free-spirited and without systems and processes or become more structured and professionally managed. Leaders need to be aware of and take steps to manage this crisis because it can have an adverse impact on the company's ability to effectively implement new systems, as well as on employee morale.

Leaders also have to focus attention on helping people, particularly the old-timers, embrace the changes that must be made in how the company operates. There is likely to be resistance to change on the part of many people who "liked things the way they were when we got started" and who tend to view the changes toward professional management as becoming bureaucratic.

Revitalization Cultural Transformations

This type of cultural transformation occurs when a business goes into decline and needs revitalization. A good example of this type, and of the cultural issues it engenders, is the turnaround of IBM during the 1990s.[3] As a result of the Great Recession of 2008–09, many companies are now engaged in this type of transformation, and undoubtedly will be for many years. In a revitalization transformation, the organization continues in the same business it has been in, but now it focuses on rebuilding itself.

During a revitalization transformation, most aspects of the real culture must typically change to support other changes that must take place in the company. It should be noted that some companies facing revitalization have a formal culture or values statement that does, in fact, reflect what the company's culture *should* be. The problem, in this case, is that there has been little effort, if any, devoted to effectively communicating and managing this culture, and as a result it is not real for employees.

One of the key cultural aspects of a revitalization transformation is to break the feeling of defeat (or even despair). Revitalization is required when an organization is suffering and experiencing loss. The losses are not only financial but also psychological. There is a different sensibility in a company that was once successful and is now experiencing decline.

This problem is exacerbated as "colleagues and friends" leave the company, some by their own choice and others by being let go. When respected and valued colleagues leave by their own volition, it creates what is called "cognitive dissonance." People reassess their own situation. Stated differently, they begin asking, "If they're leaving, why am I staying?"

Our research has identified a cultural variable that can have a positive or negative effect on this situation. In brief, the degree to which a company faces the problem of people leaving for greener pastures depends on the extent to which employees identify with the company.[4] If they feel connected, they will tend to remain even in the face of crisis. When Southwest Airlines reduced salaries after the September 11 crisis, they lost very few employees. People felt a part of something special, and it wasn't about the money.

The Impact of Culture on Amgen's Revitalization

The revitalization and related cultural change at Amgen during the early and mid-1990s is, in contrast to Southwest, an example of the impact culture can have on a company, its employees, and the ability to recover from a decline. After a period of sustained growth, increased profitability, and a related rise in stock price, Amgen began to experience decline. The drop in stock price was jarring to employees who had come to expect Amgen would continue to be successful.

During this period, some people left for (perceived) greener pastures. There was another up-and-coming biotechnology company in southern California, and many people decided to leave Amgen and join them. Some actually said "the party is over at Amgen; but Agouron is on the rise. It might become the next Amgen."

Despite the noticeable exodus of talent, some people who were loyal to Amgen were determined to help the company see better days.

The problem was that although Amgen was known for having a good (positive) culture, it was not an *effectively managed* culture. If the culture had been better managed, there would have been a greater percentage of loyalists. Fortunately for Amgen, there were enough people who identified with the company (and who therefore stayed) to create the required revitalization.

One caveat: there is nothing like a layoff to reduce loyalty to a company and dissipate the intangible asset of people's sense of identification with it. The loyalty must be perceived as reciprocal. What this means is that when a company needs to reduce its workforce, the process must be carefully managed so that its culture is not irreparably damaged.

How Disney Animation Got Reanimated

In 1984, the Animation Division of Disney, which was the historical foundation of the larger company itself, was in the doldrums. This Disney unit—which during the 1930s and 1940s had created cultural landmarks such as *Fantasia* and *Snow White and the Seven Dwarfs*—had become something of a business dwarf itself. The key problem was lack of leadership and a culture that had drifted into passivity and mediocrity. The animators (who included a young Tim Burton) were not motivated or pushed to do their best. Business practices included long lunches and midday volleyball.

The arrival of Michael Eisner together with Jeffrey Katzenberg was the catalyst for changing all of that "nonsense." They set much higher performance standards and required more task-oriented behavior. They called meetings on Sundays at 8:00 a.m. Although the animators initially rebelled against this new regime, they soon realized that they had been unleashed artistically.[5] The results included such successful animated films as *The Little Mermaid* and *The Lion King*.

The "new" Disney was not without its own cultural problems. There was great conflict between Eisner and Katzenberg—not just creative differences, but conflict over credit for the success of the films. For a while, the relationship was mediated by Frank Wells, known as Disney's peacekeeping president and COO, who unfortunately died in a tragic helicopter accident in 1994. Ultimately, Katzenberg left the company and cofounded DreamWorks as a competitor. This is yet another example of the effects of a disintegrating leadership molecule.

Business Vision Cultural Transformations

A business vision transformation occurs when an organization changes the basic concept of the business it is in. This involves changing a company's existing business vision and related strategy to fundamentally different ones. Business vision transformation is inherently risky because it involves redefining the very essence of the enterprise.

There are several examples of companies that have attempted, but not successfully accomplished, this. In fact, only a few were successful. Sears, AT&T, United Airlines, and Kodak were all unsuccessful with this kind of transformation. The driving force behind these types of transformation is generally some sort of strategic factor (technological change, demographics, competition, and the like). However, the key to making the transformation successful is typically *cultural change.*

One example of successful vision change is American Express under the leadership of Harvey Golub (described in more detail in Chapter 9). This transformation involved abandoning Jim Robinson's concept of AMEX as a financial supermarket and focusing instead on leveraging the brand as the core strategy. It should be noted that this transformation would not have been successful without the significant changes in the culture introduced by Golub, who was the ultimate leader of the company's culture.

Business Combination Cultural Transformations

A fourth type of cultural transformation occurs when a company embarks on and completes a merger or acquisition. Although a merger or an acquisition might make sense from a strategic standpoint, the primary reason for failure is typically lack of cultural compatibility.[6]

As with revitalization transformations, the Great Recession of 2008–09 has led to a number of business combinations, sometimes with strange bedfellows. During this period, Bank of America acquired Merrill Lynch and Countrywide Financial. Bank of America has long been a professionally managed company, with even a bureaucratic culture. Merrill Lynch was a classic Wall Street firm with a variety of financial services platforms. Countrywide was a classic entrepreneurial firm, still led at the time of its acquisition by the legendary, charismatic, and controversial founder, Angelo Mozilo.[7] Putting all of these pieces together in an economically sound way is without doubt a challenging exercise. It is made even more challenging by the unique aspects of each company's culture.

The integration of companies in an acquisition is an underappreciated core competency. Some companies have developed this competency and are able to fuel continued growth by way of this method. Johnson & Johnson is one of the masters at integrating successful acquisitions. J&J has successfully purchased many companies over the years: Neutrogena, LifeScan, Centecor, and others. In fact, J&J is known for the practice of looking carefully at an acquisition candidate's culture. If the culture of the potential acquisition is in conflict with J&J values (presented in the company's Credo), it will walk away.

One of the authors served as a consultant to Neutrogena after it was acquired by J&J. The CEO of Neutrogena, who was transferred from another J&J unit, was told when he got the assignment: "We put a lot of chips on the table. Don't screw it up." The translation of this somewhat colorful, but cryptic, message was clear to him, as he explained: "Hey, we paid a lot of money for this company. Bring them into the J&J way of doing things, but do not be heavy-handed while you're doing it, or you risk our investment, and by implication your career!"

There is, however, a dark side to acquisitions and mergers. It is quite tricky to make them work well. The reason most acquisitions fail is not lack of strategic fit but lack of *cultural* fit.

In one sad example, two health care companies that were competitors and also numbers one and two in their market space decided to merge and become the dominant player. Homedco and Abbey Healthcare merged to become Apria Healthcare. Although the combination made strategic sense on paper, it was doomed to failure almost from the outset. The companies were too far apart culturally to make merger an easy process. Both were actually entrepreneurial, but Abbey's culture was entrepreneurial to an extreme, while Homedco was more of an entrepreneurially oriented but professionally managed firm.

It was like the mating of a gazelle and an elephant, both of which have their virtues. Their offspring, which we might call a "gazellephant," is a phantasmagoric creature that has no real place in this world. Ultimately, the merger of equals proved too difficult to manage, and the company went private; all of the senior leaders of the company were replaced. In fairness, cultural problems were not the only issues facing the company and not the only cause of its decline; but they were enough of a distraction to make the task at hand far more difficult.[8]

Cultural Compound Transformations

A compound transformation occurs when an organization simultaneously undergoes more than one of the four primary types identified here. Clearly, a compound is even more complex than a simple cultural transformation. Nevertheless, organizations often face the need for complex, compound transformation. An organization might undergo an entrepreneurial trans-formation to professional management *and* a business vision transfor-mation simultaneously, as Disney did in the mid-1980s. IBM underwent a revitalization and business vision transformation simultaneously in the mid-1990s.[9] Probably the most common case of compound transformation occurs when a company is transforming from entrepreneurship to profes-sional management and simultaneously acquires another company.

Time Required for Cultural Change

In general, the time needed to complete a change in corporate culture de-pends on a company's size. The larger the size, the longer it takes. As a rule of thumb, if effectively managed a culture change in a relatively small com-pany (less than $10 million in revenues) will take about a year. Change in companies larger than $10 million will take at least a year, and for compa-nies exceeding $100 million, it might take more than two years.

Although this seems long to some readers, we have some empirical sup-port for these estimates. In our study of nine companies of varying sizes involved in culture change efforts, all of the successful transformations re-quired substantially longer than originally envisioned, by a factor of two or three times what was initially planned.[10] Of course, the unsuccessful changes occurred much more quickly!

Cultural Change at Emergent BioSolutions

One of the major exceptions to the relatively long time required for cultural change that we have observed was at Emergent BioSolutions, the biopharmaceutical company described in Chapter 2.

As we noted, Emergent launched a culture management initiative in 2009. The authors of this book were engaged in the initiative as consultants to assess the current culture of the company and provide feedback on its strengths and opportunities for improvement. As part of the program, a culture survey was administered to all employees to collect their input on the company's desired and current cultures. The results identified a variety of opportunities to strengthen the culture.

In November 2009, the preliminary results of the initial culture survey were presented to the company's Executive Management Committee (EMC) in a two-day meeting. The EMC's response to these survey results is notable and extraordinary. In addition to listening carefully to and discussing the results, they devoted time to identifying specific actionable items that the company and the senior leadership team could initiate to make immediate improvements in the company's culture. For example, some employees expressed concern that they were expected to check emails "twenty-four, seven." Led by the CEO, Fuad El-Hibri, and COO, Dan Abdun Nabi, the company immediately established an "email response protocol" that limited the hours for expected response. Within a matter of days, the COO issued a memo addressing the preliminary findings of the culture initiative and announcing some immediate changes in company practice. Here is a portion of the memo:

> As a first step toward addressing some of the issues raised in the survey, the following actions . . . are effective immediately:
>
> *Respect for Employees' Professional and Personal Time*
>
> *Time Management* the Culture Steering Committee and Project Team will be working toward a more expansive approach to time and meeting management, but as an important first initiative, meetings will start on time with a five minute grace period.
>
> *After Hours E-Mailing* we have heard that some employees feel that they are expected to monitor e-mails around the clock. Employees will generally not be

expected to monitor e-mails and voice-mails between 8:00 p.m. and 8:00 a.m. in each respective time zone.[11]

In our experience as consultants and facilitators of cultural change, this type of immediate response was exemplary. The message sent by the company via its COO's memo was clear; in effect, "We have listened to you, we have heard you, and we will take action ASAP to make improvements to our culture and practices." The "meta message" is commitment to positive constructive cultural change.

Culture Management Best Practices

As researchers, experienced consultants, and facilitators of culture management, we are sometimes asked for our view of the best practices we have observed with respect to what might be termed culture management tactics. Here are three best practices that can be applied in virtually any organization:

1.   Communicate, communicate, communicate.
2.   Form a culture management task force.
3.   Include culture-related questions in the employee selection process.

Let's look at each of these tactics.

Communicate

One of the most important things any company can do—regardless of where it is in the development and implementation of its culture management plan—is communicate regularly with all employees. This communication can be about the values, specific culture management issues being addressed, updates on culture management efforts, or any other topic. If employees are asked for input (say, they participate in a culture survey process), leadership needs to give them some type of response so that employees feel they have been heard.

It is also important that employees have a way to share their feedback on the process and its results. It is important to build in two-way communication. This can happen through town-hall-style meetings led by a member of senior management, through meetings between managers at all levels and their direct reports, through use of a culture task force (described below), or other mechanisms.

Another tactic, with respect to communication, is to select a "value of the month" (or quarter) on which the entire company will focus. During that month, communication efforts concentrate on this value; every time a team meets, regardless of the level in the organization, there is discussion of that value. The discussion might be programmable (human resources or the company's leadership might create a specific agenda) or nonprogrammable (the discussion might focus on what team members have been doing to live the value, or on developing an action plan to better support the value in action).

The major goal of the communication effort is to keep the values constantly in front of all employees and ensure, as a CEO once said, that they remain "fresh." The medium is also the message: "We value our culture and we want to hear from you about what we can do, or do differently, to better support it."

Form a Culture Management Task Force

A culture management task force is a defined group of people who work with leadership in developing, implementing, and monitoring performance against the company's culture management plan. The role and responsibilities of this group can vary from company to company. In some cases, for example, the task force may be asked to develop the company's culture management plan, subject to the approval of senior management (who are the ultimate owners of the plan). In other cases, the task force might be charged with developing and implementing action plans to support culture management initiatives developed by the senior leadership team. In still other cases, as with Southwest Airlines, the culture task force can take the form of a standing committee; it becomes the designated leadership of the culture management effort.

Whatever the responsibilities, the culture task force should be led or chaired by a member of the company's senior management team. Typically, this is the head of human resources, but this isn't always the case; the original culture committee at Southwest was chaired by Colleen Barrett, who was then the president. Task force membership should, ideally, include representatives from all departments and functions. This helps promote communication between the task force and all employees; the representative can take ideas from his or her department or unit to the task force and can solicit input on task force ideas from those with whom he or she works. This helps ensure that culture initiatives that are implemented will work.

Include Culture-Related Questions in the Interview Process

Interviews typically focus on assessment of skills, but cultural fit is an equal consideration, if not a more important one. Questions related to the company's culture should be included in the interview process. If feasible, they should be unobtrusive questions.

There are no right questions to ask because they must all be tailored to the company's unique culture. In some cases, questions explicitly include or focus on a company value: "Tell me how you used humor in your last job" (Southwest). In other cases, the question might be less directly related to a specific value but intended to see how the person thinks (Google). Questions that help the interviewer understand whether the person is a good fit with the culture can be quite powerful. In one company, turnover in a specific position in the first six months after hiring was more than 50 percent. When leadership realized that this might be caused by inadequate fit, they developed three questions to ask candidates that related to the culture. Turnover in this position went down to less than 10 percent.

A Strategic Lens for Culture Transformation

In Chapter 1, we indicated that culture is a strategic building block of organizations. We also examined the role of culture as part of a six-factor framework of organizational effectiveness (Exhibit 1.4). This section builds on that notion and shows how these variables can be combined into a strategic lens for planning and managing cultural transformations.

To reiterate, the six variables discussed as strategic building blocks of effective companies are markets, products and services, resources, operational systems, management systems, and culture. As noted in Chapter 8, these six critical tasks make up the Pyramid of Organizational Development (shown in Exhibit 10.1), suggesting that these tasks must be performed in a stepwise fashion to build a successful organization. In fact, the six key tasks making up the pyramid must all be developed individually and as a (holistic) system for the organization to function effectively and increase its chances of long-term success.[12]

Exhibit 10.1. Pyramid of Organizational Development.

During the initial phase of organizational or business development, the market is the primary driver of the business. Stated differently, the customers the business wants to serve determine, in sequence, the products that must be offered, the resources and operational systems required, how the management systems are designed, and how the dimensions of culture are defined. For example, if the intent of a business in the retail space is to serve budget-conscious buyers, then the products selected, the resources of the stores (including furnishings, ambiance, and so on), the operational and management systems used, and culture all must be geared to being the low-cost provider. This is the kind of organization that Walmart and COSTCO have designed and implemented. Similarly, if a service organization is operating in the same customer space (like Southwest Airlines) then again all six variables in the pyramid must be geared to achieving the overall core strategy of being the low-cost provider for budget-conscious travelers.

Culture's Role in Organizational Development and Success: The First Iteration

Culture is shown at the apex of the pyramid not necessarily because it is the most important variable (which it well might be at times) but because it is driven or affected by (and must be designed to support) the other variables below it. For example, without a market or product, a strong positive culture is relatively meaningless. This was demonstrated by the dot-com debacle in the late 1990s and early 2000s. Many firms were founded—funded with venture capital—to search for ways to create businesses leveraging the Internet. Most of these firms had great cultures but were doomed to fail because they lacked the most fundamental requirement for a successful business: a market or customer who would pay for a product or service. Some companies with great potential business concepts, such as WebVan, eToys, and Boo.com, failed to achieve "proof of concept" and ultimately disappeared.[13]

Culture's Role in Organizational Success: The Second Iteration

Although corporate culture is typically not the primary driver of initial success for a business venture, once a business is in place and has been developed then culture takes on a whole new dimension.[14] At that point, culture can assume a life of its own and become a driver of all other variables. This means that culture now becomes in some ways the base of the pyramid by having a bottom-up impact on all other variables.

A strong culture can actually overwhelm a company even in terms of products or services offered, and cause the company to be out of tune with the marketplace. The example of how IBM focused not on what customers wanted but on what IBM wanted customers to want (as described in Chapter 9) illustrates this.

A Case Study of Culture Management in Organizational Development: Haohe Construction

This section presents a case example of the process of leading cultural change and its impact on organizational effectiveness. The company is Haohe Construction, a successful business in China.

Haohe Construction was established in 1983 in the city of Guangzhou. Haohe's services include general contracting, project management, design, permitting, construction, procurement, decoration, final inspection, and acceptance. The company carries out a range of design and construction through three regional branch companies in South China, East China, and North China. It also performs complete design-and-build or EPC (engineering procurement construction) services.

Haohe's clients come from Europe, the United States, Japan, Korea, Southeast Asia, Hong Kong, and Taiwan and include many prominent companies. During the past twenty-seven years, the company has grown rapidly and successfully and has constructed more than 220 major projects.

Origins of the Cultural Change Initiative at Haohe

The CEO of Haohe, Yixiao "Kenny" Zhang, has been concerned about Haohe's culture for many years. About ten years ago, when Zhang returned to the company from abroad, he found that "integrity" was not a part of the core values of Haohe's people or its corporate culture. As he put it, "Ten years ago, first time I came back from abroad, I felt bad that people weren't ashamed of telling lies, so I put integrity in the first place in our core values."[15]

From these concerns, Zhang initiated a culture management initiative in 2003–04 at Haohe. As an initial step, he articulated a mission for the company: "Haohe's mission is to improve human beings' living and working environment." However, workers at Haohe found this to be too abstract and not directly relevant to their work, so Zhang took steps to explain the company's mission in terms that could be understood by all workers. As he relates:

> First-line managers thought it is too intangible and far from their current work. As a result, I spent time with them in illustrating what we mean by this and how it is relevant to their daily work. I explained to them that even trivial things like "spit" or leaving trash in workplace are against our mission of improving people's living and working environment and should be prevented. Those are all very tangible.[16]

The next step was for Zhang to articulate a vision for Haohe: "We set our vision as 'to be the most reliable contractor in China.'"[17].

Building on the mission, Zhan then articulated a set of core HR values for Haohe, saying, "Our HR values are integrity, passion, initiative, good quality, team work, and continued improvement."[18] To make these values real and operational in the company, Zhang spent a great deal of time communicating with his people: "I spent much time in communicating and getting midlevel and senior management aligned with our mission, vision, and core values."[19]

He worked hard to translate those values into specific norms of behavior that could be understood by all the employees. Wanting to emphasize integrity but realizing that people might be unwilling to be criticized for mistakes, he found a clever solution: "We emphasize 'forgiveness for honest mistakes' in order to promote taking initiative while retaining high level of integrity. We have demonstrated to our employees that we actually did not punish people if they made mistakes with good intention; at the same time, some people were fired for being dishonest and doing harm to the company's integrity."[20] Zhang explains the difference between an honest mistake, which can be forgiven, and a dishonest mistake for which there can be no forgiveness: "If someone does [takes or gives] a bribe or some acts against values, they get fired right away."[21] However, honest mistakes are forgiven. Zhang recalls: "One day my secretary forgot to bring me something I had asked for. I said it was 'no problem.' Everyone makes mistakes."[22]

Impact of Culture on Organizational Effectiveness, 2009–10

In 2009, Zhang attended the CEO Leadership Program offered by Cheung Kong Graduate School of Business (CKGSB). Coauthor Flamholtz was one of the instructors for this program. He was engaged by CKGSB to coach approximately forty CEOs in China as a way of helping them enhance their leadership and organizational effectiveness during a nine-month program. As part of his sessions, he had the program participants (along with their senior management teams) complete two proprietary organizational effectiveness tools: the Growing Pains Survey and the Organizational Effectiveness Survey. Developed by Flamholtz, both have been validated and demonstrated predictive validity to financial performance.

The *Growing Pains Survey* measures the extent to which a company is facing problems in making the transition to the next stage of development. Growing pains represent an early warning of problems that an organization will encounter over time. Scores on the Growing Pains Survey can range from a low of 10, which suggests that current systems are functioning reasonably well, to a high of 50, which means the company is facing very severe problems. The Growing Pains scores and their interpretations are presented in Exhibit 10.2.

Score Range	Color	Interpretation
10–14	Green	Everything is OK
14–19	Yellow	Some things to watch
20–29	Orange	Some areas need attention
30–39	Red	Some very significant problems
40–50	Purple	A potential turnaround situation

Exhibit 10.2. Growing Pains Survey score interpretation.

The *Organizational Effectiveness Survey* consists of sixty-five items intended to assess the extent to which the systems, processes, or structures at each level in the Pyramid of Organizational Development (Exhibit 10.1) have been designed and are functioning effectively in meeting the company's needs (given its stage of development). As previously discussed, our research and experience suggest that for an organization to have the highest probability of success over the long run, it needs to effectively manage all six levels in this pyramid plus financial results—individually, and as a system. Respondents are asked to score each item according to how they feel it describes their company at the current time. The five-point response scale ranges from "to a very great extent" to "to a very slight extent." This qualitative scale is converted to a five-point numerical scale, with 5 = "to a very great extent" and 1 = "to a very slight extent."[23] A computerized analysis is performed on survey data to generate the mean scores. Mean scores range from 1 to 5 and are color-coded to indicate the extent to which the company has developed the infrastructure needed to support its current and future operations. Exhibit 10.3 shows the range of scores and their interpretation.

Haohe's Organizational Effectiveness Survey Scores

As part of his participation in the CKGSB CEO Leadership Program, Zhang and five members of his team completed both the Growing Pains and Organizational Effectiveness Surveys, first in July 2009 and then again in February 2010. The results of both administrations are presented in Exhibits 10.4 and 10.5, respectively.

Score Range	Color	Interpretation
4.5–5.0	Green	To a very great extent
4.0–4.4	Yellow	To a great extent
3.0–3.9	Orange	To some extent
2.0–2.9	Red	To a slight extent
1.0–1.9	Purple	To a very slight extent

Exhibit 10.3. Organizational Effectiveness Survey mean score interpretation.

	Rank		Score		
Growing Pains	**2009**	**2010**	**2009**	**2010**	**Change**
There are too few good managers.	1	1	35.0	33.3	–
People feel that there are not enough hours in the day.	8	1	26.7	33.3	+
People are spending too much time putting out fires.	3	3	31.7	30.8	–
Everyone feels "I have to do it myself if I want to get it done correctly."	4	4	30.0	30.0	0
Most people feel our meetings are a waste of time.	6	5	28.3	28.3	0
The company has continued to grow in sales but not in profits.	4	6	30.0	25.8	–
Many people are not aware of what others are doing.	2	7	33.3	25.0	–
When plans are made, there is very little follow-up and things just don't get done.	8	7	26.7	25.0	–
Some people have begun to feel insecure about their place in the company.	6	9	28.3	22.5	–
People have a lack of understanding of where the company is headed.	10	10	25.0	17.5	–
Overall	–	–	29.5	27.2	–

Exhibit 10.4. Haohe Construction Growing Pains Survey: results 2009 vs. 2010.

Pyramid Level Plus Financial Results	Mean		Change
	2009	2010	
Markets	3.5	3.8	+
Products and services	3.1	3.6	+
Resources	3.2	3.8	+
Operational systems	3.2	3.8	+
Management systems	3.3	3.8	+
Culture	3.5	3.8	+
Financial results management	3.3	4.0	+
Overall	3.3	3.8	+

Exhibit 10.5. Haohe Construction Organizational Effectiveness Survey: results 2009 vs. 2010.

It is clear from these data that in 2009 Haohe was experiencing some growing pains. Fifty percent of the individual growing pains were in the "red zone," clearly indicating the need for action to improve Haohe's organizational systems and culture. Organizational Effectiveness Survey results suggested there were opportunities to further refine the systems and processes at all levels of the Pyramid of Organizational Development.

By February 2010, there were significant improvements in the results of both surveys. As seen in Exhibit 10.4, seven of the ten individual growing pains became less severe, with the most significant improvements related to growth in sales (and in profits), people being aware of what others are doing, and people understanding where the company is heading. Scores for all three of these growing pains show a qualitative difference in scoring range between the two administrations of the survey, moving into a different color band. Only one growing pain ("People feel that there are not enough hours in the day") was more severe on the second administration, showing a qualitative increase from the "orange" zone to the "red."

Organizational Effectiveness Survey scores, as seen in Exhibit 10.5, show improvement overall and on all seven dimensions. The most significant improvement is in the financial results management dimension, where the score moved from "orange" to "yellow." The 2010 score indicates that Haohe has now developed the processes needed to support effective financial results management.

Statistical Analysis of Results

Following the second administration of the surveys, a test of statistical significance was performed on the data to better understand the significance of the improvements in the survey results.[24] The tests found that improvement in the overall growing pains score was not statistically significant. However, improvements in scores for two growing pains ("When plans are made, there is very little follow-up and things just don't get done" and "Some people have begun to feel insecure about their place in the company") were found to be statistically significant at the 0.05 level, indicating that there is less than a 5 percent probability of these improvements happening simply by chance alone.

The statistical test results for the Organizational Effectiveness Survey indicate that improvement in the overall score was statistically significant at the 0.05 level. In addition, the improvements in the resources, operational systems, management systems, culture, and financial results management dimensions were also statistically significant at the 0.05 level.

What Did Zhang Do to Create This Difference?

Asked what he did to create this difference, Kenny Zhang replied: "We did not do a formal plan for culture management. However, since the session on culture by Professor Flamholtz, I did follow-ups to emphasize the importance of our culture and make sure people understood our values."[25] Reflecting on his attempt to change the culture at Haohe, Zhang had this to say: "Generally speaking, we need to spend six or seven years to change the corporate culture. In the first two or three years, the company went downward and some important people in the company left. In last three years, we made big progress."[26]

Zhang also talked about the influence of his personal beliefs and style in the transformation of his firm's culture. The original impetus for change grew out of a personal tragedy:

> When my family member died, I thought about the meaning of life. I reflected
> that I was pushing people to change too much and concluded that if I expected

to convince others to change, I needed to take a lead to change. Since then, things got back on the right track. In a word, if you want to change your company, you must start to change yourself first.[27]

Initially, people at Haohe (especially the founders) had a tough time changing the culture. Although some key members left, one decided not to leave and joined Zhang in believing in change. Zhang credits the persistence of his beliefs in the necessity of culture change as being crucial to its ultimate success:

> Some people asked me how I could be so confident in change. For my part, I just continued to believe in the part of change, and the team got stronger and stronger. I also made effort to strengthen the leadership of new leadership team who has no experience. I tried to share all experience whenever I got chance to and follow up details. That is why we improved so much.[28]

Conclusion: Corporate Culture, a True Strategic Asset

Corporate culture: you cannot see it, touch it, smell it, taste it, or hear it, but it is there. It pervades all aspects of organizational life and has a profound impact on organizational success and failure. If managed correctly (as we have shown in Chapters 4 through 8), it is a real economic and strategic asset. If managed incorrectly or allowed to deteriorate (recall instances in Chapter 9), it can become a true liability or strategic disadvantage.

As we have seen, management of corporate culture is very complex. But there are clear examples of companies that have mastered the process of culture management. We have shown that corporate culture can have a significant impact on various aspects of organizational operations. We have also shown how companies can master aspects of corporate culture management and create strategic (competitive) advantage, as well as enhance the bottom line.

For companies large and small, wherever they are located in the world, and no matter what industry they operate in, corporate culture can become a true asset. To accomplish this, the company culture needs to be embedded in *everything* it does. The ultimate goal is to have every employee understand, embrace, and live by the company's culture. How do you know that you and your company have been successful in these efforts? When you can ask any employee in the company what its values are and the person can accurately tell you what they are and how what he or she is doing reflects these values. And when you can ask any customer to describe what your company is like and the response reflects the value you place on customer service. This is the case at Ritz-Carlton, Southwest Airlines, and Walmart, and at other companies where culture is intangible but still a true strategic and economic asset.

We hope this book helps companies and their leaders better understand how to master the process of culture management and transform their culture into a true invisible asset and ultimate source of sustainable competitive advantage.

Notes

Preface

1. Jay B. Barney, "Organizational Culture: Can It Be a Source of Sustained Competitive Advantage?" *Academy of Management Review*, 11(3), 1986, 656–665; Daniel Denison, *Corporate Culture and Organizational Effectiveness* (New York: Wiley, 1990); Caren Siehl and Joanne Martin, "Organizational Culture: A Key to Financial Performance?" in *Organizational Climate and Culture*, ed. Benjamin Schneider (San Francisco: Jossey-Bass, 1990), 241–281; John P. Kotter and James L. Heskett, *Corporate Culture and Performance* (New York: Free Press, 1992).

2. Flamholtz has proposed that corporate culture is an asset in the accounting sense. See Eric Flamholtz, "Conceptualizing and Measuring the Economic Value of Human Capital of the Third Kind: Corporate Culture," *Journal of Human Resource Costing and Accounting*, 9(2), 2005, 78–93.

3. See, for example, Joanne Martin, *Cultures in Organizations: Three Perspectives* (New York: Oxford University Press, 1992); Kotter and Heskett, *Corporate Culture and Performance*; Joanne Martin, *Organizational Culture: Mapping the Terrain* (Newbury Park, CA: Sage, 2002); Edgar H. Schein, *Organizational Culture and Leadership* (San Francisco: Jossey-Bass, 2004); Terrence E. Deal and Allan A. Kennedy, *Corporate Cultures* (New York: Basic Books, 2000).

4. This implies that these five dimensions must all be included in corporate culture statements and must be explicitly treated as part of the overall culture management process.

5. Chapter 10 focuses on the process of managing change in corporate culture. This should not be confused with the process of managing one of the specific dimensions of culture, the innovation and change dimension, which is the subject of Chapter 7.

6. See note 3 for several significant previous contributions to the literature. Others are cited throughout this book.

7. The authors' firm, Management Systems Consulting, was founded in 1978.

Chapter 1

1. The companies in question are Walmart, Starbucks Coffee, Southwest Airlines, Google, GE, General Motors, and Toyota.

2. Technically, from an accounting standpoint culture can be an asset but cannot be a true liability. The term *liability* is used here in its colloquial sense to connote a limitation or handicap.

3. Don Soderquist, *The Wal*Mart Way: The Inside Story of the Success of the World's Largest Company* (Nashville: Thomas Nelson, 2005). Regarding various forms and punctuation of the corporate name, here is what appears on the company website:

> Wal-Mart Stores, Inc. (NYSE: WMT) is the legal name of the corporation. The name "Walmart," expressed as one word and without punctuation, is a trademark of the company and is used analogously to describe the company and its stores. Use the legal name when it is necessary to identify the legal entity, such as when reporting financial results, SEC filings, litigation or governance matters.

4. Howard Behar, with Janet Goldstein, *It's Not About the Coffee* (New York: Portfolio, 2008).

5. *2008 Southwest Cares Report: Doing the Right Thing,* http://www.southwest.com/about_swa/southwest_cares/southwest_cares.html.

6. Southwest experienced its first loss in seventeen years in late 2009.

7. Warren Bennis, "Google's Growth Engine," *CIO Insight,* June 2004, 25.

8. Adam Lashinsky, "Back2Back Champs," *Fortune International* (Europe), 157(2), 2008, 60.

9. Robert Slater, *Jack Welch and the GE Way* (New York: McGraw-Hill, 1999).

10. Coco Masters, "Toyota's President Facing Trial by Fire," *Los Angeles Times,* Business Section, February 6, 2010, B-2.

11. Jay B. Barney, "Organizational Culture: Can It Be a Source of Sustained Competitive Advantage?" *Academy of Management Review,* 11(3), 1986, 656–665; Daniel Denison, *Corporate Culture and Organizational Effectiveness* (New York: Wiley, 1990).

12. According to William Worthington and colleagues, *strategic assets* are defined as "the key knowledge, technology, competencies, and other resources needed to excel in the venture's business." See William J. Worthington, Jamie D. Collins, and Michael A. Hitt, "Beyond Risk Mitigation: Enhancing Corporate Innovation with Scenario Planning," *Business Horizons,* 52, 2009, 465.

13. See Caren Siehl and Joanne Martin, "Organizational Culture: A Key to Financial Performance?" in *Organizational Climate and Culture,* ed. Benjamin Schneider (San Francisco, Jossey-Bass, 1990), 241–281; John P. Kotter and James L. Heskett, *Corporate Culture and Performance* (New York: Free Press, 1992).

14. Linda Smircich, "Concepts of Culture and Organizational Analysis," *Administrative Science Quarterly,* 28, 1983, 339–358.

15. We will provide a more formal definition of *culture* in Chapter 2.

16. Simon Properties is the developer of the largest shopping mall in the United

States, the Mall of America, located in suburban Minneapolis. The company is listed on the New York Stock Exchange.

17. Guy S. Saffold III, "Cultural Traits, Strength, and Organizational Performance," *Academy of Management Review*, 13, 1988, 546–558.

18. Strong cultures can be either positive or negative.

19. The author's next car purchase was a Mercedes, not another Jaguar!

20. Kotter and Heskett, *Corporate Culture and Performance*, 16.

21. Other highly successful companies where culture is thought to play a considerable role are IBM, Hewlett-Packard, Southwest Airlines, Nestle, Toyota, Johnson & Johnson, Berkshire Hathaway, Tsingtao, and PIMCO.

22. Howard Schultz and Dori Jones Yang, *Pour Your Heart into It* (New York: Hyperion, 1997).

23. Howard Behar with Janet Goldstein, *It's Not About the Coffee* (New York: Portfolio, 2008).

24. Business Enterprise Trust Awards, Business Enterprise Award, "Howard Schultz," Video 994-515 (Boston: Harvard Business School, 1994).

25. Google, Inc., Amendment No. 9 to Form S-1 Registration Statement filed August 18, 2004.

26. Soderquist, *Wal-Mart Way*.

27. Ibid., 32.

28. They are actually very similar (in fact, they are almost identical) to the three key values that make up the cultural foundation of another great company, IBM.

29. See, for example, the documentary titled *Wal-Mart: The High Cost of Low Prices*, dir. Robert Greenwald, 2005. See also *Beth Dukes et al. vs. Wal-Mart Stores, Inc.* Ninth Circuit U.S. Court of Appeals, Nos. 04-16688 and 04-16720, December 6, 2004.

30. This is consistent with the "resource based view" of strategy. See Jay Barney, "Firm Resources and Sustained Competitive Advantage," *Journal of Management*, 17(1), 1991, 99–120.

31. Kotter and Heskett, *Corporate Culture and Performance*.

32. For a detailed discussion of their methodology, see ibid., 18–20.

33. Ibid., 21.

34. Eric Flamholtz, "Corporate Culture and the Bottom Line," *European Management Journal*, 19(3), 2001, 268–275.

35. Although there are several potential measures of financial performance that might be used (such as ROI, "EVA" or economic value added, cash flow, etc.), this particular study used EBIT because it was the performance measure actually employed to evaluate and rank the divisions monthly in this company.

36. Interestingly, the only research on culture management cited in *Beth Dukes et al. vs. Wal-Mart Stores, Inc.*, Ninth Circuit U.S. Court of Appeals, Nos. 04-16688 and 04-16720, December 6, 2004, op. cit., is this study by Eric Flamholtz.

37. Eric G. Flamholtz and Yvonne Randle, *Growing Pains*, 4th ed. (San Francisco: Jossey Bass, 2007).

38. Eric G. Flamholtz and Zeynep Aksehirli, "Organizational Success and Failure: An Empirical Test of a Holistic Model," *European Management Journal*, 18(5), 2000, 488–498; Eric G. Flamholtz, "Towards an Integrative Theory of Organizational Success and Failure: Previous Research and Future Issues," *International Journal of Entrepreneurship Education*, 1(3), 2002–03), 297–319; Eric Flamholtz and Stanford Kurland, "Strategic Organizational Development, Infrastructure and Financial Performance: An Empirical Test," *International Journal of Entrepreneurial Education*, 3(2), 2005, 117–142.

39. Louis V. Gerstner, *Who Says Elephants Can't Dance? Inside IBM's Historic Turnaround* (New York: HarperCollins, 2002).

40. The difference between humans and chimpanzees in terms of DNA is about 1 percent.

Chapter 2

1. Others agree with this notion. See, for example, Terrence E. Deal and Allan A. Kennedy, *Corporate Cultures* (New York: Basic Books, 2000), 21.

2. Linda Smircich, "Concepts of Culture and Organizational Analysis," *Administrative Science Quarterly*, 28, 1983, 339–358. Also, some books about culture do not actually define the concept formally. For example, see Joanne Martin, *Cultures in Organizations: Three Perspectives* (New York: Oxford University Press, 1992).

3. This is called the "Credo" by Ritz Carlton. See Joseph A. Michelli, *The New Gold Standard* (New York: McGraw-Hill, 2008), 23.

4. This is called the "Motto" by Ritz Carlton. See ibid., 26.

5. This is called the "Three Steps of Service" by Ritz Carlton. See ibid., 30–31.

6. Li-Ning company website: http://www.lining.com/EN/company/inside-1_3.html.

7. http://corporate.disney.go.com/careers/culture.html.

8. The scientific meaning of the term *general importance* is that something can be generalized to people or organizations broadly and is not specific to a single person or organization.

9. Eric Flamholtz, "Corporate Culture and the Bottom Line," *European Management Journal*, 19(3), 2001, 268–275; Eric G. Flamholtz and Rangapriya Narasimhan-Kannan, "Differential Impact of Culture upon Financial Performance: An Empirical investigation," *European Management Journal*, 23(1), 2005, 50–64.

10. These five areas or "clusters" have been identified by means of empirical research. See ibid.

11. As can be easily seen, the Walt Disney Company does not include all of the five key dimensions of culture. Specifically, it is silent with respect to treatment of people or employees.

12. As discussed in Chapters 7 and 8, it is hoped that Toyota's culture has not

morphed into a variation of the dysfunctional culture that brought U.S. car manufacturers to the brink of bankruptcy.

13. David Sarno, "Apple Tops Microsoft as King of the Tech World," *Los Angeles Times*, May 27, 2010, A1.

14. Ibid., p. A13.

15. Rensis Likert is the developer of the "Likert scale." This was done is his Ph.D. dissertation at Columbia University, titled "A Technique for Measuring Attitudes."

16. Items can also be "reverse scaled" to check for respondent bias.

17. This Appendix draws on Eric Flamholtz, "Culture and the Bottom Line."

18. The regression equation describing the relationship among variables in the exhibit is $y = 0.3888 \times -18.015$. $R^2 = 0.4552$ and was statistically significant at the 0.05 level. This means that approximately 46 percent of EBIT is explained by the variable of corporate culture, or cultural buy-in.

Chapter 3

1. Data derived from numerous sources, including www.myspace.com/youdrink coffee/blog and Joseph A. Michelli, *The Starbucks Experience* (New York: McGraw Hill), 2007.

2. Wooden Global Leadership Awards Presentation, Anderson School of Management, UCLA, May 28, 2008.

3. Elinor Mills, "Meet Google's Culture Czar," http://news.cnet.com/Meet-Googles -culture-czar/2008-1023_3-6179897.html.

4. Disney has carefully used language as a supporting tool of its culture management process. It created a special language to communicate its values and support the cultural focus. Employees are all called "cast members," and customers are called "guests."

5. Language is a key indicator of culture. The word *bootleg* has defined cultural meaning at 3M, as discussed in Chapter 7.

6. Osmosis is a passive biological process that occurs when water moves across a partially permeable membrane. *Cultural osmosis* is defined as transmission of cultural values to people without an active intention to do so.

7. See Eric G. Flamholtz and Yvonne Randle, "Corporate Culture Management," *Growing Pains: Transitioning from an Entrepreneurship to a Professionally Managed Firm*, 4th ed. (San Francisco: Jossey-Bass), 2007, 298–331.

8. Schwarzenegger played the title role of "the Terminator" in the now classic movie with that name.

9. Wooden Global Leadership Awards Presentation, May 28, 2008.

10. Eric G. Flamholtz and Yvonne Randle, "Leading Change," in *Leading Strategic Change* (Cambridge, UK: Cambridge University Press, 2008), 49–66.

11. Ibid.

12. Personal communication with Eric Flamholtz, May 2008.

13. See Eric G. Flamholtz and Yvonne Randle, "Organizational Structure," *Growing Pains*, 188–213.

14. The stages of corporate growth presented here draw on Eric G. Flamholtz and Yvonne Randle, "Identifying and Surviving the First Four Stages of Organizational Growth," *Growing Pains*, 26–47.

15. During the remainder of this discussion, we will refer to "the" founder, while recognizing that it might actually be more than one person.

Chapter 4

1. Business Enterprise Trust Awards, Business Enterprise Award, "Howard Schultz," Video 994-515 (Boston: Harvard Business School, 1994).

2. Joseph A. Michelli, *The Starbucks Experience* (New York: McGraw-Hill, 2007), 35.

3. Ibid., 35.

4. Howard Schultz Presentation, Wooden Global Leadership Awards Presentation, Anderson School of Management, UCLA, May 28, 2008.

5. In 2014, Disney will open a theme park in Shanghai, China.

6. The Walt Disney Company reports combined numbers for theme parks and resorts.

7. The "under park" is the area located at ground level under the theme park itself, which is actually elevated.

8. Allan Cohen, James Watkinson, and Jenny Boone, "Herb Kelleher Talks About How Southwest Airlines Grew from Entrepreneurial Startup to Industry Leadership," *Babson Insight*, March 2005, 3.

9. Ibid., 2.

10. "Bibliography." http://www.southwest.com/about_swa/press/bibliography.html.

11. "The Mission of Southwest." http://www.southwest.com/about_swa/mission.html.

12. "Customer Service Commitment." http://www.southwest.com/about_swa/cus tomer_service/csc.pdf.

13. Debby Gibson, "Southwest Airlines Succeeds Through Self-Expression," *Larson-Allen EFFECT*, Winter 2001, 13.

14. For a number of years, Kelleher served as CEO and Colleen Barrett served as president. As of 2010, Gary Kelly held both the CEO and president titles.

15. U.S. Chamber of Commerce, Business Civic Leadership Center website, "Southwest's Secret to a Positive Corporate Culture: Its Employees." http://uschamber.com/bclc/profiles/southwest.html.

16. "Culture." http://corporate.disney.go.com/careers/culture.html.

Chapter 5

1. Howard Schultz, Harvard Business School Video 994-515 (Boston: Harvard Business School Publishing, 1994).

2. See the six guiding principles of Starbucks listed in Chapter 3.

3. Sharon Elliott, who joined Starbucks as vice president of human resources in 1995, championed this principle. It was added to the original five about a year later.

4. http://money.cnn.com/magazines/fortune/best companies/2010/full_list/

5. Howard Schultz Presentation, Wooden Global Leadership Awards Presentation, Anderson School of Management, UCLA, May 28, 2008.

6. http://www.merriam-webster.com/dictionary/google.

7. Mark Veverka, "Google Searches for Another Winner," *Barron's*, Nov. 2, 2009, 26.

8. Thomas S. Eisenmann and Kerry Herman, "Google Inc.," Case 9-806-105 (Boston: Harvard Business School Publishing, Revised, November 9, 2006), 5.

9. Ibid., 6.

10. Ibid., 6.

11. Robert G. Hagstrom, *The Warren Buffet Way* (New York: Wiley, 1994).

12. Elinor Mills, "Meet Google's Culture Czar," http://news.cnet.com/Meet-Googles -culture-czar/2008-1023_3-6179897.html.

13. Ibid.

14. Ibid.

15. Fred Vogelstein, "Search and Destroy," *Fortune*, May 2, 2005, 73.

16. Don Soderquist, *The Wal*Mart Way* (Nashville: Thomas Nelson, 2005).

17. Ibid., 30.

18. Ibid., 32.

19. Ibid., 36.

20. "The Mission of Southwest," http://www.southwest.com/about_swa/mission. html.

21. Allan Cohen, James Watkinson, and Jenny Boone, "Herb Kelleher Talks About How Southwest Airlines Grew from Entrepreneurial Startup to Industry Leadership," Babson *Insight*, March 2005, 4.

22. "Nuts About Southwest," http://www.blogsouthwest.com/.

23. Kevin and Jackie Freiberg, *Nuts! Southwest Airlines' Crazy Recipe for Business and Personal Success* (New York: Broadway Books, 1996), 68.

24. Ibid.

25. Cohen, Watkinson, and Boone, *Insight*, 5–6.

26. Ibid., 7.

Chapter 6

1. This phenomenon is also true in certain national cultures. For example, there is no word in the Italian language that corresponds to the concept of accountability. It can hardly be a concept that drives behavior if no word exists for the construct!

2. This dimension of culture was identified by the method of factor analysis as described in Eric G. Flamholtz and Rangapriya Narasimhan-Kannan, "Differential Impact of Culture upon Financial Performance: An Empirical Investigation," *European Management Journal* 23(1), 2005, 50–64. Since the cultural dimension of performance stan-

dards and accountability is of great importance in and of itself and because it amounts to an independent statistical factor, we are treating it in a chapter separate from the people orientation dimension.

3. For a discussion of Deming, see W. Edwards Deming, *Out of the Crisis* (Boston: MIT Press, 1986).

4. "HP Corporate Objectives and Shared Values," http://www.hp.com/hpinfo/abouthp/corpobj.html.

5. Data derived from numerous sources, including the Hewlett-Packard website (www.hp.com/hpinfo/about hp/corpobj.html).

6. Source of quote: ibid. Data derived from numerous sources, including the Hewlett-Packard website (www.hp.com/hpinfo/about hp/corpobj.html).

7. Source of quote: ibid.

8. Gregory C. Rogers, "Human Resources at Hewlett-Packard (A)," Case 9-495-051 (Boston: Harvard Business School Publishing, Rev. November 1, 1995), 10.

9. Ibid., 6.

10. Ibid., 9.

11. Source for all Smartmatic data in lists and Exhibit 6.1 is internal documentation.

12. Personal communication to the authors, October 29, 2009.

13. A "system" is a set of interrelated parts designed to achieve a specific purpose.

14. Smartmatic "Performance Management System" (document), 1.

15. Ibid., 2–3.

16. Ibid., 4.

17. This is consistent with the GE approach described in Chapter 1.

18. Personal communication to the authors, October 29, 2009.

19. Ibid.

20. For most of the company's history, its legal name was Unitech Systems. This name was changed to Infogix in 2005. We shall use the name Infogix throughout this discussion.

21. See Deming, *Out of Crisis*.

22. Ibid.

23. W. Edwards Deming, *The New Economics for Industry, Government, Education,* 2nd ed. (Boston: MIT Press, 2000).

24. Ibid.

25. Ibid.

26. See W. Edwards Deming, *Out of the Crisis* (Boston: MIT Press, 1986).

27. For a more complete discussion of the impact, see Eric G. Flamholtz and Yvonne Randle, "Leading Strategic and Organizational Change at Infogix," in *Leading Strategic Change* (Cambridge: Cambridge University Press, 2008), 155–167. The chapter was coauthored with Madhavan Nayar, company leader at Infogix.

28. In March 1999, Nayar attended a Forbes Presidents Conference where he heard Eric Flamholtz make a presentation about a framework for building successful organi-

zations. In late 1999, he invited Flamholtz to work with Infogix and apply his approach. Although Flamholtz's approach was more consistent with a classic management-by-objectives approach, he was interested in learning more about application of the Deming approach and was willing to experiment with tailoring his approach to fit a Deming culture. Working together, Flamholtz and Nayar began to develop a modified management system at Infogix. A key aspect of the management system developed at Infogix was creation of a "performance optimization system" that was consistent with the Deming philosophy as applied at Infogix but incorporated some of the methods used by Flamholtz at other companies to help manage performance.

29. Eric G. Flamholtz and Yvonne Randle, *Growing Pains*, 4th Edition (San Francisco: Jossey-Bass, 2007), 266–268.

30. Problems of this kind have led to development of laws such as Sarbanes-Oxley, which try to enhance the credibility of internal control systems and punish people and companies for violations.

31. Personal communication with the authors.

Chapter 7

1. James C. Collins and Jerry I. Porras, *Built to Last* (New York: HarperCollins, 1994).

2. Our view that change and innovation must be managed effectively for long-term organizational health is clearly supported in the literature. See, for example, Donald F. Kuratko, "The Entrepreneurial Imperative of the 21st Century," *Business Horizons*, 52, 2009, 421–428; and Jeffrey S. Hornsby and Michael G. Goldsby, "Corporate Entrepreneurial Performance at Koch Industries: A Social Cognitive Framework," *Business Horizons*, 52, 2009, 413–419.

3. In Chapter 10, we deal with the overall process of leading change in corporate culture. This should not be confused with management of the specific innovation and change dimension of culture, one of the five core dimensions of culture.

4. See Eric G. Flamholtz and Yvonne Randle, *Leading Strategic Change* (Cambridge, UK: Cambridge University Press, 2008).

5. We will treat these two aspects of culture as separate and independent rather than as interchangeable.

6. This case draws on information furnished in the "Smartmatic Profile." The authors are indebted to Antonio Mugica, CEO; Victor Ramirez, VP international human resources; and Samira Saba for assistance in preparation of this case example.

7. Personal interview with Antonio Mugica, October 16, 2009. All quotes from Mugica in this section are from the same interview.

8. Ibid.

9. Ibid.

10. Although the process of innovation at 3M is by now well known to some people, it is still one of the iconic examples of how to stimulate innovation in large, established companies. For this reason, we have included it here.

11. "The Mission of Southwest." http://www.southwest.com/about_swa/mission.html.

12. "The Freedom to Create and Innovate." http://www.southwest.com/careers/freedom_innovate.html.

13. Allan Cohen, James Watkinson, and Jenny Boone, "Herb Kelleher Talks About How Southwest Airlines Grew from Entrepreneurial Startup to Industry Leadership," Babson *Insight*, March 2005, 5.

14. Ibid., 3.

15. Kevin and Jackie Freiberg, *Nuts! Southwest Airlines' Crazy Recipe for Business and Personal Success* (New York: Broadway Books, 1996), 84.

16. Cohen, Watkinson, and Boone, "Herb Kelleher Talks," 4.

17. Cheryl Hall, "Southwest Airlines Chief Is Flying High," *Los Angeles Times*, Business Section, May 3, 2010.

18. Ibid.

19. Freiberg and Freiberg, *Nuts*, 192.

20. "Southwest Airlines Founder Herbert D. Kelleher to Receive Innovation Award at TravelCom '09," *eTurboNews*, February 5, 2009.

21. "American Advertising Federation to Present Award to Southwest Airlines," ILA 2010 Award Press Release, February 2, 2010.

22. Jeffrey K. Liker and Michael Hoseus, *Toyota Culture: The Heart and Soul of the Toyota Way* (New York: McGraw-Hill, 2008), 324.

23. Ibid., 324.

24. Jerry Hirsch and Coco Masters, "Sorry Won't Be Last Word on Toyota," *Los Angeles Times*, February 6, 2010, A-1.

25. Coco Masters, "Toyota's President Facing Trial by Fire," *Los Angeles Times*, Business Section, February 6, 2010.

26. Satoshi Hino, *Inside the Mind of Toyota: Management Principles for Enduring Growth* (Florence, Kentucky: Productivity Press, 2006).

27. Ralph Vartadebian and Ken Bensinger, "Toyota Chief Sorry for Safety Lapses," *Los Angeles Times*, February 25, 2010, A-1.

28. Ken Bensinger, "Toyota's Focus Was Recall Costs," *Los Angeles Times*, February 22, 2010, A-1.

29. Ibid.

30. Stan Gwizdak and Dennis McRae, "What Went Wrong at Toyota?" http://www.industryweek.com/articles/what_went_wrong_at_toyota_21260.apx, March 6, 2010.

31. Bensinger, "Toyota's Focus Was Recall Costs," A–1.

32. Jerry Hirsch, "Toyota's Rivals Rush to Fill the Void," *Los Angeles Times*, Business Section, February 23, 2010, B-1.

33. http://www.ge.com.

34. Robert Slater, *Jack Welch and the GE Way* (New York: McGraw-Hill, 1999).

35. Ibid., 92.

36. Ibid., 53.

Chapter 8

1. It should be noted that communication in this chapter refers to the overall "systems, processes, structure, etc." that promote the flow of information throughout a company. This can include, but is not limited to, information related to a company's values. In brief, communication is a culture management tool (as identified in Chapter 3), but this is not the only role that communication systems, processes, and the like play within a company.

2. Allan Cohen, James Watkinson, and Jenny Boone, "Herb Kelleher Talks About How Southwest Airlines Grew from Entrepreneurial Startup to Industry Leadership," Babson *Insight*, March 2005, 4.

3. Ibid.

4. Kevin and Jackie Freiberg, *Nuts! Southwest Airlines' Crazy Recipe for Business and Personal Success* (New York: Broadway Books, 1996), 86.

5. Ibid., 87.

6. This case example draws on an earlier version that appeared as an article. See Madhavan Nayar and Eric G. Flamholtz, "The Transformation from Entrepreneurship to Professional Management at Unitech Systems," *International Journal of Entrepreneurial Education*, 3(2), 2005, 169–184.

7. Both the planning process and the Pyramid of Organizational Development are described in Eric G. Flamholtz and Yvonne Randle, *Growing Pains*, 4th Edition (San Francisco: Jossey-Bass, 2007). The pyramid framework is also discussed in Chapter 10 of this book.

8. Eric G. Flamholtz, "Towards an Integrative Theory of Organizational Success and Failure: Previous Research and Future Issues," *International Journal of Entrepreneurship Education*, 1(3), 2002–03, 297–319.

9. "Southwest's Secret to a Positive Corporate Culture: Its Employees," Business Civic Leadership Center, U.S. Chamber of Commerce, http://www.uschamber.com/bclc/profiles/southwest.html, 2005.

10. Freiberg, *Nuts*, 88.

11. Ibid., 77.

12. Eric Schmidt and Hal Varian, "Google: Ten Golden Rules," *Newsweek*, December 2, 2005.

13. Michael Arrington, "Why Google Employees Quit," TechCrunch, http://techcrunch.com/2009/01/18/why-google-employees-quit/, January 18, 2009.

14. "Goodbye Google," http://stopdesign.com/archive/2009/03/20/goodby-google.html.

15. Communication as a tool for culture management was examined in Chapter 3.

16. "Benefits—The Freedom to Stay Connected," http://www.southwest.com/careers/freedom_connected.html.

17. "Open Door," "Sundown Rule," and "Grass Roots Process," http://walmartstores.com/About Us/286.aspx, /294.aspx, and /284.aspx.

18. Don Soderquist, *The Wal*Mart Way* (Nashville: Thomas Nelson, 2005), 62.

19. Ibid., 63.

20. Robert Reiss, "How the Ritz-Carlton Stays at the Top," Forbes.com, http://www.forbes.com/2009/10/30/sim-cooper-ritz-leadership-ceonetwork-hotels.html, October 30, 2009.

21. Jennifer Robinson, "How the Ritz-Carlton Manages the Mystique," http://gmj.gallup.com/content/112906/how-ritzcarlton-manages-mystique.aspx, November 29, 2006.

22. BusinessDictionary.com.

23. *2008 Southwest Cares Report: Doing the Right Thing*, http://www.southwest.com/about_swa/southwest_cares.html.

24. Ibid., 10.

25. Ibid., 12.

26. Cohen, Watkinson, and Boone, Babson *Insights*, 8.

27. *2008 Southwest Cares Report*, 4.

28. See http://www.starbucks/responsibility/learn-more/starbucks-shared-planet.

29. See http://www.starbucks.com/responsiblity/learn-more.

30. "Environmental Mission Statement," http://www.starbucks.com/mission/default.asp.

31. "Our Responsibility," http://www.starbucks.com/sharedplanet/ourResonsibility Internal.aspx.

32. Ibid.

33. http://www.starbucks.com/responsibility/community/community-service.

34. Personal communication to authors from Robert Befus, CEO, Interactive Holdings, February 8, 2010.

35. Ibid.

36. Ibid.

Chapter 9

1. As noted previously in this book, we are not using the terms *asset* and *liability* with their technical accounting denotations but in a more colloquial sense.

2. Ralph Vartabedian and Tom Hamberger, "AIG Woes Could Be Just the Start: Critics Say AIG Took Too Many Investment Risks," *Los Angeles Times*, March 30, 2009, A1, A14.

3. Jeffrey S. Young and William L. Simon, *iCon: Steve Jobs* (New York: Wiley, 2005).

4. Jim Puzzangherra, "Financial Crisis: Why AIG Is Still Getting Rescue Funds," *Los Angeles Times*, Business Section, 4.

5. Heidi Suzanne Nelson, "American International Group, Inc.," case 9-200-026 (Boston: Harvard Business School, December, 1999).

6. Brady Dennis and Robert O'Harrow, Jr., "Financial Crisis: Complex Deals Led to AIG's Undoing," *Los Angeles Times*, Business Section, January 1, 2009, 1, 4.

7. Ibid., 4.

8. Nassim Nicholas, *The Black Swan: The Impact of the Highly Improbable* (New York: Random House, 2007).

9. Dennis and O'Harrow, 1, 4.

10. Ibid., 4.

11. Credit default swaps were a complex financial transaction in which debt was layered into bondlike securities and sold in pieces.

12. Dennis and O'Harrow, 1, 4.

13. The term *mainframe guys* was actually in use at IBM. The authors do not intend any gender disrespect by using this term, and perhaps women will be pleased to be excluded from this particular reference!

14. Louis V. Gerstner, *Who Says Elephants Can't Dance: Inside IBM's Historic Turnaround* (New York: HarperBusiness, 2002), 182–199.

15. Artemis March, under the supervision of David A. Garvin, "Harvey Golub: Recharging American Express," case 9-396-212 (Boston: Harvard Business School, March 19, 1996), 3.

16. Ibid.

17. Ibid.

18. Ibid.

19. Ibid.

20. Ibid.

21. Ibid.

22. Ibid., 11.

23. Ibid., 10.

24. Ibid., 12.

Chapter 10

1. Arthur R. Pell, *The Complete Idiot's Guide to Human Resource Management* (New York: Alpha Books, 2001), 120.

2. Amgen video "Introduction to Amgen," 1994.

3. See Louis V. Gerstner, Jr., *Who Says Elephants Can't Dance: Inside IBM's Historic Turnaround* (New York: HarperCollins, 2002).

4. See Eric G. Flamholtz and Rangapriya Narasimhan-Kannan, "Differential Impact of Culture upon Financial Performance: An Empirical Investigation," *European Management Journal*, 23(1), 2005, 50–64.

5. John Horn, "When Disney Became Reanimated," *Los Angeles Times*, Section D, January 10, 2010, D 4.

6. Julie Creswell, "Killer Deals: When Bad Mergers Happen to Good Firms," *Fortune*, May 1, 2000, 46.

7. Even though Mozilo left after the acquisition was consummated, the imprint of his culture will be in place for former Countrywide employees who are now employed by Bank of America.

8. The company also faced a drastic decline in revenues because of changes in Medicare reimbursement policies.

9. See Gerstner, *Who Says Elephants Can't Dance*, 2002.

10. See Eric G. Flamholtz and Yvonne Randle, *Leading Strategic Change* (Cambridge, UK: Cambridge University Press, 2008).

11. Data from portion of internal memo, by Dan Abdun Nabi, Emergent BioSolutions, October 16, 2009; used with permission.

12. For a discussion of this framework, see Eric G. Flamholtz and Yvonne Randle, *Growing Pains, 4th Edition* (San Francisco: Jossey-Bass, 2007).

13. WebVan was an online "credit and delivery" grocery business that went bankrupt in 2001. Headquartered in Silicon Valley, it delivered products to customers' homes within a thirty-minute window of their choosing. At its peak, it offered service in ten major U.S. markets. In June 2008, CNET hailed WebVan as "one of the greatest dotcom disasters in history" (as cited by Wikipedia).

14. There are possible exceptions. For example, Starbucks is about the "experience" of the customer at its cafes, and this is driven to a great extent by culture.

15. Personal communication with Kenny Zhang, April 12, 2009.

16. Zhang, personal communication, March 15, 2009.

17. Ibid.

18. Ibid.

19. Ibid.

20. Ibid.

21. Zhang, personal communication, April 12, 2009.

22. Ibid.

23. See Rensis A. Likert, "A Technique for the Measurement of Attitudes." *Arch. Psychol.*, New York, 1932, 140, 1–55. See also Peter H. Rossi, James D. Wright, and Andy B. Anderson, *Handbook of Survey Research* (Orlando: Academic Press, 1983), 252–255.

24. The statistical test used was the Wilcoxon Matched Pairs Signed-Rank Test. See Sidney Siegel, *Nonparametric Statistics for the Behavioral Sciences* (New York: McGraw-Hill, 1956), 75–83.

25. Zhang, personal communication, April 12, 2009.

26. Ibid.

27. Ibid.

28. Ibid.

Index

Page numbers in *italics* indicate tables, charts, and graphs. Terms and corporations beginning with numbers are alphabetized as if spelled out; 3M, for instance, will be found in the Ts.